T H E
PRICING
DECISION

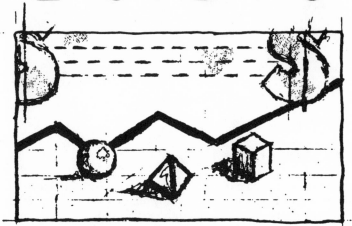

A Strategic Planner for Marketing Professionals

DANIEL T. SEYMOUR
EDITOR

PROBUS PUBLISHING COMPANY
Chicago, Illinois

© 1989, Daniel T. Seymour

ALL RIGHTS RESERVED. No part of this publication may be reproduced, stored in a retrieval system, or transmitted by any means, electronic, mechanical, photocopying, recording or otherwise, without the prior written permission of the publisher and the copyright holder.

This publication is designed to provide accurate and authoritative information in regard to the subject matter covered. It is sold with the understanding that the publisher is not engaged in rendering legal, accounting or other professional service.

FROM A DECLARATION OF PRINCIPLES JOINTLY ADOPTED BY A COMMITTEE OF THE AMERICAN BAR ASSOCIATION AND A COMMITTEE OF PUBLISHERS.

Library of Congress Cataloging-in-Publication Data Available

ISBN 1-55738-032-5

Printed in the United States of America

1   2   3   4   5   6   7   8   9   0

DEDICATION

To Margit, Ruth, Egon, Stunzi and the little one.

CONTENTS

PREFACE

A recent edition of the *Los Angeles Times* ran two seemingly unrelated articles—one on going to college and the other on hair styling. The college article had an accompanying picture of a campus with the ever present clocktower building and a troop of students crisscrossing in the foreground. The hair styling article, in contrast, highlighted its text with a series of perfectly coiffured actresses. But in spite of the different pictures being portrayed, both articles were really concerned with the identical topic—*how much do I have to pay for this*? Indeed, the cost of good grooming is assessed in the first paragraph: "Welcome to Los Angeles, city of angels and heavenly hair styles, where the $100-and-up cut has taken hold." Access to the college of your choice and its attendant price tag is equally well defined in the other opening paragraph: "The study released today by the College Board showed that average tuition and fees for 1988-89 will be $156 at four-year public colleges and universities, an increase of 5% from the previous year. Students at four-year private schools will pay $7,693, a hike of 9%." Price, or the cost to obtain a good or service, is truly one of the most pervasive concepts in our culture. From hair cuts to higher education, from the cost to obtain an illegal drug in a back alley to the cost attached to a blue-chip stock on Wall Street, the value of a commodity is defined in terms of its price.

In addition to its pervasiveness, price also has another interesting characteristic; it has distinctly different meanings. From a *consumer's point of view*, a purchase decision is based on the perceived value of the product or service, or what he or she is willing to "give up." Because value is subjectively perceived by users, it is likely that individual consumers will perceive different values in the same product or service. Such perceptual differences are the

vii

economic rationale for price differentials. The act of pricing, from the *seller's point of view*, is an attempt to put a number on value. But there are differences here as well. Sellers view price in several different ways: as expected revenues; as an accumulation of costs; and as a marketing feature (in the same regard as advertising or a distribution channel). Different sellers, therefore, can establish different prices for essentially the same product based on their own order of priorities, perspectives and competing objectives. Price, therefore, has two dominant qualities in a modern society—universality and multiformity. It is at once both ubiquitous and has multiple meanings and forms.

Given such Medusa-like qualities, it is only appropriate that this book take an equally diverse approach to pricing. Within an organization the pricing decision can be viewed as a single beam of light striking a prism. While the decision itself is essentially straightforward, the refraction of light by the prism presents myriad interpretations and perspectives. Many individuals within an organization see the impact of price in unique ways. A corporate accountant is concerned that the price of a good or service covers the costs associated with producing it and returns a fair profit. A marketing researcher views the pricing decision in terms of his or her understanding of consumer price points. Salesmen are interested in price as a strong selling proposition while a manufacturing engineer often sees pricing as a constraint that limits design features and materials. The corporate executive, of course, has still another perspective—usually focusing on the relationship of price to a more comprehensive business strategy. Each individual has a stake in pricing and each is directly affected by the results of pricing decisions.

In order to reflect these diverse viewpoints a broad spectrum of authors contribute their unique expertise to the discussion of pricing in the following pages. Practitioners from various levels of organizational responsibilities discuss the pricing decision from their own corporate vistas. From a pricing manager to a vice president of marketing, the scenery is presented according to the demands of the position. Consultants in both marketing research and management strategy also contribute their expertise to this book. Being intimately involved with a broad array of pricing problems, each consultant/author brings his or her own battle record, biases and beliefs into their writing. And finally, academics have the perspective and objectivity to survey a broader landscape. The academic authors offer powerful generalizations that transcend specific situations and industries. This mix of authors and their experiences provide the prism of views that make this book so useful for anyone involved in *the pricing decision.*

The book is divided into two sections: *Price Planning* and *Price Strategies.* The eight chapters that are contained in Section I focus on general issues that are generic to an organized approach to price decision-making. As such, the topics that are discussed, from cost accounting and legal issues to business strategies, have broad applicability across virtually all organizations and situations. Section II contains ten chapters. In contrast to the initial section, however, these chapters develop a more precise understanding of pricing within the context of specific organizations. The authors use actual case examples within designated industries to illustrate pricing strategies for both products and services—from electronics and pharmaceuticals to hotels and the performing arts.

Chapter One, "A Strategic Approach to Price Planning," presents an expansive framework for the decision maker. The approach is to argue that pricing is a series of decisions that, if properly conducted, proceed from the general to the specific. The process begins with a definitive choice of target markets for the product or service. Each of the remaining five stages tends to further limit the pricing band until the decision maker is required to make a narrow tactical choice among the remaining price points. The approach that is enumerated in the lead chapter sets a context for all pricing planning decisions.

"Using Pricing as a Strategic Weapon," by Andrew A. Stern of Booz, Allen & Hamilton, is the title of Chapter Two. This pivotal chapter details the critically important link between pricing and an organization's more general business strategy. The primary notion is that strategic pricing can be one of a business' most potent competitive weapons, but that pricing is often not fully integrated into a comprehensive strategic planning process. Four key steps are enumerated to realizing the benefits of strategic price planning.

Chapter Three, "The Economics of Price: Measuring Elasticities," by John Morton of Total Research Corporation, directly addresses the dynamics of the marketplace. The relative influence of price increases and decreases by a company and its competitors on revenues is one of the most difficult questions that marketing executives face. This chapter reviews the problems inherent in measuring the affect of price changes and describes a series of behavioral models that have proven useful in many business situations.

Chapter Four, by J. Stanton McGroarty of Ingersoll Engineers Incorporated, is titled "The Power of Functional Costing in the Pricing Decision." This chapter also takes a strategic approach to pricing. The premise that drives the chapter is that traditional approaches to the development of cost information are so riddled with assumptions and difficulties as to make the resulting data virtually useless to the pricing decision-maker. Functional costing methods are presented as an alternative.

"Consumer Behavior Foundations for Pricing," Chapter Five, is authored by Jerry N. Conover of Northern Arizona University. In this chapter the author argues that an understanding of the factors influencing consumer responses to price is essential for effective management of pricing strategies. The chapter outlines an information processing view of consumer behavior and provides a detailed discussion of several of the most important areas involved in developing a strong consumer or demand perspective.

Chapter Six, "Legal Considerations in Pricing Decisions: 'Predatory Pricing,'" approaches price planning from still another perspective. Kevin J. O'Connor of the Wisconsin Department of Justice focuses on the legal restraints on pricing policies of the individual firm. Of specific importance is the inclusion of a thorough enumeration of guidelines useful in the avoidance of lawsuits directed at aggressive pricing and promotional campaigns.

William H. Redmond of Bowling Green University is the author of Chapter Seven—"Analyzing an Industry: Price Levels, Price Structures and Price Changes." This chapter looks at the pricing decision from a competitive viewpoint. The goal of the chapter is to achieve better price planning through a more informed understanding of the current and future competitive environment.

The means to this goal, as outlined in the chapter, is a systematic evaluation of competitive prices along with guidelines for making sense of "why the competitors do what they do."

Chapter Eight, "Pricing Analysis Using Spreadsheets," contributed by Michael V. Laric of the University of Baltimore and ECOMARES International Ltd., reviews the benefits of using computers and spreadsheets for pricing analyses. In addition, a series of a specific models for doing cost-based breakeven analysis, quantity discounts, experience curve pricing and other analyses are fully enumerated and explained. In contrast to the more general chapters in the section, this chapter presents the reader with an overview of some of the specific computational tools that are useful in price planning.

The initial chapter of the *Price Strategies* section of the book, "Creative Pricing of Products and Services: Principles, Analysis and Applications" written by Gerard J. Tellis of the University of Iowa, is a comprehensive review of pricing strategies. The strategies are presented in Chapter Nine in comparable terms, emphasizing the principles underlying each and demonstrating the relationship among the strategies, the circumstances in which each can be used, and the legal and policy implications of each. Specific examples are developed to elaborate on the strategies and their application. This chapter is particularly important to the reader because it offers a unifying classification of pricing strategies.

Chapter Ten, "Implementing Proactive Pricing: Navistar International Corporation," is contributed by Steven R. Hyde of Navistar International. This chapter details a situation in which fundamental changes in Navistar's core business of medium and heavy duty trucks required the company to transform its corporate strategy. As part of that new strategy, Navistar needed to develop a way to manage a transaction-based pricing approach to market share and profit margin objectives. The implementation of transaction-based pricing, and the fundamental changes required in Navistar's organization and information systems, form the basis for a proactive approach to pricing.

The following chapter, Chapter Eleven, is authored by Margaret Shaw of the University of Massachusetts, Amherst and William H. Heck of Hotels of Distinction. "Managing Demand and

Adjusting Inventory: Pricing Strategies in the Hotel Industry" is a critical examination of pricing as a function of supply and demand. Specifically, the authors review the pragmatic problems of using the price variable to respond to a volatile demand when faced with a set supply (of rooms). Throughout the chapter, specific case examples are drawn from hotels in the Boston marketplace.

"Pricing, Product Differentiation and the Dominant Firm: Borden's ReaLemon Foods," Chapter Twelve, is contributed by David I. Rosenbaum and Phil Hall of the University of Nebraska, Lincoln. This chapter describes how one leading firm used a promotional pricing strategy designed to maintain market dominance. The economic model that is provided details the effects that product differentiation and promotional pricing can have under particular industry conditions.

Chapter Thirteen, "Small Business, Big Opportunity: Developing a Successful Pricing Strategy," is written by Matthew W. Pierson of CYPLEX, a manufacturer of communication devices used in automation systems. While many of the chapters use mid- to large-sized firms as examples, this chapter involves a discussion of pricing strategies available to smaller manufacturing companies. A number of case studies are developed in the chapter in order to describe in detail the unique problems and opportunities faced by these companies.

The author of Chapter Fourteen, Oliver Chamberlain of the Center for the Performing Arts at the University of Lowell, provides a stark transition from manufacturing in "Pricing the Performing Arts." This chapter discusses the considerations of cost, demand and competition and their application to pricing the performing arts. The results of a survey of arts administrators are presented, as well as a systematic approach to integrating pricing information, decisions and communication actions into the financial and marketing management systems of arts organizations.

Chapter Fifteen, "Pharmaceutical Pricing: Strategies in a Regulated Industry" by Jane Osterhaus of Glaxo Inc., reviews a somewhat different consumer product—prescription pharmaceuticals. In this situation the ultimate consumer does not decide what drug to take, a physician prescribes it. This relationship, coupled with the fact that the drug industry is highly regulated, creates a unique environment in which to make pricing decisions.

"Pricing in Smaller Service Firms: Cassette World Inc.," Chapter Sixteen, is contributed by John Y. Lee of California State University, Los Angeles. This chapter is concerned with the unique pricing problems of smaller service firms. In particular, the chapter details the difficulties associated with conventional cost accounting systems as the basis for price-setting. A case study is used to explore methods for generating reliable cost information and allocating indirect costs.

Chapter Seventeen, by Deborah Ferro of L'oreal, "Pricing in Today's Hair Care Industry: Who's in Charge?," is an interesting look at the dynamics involved in consumer product pricing. With the shift toward national retail chains the power to control prices in the channel has shifted away from manufacturers. In order for manufacturers to compete effectively they must approach the price decision in a new way. This chapter enumerates a three-stage methodology for developing a strategic pricing effort in a highly competitive environment.

The final chapter in the book, Chapter Eighteen, "Pricing in the New Hospital Marketplace," is authored by Jack Zwanziger of the Rand Corporation. One of the most dynamic environments today is the hospital and health care industry. This chapter explores how a changing market can demand major shifts in pricing strategies. Specifically, three case stories (a university hospital, a community hospital, and a rural hospital) are used to integrate a discussion of pricing hospital services.

Any introductory textbook on marketing begins with an important caveat. It is always mentioned that while the functional aspects of marketing can be assigned to specific people within an organization, the success of the company is dependent upon everyone developing a market orientation. Everyone shares responsibility for the generation of a product or service that has quality features and is attractive to a targeted group of potential customers. Pricing, as one of the marketing variables, also extends beyond a single individual or unit within an organizational structure. Whether price is used to signal the value of a college education or to cover the cost of a hair stylist's time, the very nature of pricing has the broadest possible impact on the organization and its ultimate success or failure. It is this dynamic and comprehensive perspective that inspired the development of *The Pricing Decision* and it is this same perspective that makes it a unique contribution to the strategic thinking of decision makers.

Daniel T. Seymour

SECTION I

PRICE PLANNING

CHAPTER ONE

A STRATEGIC APPROACH TO PRICE PLANNING

DANIEL T. SEYMOUR

DANIEL T. SEYMOUR

Daniel T. Seymour is Visiting Scholar at the University of California, Los Angeles and the president of Seymour Associates, a market information consulting firm. In addition to having held faculty positions at the University of Rhode Island and the College of William and Mary, Dr. Seymour has also worked in the financial services industry. He is a frequent contributor to a wide variety of marketing publications and is the author of *Marketing Research: Qualitative Methods for the Marketing Professional* (Probus 1988). Dr. Seymour has a B.A. from Gettysburg College and an M.B.A. and Ph.D. from the University of Oregon.

CHAPTER ONE

There is a yin and yang to pricing. In spite of improved cost accounting procedures, more extensive market analyses, and a wealth of information technologies, a manager's pricing decision is often based upon one *passive* factor—the cost involved in producing the product or service. On the other hand, *active* discussions of pricing, especially among academics, often result in mechanical pricing formulas or comprehensive lists of factors that need to be collectively weighed before judgment can be applied. This exhaustive procedure often stretches the boundaries of common sense and reduces pricing to a herculean number-crunching task. The approaches are both underwhelming and overwhelming.

This introductory chapter takes an intermediate approach, one which entails the presentation of a planning framework that affirms the notion that price setting is not a single decision but a series of decisions that result in a continual narrowing of choices. It does not, however, attempt to devine a universal pricing model that accounts for all the complexities inherent in setting a price. The procedure offered in this chapter is rooted instead in the everyday sensibilities of the managerial decision maker—What market niche do I choose to pursue? What image am I trying to reinforce? What unique product or service attributes do I have to offer? And in that sense the goal of this chapter is quite limited: to offer a more strategic approach to price planning.

The Incline of Price

In the large scheme of things, is the decision of what to charge for a particular product or service all that important? Apparently, the answer to that question has changed over time. Twenty-five years ago a study of industrial and consumer goods manufacturers attempted to answer the question, "What are the key policies and procedures common to successful marketing management in various industries?"[1] The resulting rank ordering of marketing success factors was headed by (1) product research and development, followed by (2) sales research and sales planning, (3) management of sales personnel, (4) advertising and sales promotion, and (5) product service. "Pricing" ranked sixth in importance. A decade-long comparison of the results of the American Marketing Association's *Survey of Marketing Research*, however, illustrates the change in the price variable over a relatively short span of time. In 1973 the survey of the research activities of all respondent companies indicated that 56 percent were doing pricing studies, including a 70 percent rate for consumer companies.[2] The 1983 survey indicated that 83 percent of the companies were engaged in pricing studies while the consumer company rate had risen to 91 percent.[3] This steady incline of price as a decision variable is reinforced by a recent (1987) national survey report that ranks pricing first among marketing executive "pressure points."[4] There seems to be little doubt that pricing and price competition has become a leading cause of ulcers among industry decision-makers.

But while the incidence of pressure, pain, and discomfort has risen sharply, there is scarce evidence to suggest that a broad set of remedies has emerged. For example, almost fifty years ago the authors of a historic study of corporate strategy found that cost-plus pricing was used by about 80 percent of their sample.[5] In spite of the fact that the intervening years have seen countless references made to the fact that cost-plus pricing pays insufficient attention to environmental dynamics, it remains the predominant price-setting methodology. There is even some reason to suggest that as the environment becomes more complex and more dynamic, reliance on cost-plus pricing has become even greater. A recent study of pricing methods found that 92 percent of the sample used cost- plus pricing either some or all of the time.[6] In order to ascertain why cost-plus pricing has remained so entrenched, the authors of the study asked the cost-plus users in the sample to consider a list of factors that would explain their firm's use of the method. The notion that it was the "most profitable technique" ranked eighth as a reason for its use. Such reasons as "less expensive," "periods of price stability," "industry standard," and "simplicity" all received considerably more attention. Interestingly, in spite of an era in which pricing has taken on greater importance, practitioners appear to be relying to a great degree on an approach that ignores competitors' prices and customer perceptions of the product or service's value.

A pricing system that is based upon ease of implementation, for example, not only endangers profitability but also puts the continuing existence of the organization at risk. The rise and fall of one of *INC.'s* 1984 list of the 500 fastest-growing companies is illustrative.

Contextural Design was formed in the fall of 1977 by four partners, all in their twenties, in North Carolina. The company designed and manufactured furniture—a line of unfinished components which were then shipped to some 800 furniture-in-parts outlets throughout the country. The foursome struck upon a strong combination of good product quality and lower price levels as the key to success. The designing and crafting of their own parts would enable them to control not only materials and manufacturing costs, but the quality and integrity of the products as well. The pricing formula—direct labor and raw materials multiplied by two—was used because it would not only take care of overhead but return a comfortable net profit as well. The result led to a credible wholesale price, and for five years, the straightforward arithmetic showed signs of working. By 1983, revenues were compounding so briskly that the corporation placed #177 on *INC.'s* 1984 listing of the country's 500 fastest-growing private companies.

Retail sales kept the partners busy moving furniture onto the shipping dock, and a New York city financial firm was factoring—or purchasing accounts receivable at a discount—Contextural Design's mushrooming receivables, thereby producing a significant cash flow. But by the end of 1984 it became obvious that something was wrong. In spite of the fact that sales had increased to almost $2.5 million, payables of almost one-half million were still on the books but receivables were low because the funds had already been advanced by the factor. The next interim report, six months into fiscal '85, revealed a continuing slide. Again, sales were up by almost 20 percent but there was a loss of about 6 percent with payables still escalating. Lumber brokers began to push for their payments and the factoring company trimmed Contextural Design's line of credit to zero. The company struggled to stay in business for almost one more year before being forced to sell its assets to another furniture design company.

While financing rapid growth through borrowing on receivables had concealed the severity of the difficulties facing the company, the plain fact was that true costs exceeded sales revenue. One Coopers & Lybrand report indicated early in 1983 that the actual labor costs, overhead allocation, and materials costs were all underestimated. For example, the company should have calculated the allocation to overhead at $1.50 for every $1.00 of actual labor as opposed to its being virtually ignored in their original pricing formula. But perhaps even more revealing was the fact that a modest five percent price increase in 1983 might have saved the company. The partners, however, were fearful that their untested market wouldn't support a price hike and that it would cut volume. In fact, after the demise of Contextural Designs one of the partners observed that while the seat-the-pants bookkeeping failed to raise the necessary warning flags, the real problem was pricing. "There never was a market analysis of price, never any consideration of what the market would bear. That's what was so crazy."[7]

A more comprehensive approach to pricing is advocated in this chapter. This advocacy is based upon the belief that the strategic value of the pricing decision has increased in recent years due to market segmentation, product differentiation and environmental factors. Specifically, the realization that different market segments have different price elasticities has helped to fuel the fragmentation of markets. Early on the airline industry learned that they could not survive by treating all their customers the same. Were every traveler required to purchase first class service at a premium price, they would soon be suffering for lack of customers. Were every traveler charged a discount rate, their planes would be full but they would be suffering from lack of revenues. As these different segments emerge and evolve, companies need to be aware of how they respond to various price levels.

The obvious complement to market segmentation is product differentiation. As segments are identified, companies hasten to modify their current product or service accordingly. A different set of attributes or features is offered, thereby creating a product line—as opposed to a single brand. The strategic value of pricing has also increased due to the fact that the price established for one product affects not only the demand for that product, but also the demand for other products offered by the same organization. Product line pricing, therefore, requires that companies need to understand not only the isolated relationship between a product and a market segment but also the more comprehensive relationships of different products over a broad range of segments.

The increased strategic value of pricing can also be attributed to a more hostile and turbulent environment. In general, the significance of price has been enhanced by the need to react to rising costs, unstable domestic and world demand, intense home and foreign competition, fluctuating currency values and interest rates, and governmental regulations. As such unpredictability increases, the value of price as a strategic weapon increases as well, since it can be adjusted more quickly and more easily than product, promotion or distribution modifications.

Finally, in the midst of all this change it must be remembered that the most basic strategic value of price has not changed at all. While managers can squeeze out more production efficiency, develop new product concepts, negotiate more favorable distribution channels, and create more effective advertisements, price remains the only variable that directly generates revenue, all others being cost creation variables. And as the partners in Contextural Design eventually realized, the strategic value of the revenue generation potential of price can often be the difference between success and failure.

The Positioning of Price

Problem solving is confusing and, as such, the tendency is to minimize confusion by latching on to the first best solution. The price decision is problem solving at its "messiest." And consequently, it is one of the most difficult choices that management is called upon to make. It follows, then, that the complexity of the problem often leads to simplification—for example, the reliance on cost-plus pricing procedures. The dominant cause of this complexity in pricing is the strong interaction of a host of internal and external factors. These factors often push and pull "price" in many contradictory directions. For instance, while the cost to produce a product plus a satisfactory profit margin could result in a fairly low price, the unique product features may suggest a considerably higher price. Or perhaps the image of a company is such that a premium price for its products is expected, yet several strong retailers refuse to stock the product unless it can be brought in at a much lower price point. Another situation may call for the introduction of a new product with a penetration price, but it is feared that in a highly competitive industry such a strategy may be the first salvo in a price war among competitors. Figure 1 presents a simplified planning framework that captures these interrelationships.

The basic thrust of the planning framework is that management should choose a price that is consistent with the overall positioning of the product or service. The six stages of the product/service position represents a sequential set of decisions that act to frame or limit choices. From the designation of a market niche to the establishment of a specific price, each stage is the logical antecedent of the next. For example, the ability to create a favorable brand image does not occur in a vacuum. It is dependent upon previous knowledge of a market niche and those qualities and cues which signal "value" to that segment of the market. Each subsequent stage acts to further qualify the price decision and, consequently, enables decision-makers to focus their attention on a more manageable set of pricing options. The resulting sequential analysis, modified by cost-related factors, anticipated competitive reactions, prevalent channel trade practices and legal considerations, creates a broad strategic context for the

Figure 1

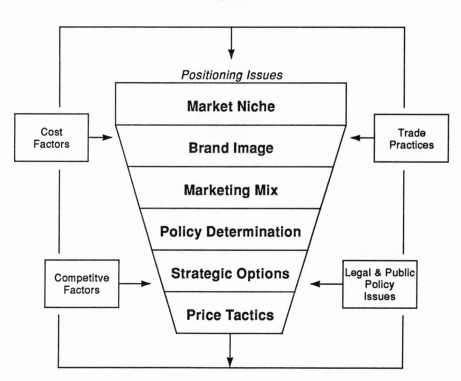

pricing decision. The remainder of this chapter offers specific examples and explanations of this multi-stage approach to pricing.

Market Niche

The initial and most fundamental pricing decision that management must make is which market segment it will attempt to cultivate. Such descriptors as demographics, geographics, socio-economic variables, life style, and family life cycle have been regularly used by marketers to label consumer segments with a unique set of needs and wants. These needs and wants are satisfied on the basis of value—a subjective interpretation of what a product or service is worth to the consumer. The company or producer, in turn, attempts to place a more objective measure of value on the product or service; that is, the price. Because value is subjectively perceived by users, it is likely that they will perceive different values in the same product. And it follows that different groups, or segments, will place different values on the same product—some will see the stated price as too expensive or too cheap, or just about right. The perceived product value depends on what consumers expect to achieve from the purchase, as compared to what can be achieved by purchasing an alternative product, or by not purchasing at all. Such perceptual differences form the basis for both product and price differentiation. Successful companies differentiate their products and services from the competition in order to allow customers to see the value of the stated price—*because price really comes down to what a consumer is willing to pay.*

Given the matching of a market segment or niche with a specific product or service, the question remains as to what consumers are willing to "give" in order to get the product or service. There is strong evidence, both intuitive and empirical, to suggest that the "give" falls into a range that has both upper and lower limits. The upper limit represents the maximum expenditure a consumer is willing to make. A product or service that exceeds this price is excluded from consideration based solely upon the price. The presence of an upper limit follows from consumer research that has verified the existence of non-compensatory decision rules. While many consumer choices involve compensation—the willingness to pay more or less depending upon the product features—there is a point at which no amount of additional or distinctive product features can compensate for its excessively high price: too much would have to be given. The lower limit is a minimum threshold. Price is often used as a cue to infer the value of different product attributes. As such, there exists a lower limit that reflects the cue properties of price. Specifically, a product that is very cheap "must have something wrong with it."

The resulting price band sets an initial broad spectrum of pricing freedom. One way to represent this price band is as a normal frequency distribution curve—order frequency plotted against price. At the upper limit and lower limit of the price band the unit sales are significantly less than they are at the median price point. The ice cream industry provides a simple illustration of how the price band (normal frequency distribution) can vary between market segments (Figure 2).

In the case of the generic ice cream product, the equivalent of a commodity, the consumer price band is extremely narrow—plus or minus two or three cents per serving. But in the speciality segments the price band widens to plus or minus 10 cents a serving. This range of prices depends partly on the way consumers perceive the relative value of different brands of ice cream that are sold in that segment and partly on the competitive intensity in each segment.

The distinctiveness of these price bands is a very real phenomenon. It is something that concerns marketers as they try to develop unique product benefits in order to expand the range and hence increase their degree of pricing freedom. Recent attempts to establish a second tier in the soft drink category illustrates the connection between market segments, product features, and price bands.

> The addition of juice to soft drinks has effectively sparked sales in a consumer marketplace that has a significant "health and fitness" segment. But along with boosting sales, the added juice has also resulted in higher concentration and production costs for bottlers. Given the double-edged sword of consumer acceptance and higher production costs, it is in-

Figure 2

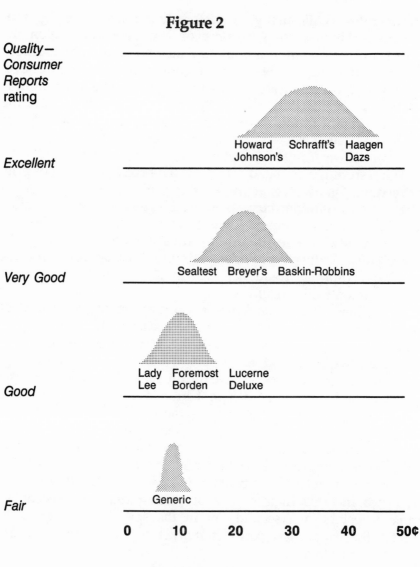

Quality—
Consumer
Reports
rating

Excellent

Very Good

Good

Fair

Consumer Price—Cents per 4-ounce serving

evitable that bottlers attempt to establish a two-tier market. General Cinema Corporation (GCC), a bottler of Slice first introduced their 10 percent juice-added formula at a standard rate—and in some cases even discounting off of that rate to encourage trial. This reinforced an already ingrained expectation among shoppers about paying one across-the-board price for regular, diet—and now juice-added—soft drinks.

But GCC believes that the consumer will pay a premium for their products. The president of GCC, Robert Tarr, identified the added value of juice-added soft drinks as the major factor behind his company's move to two-tier—"A 10-cent to 15-cent premium per retail purchase unit should not discourage consumption. As a matter of fact, it may even reinforce the products' deserved quality image, resulting in the margin relief necessary to properly service them in the market." Others, however, see the 10 percent formulation as being merely cosmetic, and that higher juice percentages are necessary to parlay health benefits into a higher retail price. One franchise company executive explains, "When you start getting into the higher percentages of juice, then the added value might be there. There are a lot of people who feel that you have to get to the 50 percent and over level before the consumer says, 'Now I'm drinking something that's really good for me'."[10]

General Cinema Corporation, by pursuing a more health- and fitness-oriented segment, is attempting to broaden a price band. When a company has specific knowledge regarding market segments and why consumers buy, it can begin to manipulate product features, advertising, image, and other variables in order to define more sharply its pricing options.

Brand Image

Once a submarket or niche has been defined by management, it must begin to establish the means by which the markets will be cultivated. The most general idea that a consumer has about a product or service is the rather vague notion of image. This "impression" represents a feeling or a perception that is not solely grounded in specific product attributes. It is a culmination of broad experiences that results in a basic belief. Management's selection of its company and brand image should be dictated by the types of customers it is trying to attract. Submarkets, therefore, may be likened to targets at which the seller is firing, and "images" are powerful weapons that can be used to create favorable attitudes and opinions. It should also be noted that the mere size of the weapon is secondary to the aim. A recent survey of 1,000 consumers by Landor Associates, an image and design consulting firm, found that the most famous brands aren't necessarily the most favored.[11] When consumers were asked how highly they regarded brands, Playboy, Greyhound and Weight Watchers all placed in the bottom 70 in a list of over 600 names. The high-profile/low-esteem gap is especially a problem for cars (Volkswagen and Pontiac) and fast-food restaurants (Dairy Queen and Taco Bell). In contrast, some brands are blessed with powerful images—both high recognition and high esteem. The top brands include, Campbell, AT&T, McDonald's, American Express, Kellogg and IBM.

Much of our approach to the marketing of goods and services is based upon the mistaken notion that consumers engage in comprehensive problem solving—they gather appropriate information and make comparisons among different brands. The problem is that today's real-world consumer usually doesn't suffer from lack of information concerning purchase alternatives, but rather is overwhelmed with choices. This information overload often results in various types of simplification strategies. For example, brand loyalty is based upon a belief system that is built up around a brand by a consumer. When the consumer is faced with a choice situation, the belief that the product or service has a strong reputation or has performed well in the past will tend to limit information-gathering on alternative choices. Such strong images can even go well beyond the immediate product or service to include an extended product line. For example, it was noted in the Landor image survey that brands such as RollsRoyce, Hilton and Cadbury have positive images but suffer from low visibility. In these instances it was suggested that such names (images) might be ripe for extension to other products—Rolls-Royce watches, perhaps, or Hilton sportswear.

Given a specific market niche, therefore, brand image acts to place the product or service within a price band. This is because external stimuli such as price exert only indirect effects, not direct effects, upon behavior. The external stimuli is modified as a raw unit of information as it is encoded by the consumer. In our case, a price stimulus is encoded as a psychological price, and then integrated with other information. Purchase, the behavioral act, is not based upon the external price but rather the internal, psychological price after encoding and integration. For example, an external price of $150 for a hotel room may be assigned a meaning of "expensive" when being encoded. But when that psychological price is integrated with other information, in this case the reputation and esteem of Hilton, it may very well result in purchase behavior. Brand image, therefore, influences the effective placement of a product or service within a price band.

From a deluxe hotel to a bag of onions, the role of brand image in pricing is a critical factor, one that must be carefully planned and effectively implemented:

Art Caston and his fellow Imperial Valley farmers knew they were getting a raw deal. Onion growers in Georgia were regularly pulling in $25 and more a bag for their sweet onions, but Californians were selling theirs for break-even prices of $4.50. Somehow, the Georgia growers and their cronies in Texas, Washington and even Hawaii had convinced the public into thinking that their onions were different. But Caston knew better. Believing their onions were as sweet as anyone's, they gathered a group of esteemed food critics at Charlie's restaurant in El Centro and held their first annual sweet onion challenge in 1985. When Imperial Valley sweet onions won and were declared the best onions in the country, the losers cried foul and demanded a rematch. So in 1986, onion aficionados fought it out in McAllen, Texas, home to the famous Texas 1015 sweet onion. Again, Imperial's sweet onion came out number one.

Able to claim the best sweet onion on the market, the Californians formed the Imperial Valley Sweet Onion Commission, established quality standards, developed a label, created a marketing strategy and set their sights on the top-dollar Vidalia sweet onion market. During the 1987 season, as bad weather conditions cut into the supply of Texas and Georgia onions, Imperial Valley sweet onions sold for $15 per 50-pound bag, the highest price ever in the short, sweet history of the commission. "They're not too happy with us back in Vidalia, Georgia," chuckles Caston. "But, heck, for years we've produced wonderful, sweet onions. The problem was, nobody knew about them. Now we've got some name recognition and an identity. It just shows that there's more to farming than growing a good crop."[12]

Imperial Valley sweet onions serve to reinforce a notion that has been confirmed in numerous pricing studies: the development of a unique brand identity instills loyalty in consumers and lowers price sensitivity. As such, brand image helps define the price range within which a company can successfully price its products or services.

Marketing Mix

Our initial emphasis in this price planning framework has been on how market niche and brand image decisions influence two price limits—the upper limit above which the product is judged to be "too dear" and the lower limit below which the quality of the product is inferred to be suspect. But the fact is that most consumers do not choose to purchase a product or service solely on the basis of price. Price, therefore, is an evaluative criterion in the same sense as are product features. It is also true that producers or manufacturers have choices as to the role and relationship that price should play in their offerings to the marketplace. The price question is one of many: How heavily do I advertise? What product attributes do I feature? How many salesmen do I maintain? How extensively should I distribute the product? People Express, for example, relied on price as its lead variable—almost to the exclusion of the other marketing variables:

> In the aftermath of deregulation, People Express' emphasis on low price broadened the air traveler market. But a large portion of People Express customer base also reflected the nature of the role price played in the company's strategy. The "discount" airline's customers, consequently, were almost solely rate- driven. While rates that were often less than half of the competition's drew attention, other standard service variables were unbundled—cold meals ($6), soft drinks (50¢) and luggage handling ($3 per bag). As losses mounted to $130 million in the first half of 1986, the company continued to use a price appeal to boost traffic by cutting fares still further. After having been acquired by Texas Air Corporation, People Express was folded into Continental and its planes painted Continental's colors. Without discount fares there was no reason for People Express to maintain its identity since its customers evaporated quickly. As one former executive pointed out, People Express disappeared because, "Analysis said no consumer loyalty is left to exploit."[13]

The degree to which a firm choses to emphasize price *vis a' vis* other controllable variables such as advertising and promotion, brand features or a distribution network, is dependent upon a number of factors—for instance, the life cycle stage of the product or service. The relative importance of marketing activities and their relationship to one another tends to shift as a product moves from its introductory stage to growth, maturity and then decline. In the introductory stage of a product or service the price variable is extremely important. Since a new product almost always enjoys its greatest degree of differentiation in its introductory stage, demand is usually more price inelastic than at any other stage. Also, costs are high due to relatively low output rates and greater margins are required to support heavy promotional expenditures. The two dominant pricing strategies for introducing a new product are skim pricing and penetration pricing. A skimming strategy takes advantage of the lack of price sensitivity by attracting the innovators at the top of the product's demand curve and it assumes that additional layers of customers can be peeled off one at a time. After those who are willing to pay an initial high price have bought, price can be lowered to appeal to the next layer. If, in contrast, management believes that the segment of customer willing to pay a premium price is too limited, a penetration price may be adopted. A lower price may enable the company to attract a large volume of customers quickly, which could lead to declining unit production and distribution costs. In addition to the price variable, the promotion variable is at its highest ratio to sales in the introductory stage. A high level of promotional effort is required to inform potential customers of the new product or service, to induce trial of the product, and to secure initial distribution. Relative to price and promotion, the product mix and level of distribution activity tends to be limited in the introductory stage. There is usually only one basic model and the distribution is selective.

If the new product satisfies the market's needs, sales will climb as early adopters are replaced by broader segments of the target market. This growth stage is characterized by a shift in marketing activities. For instance, while the level of promotion activity may remain the same, the emphasis usually shifts from building awareness to persuasive advertising. Price skimmers will also be ready to shift to lower prices in order to attract the next layer of price-sensitive buyers into the market. The real emphasis in the growth stage, however, shifts away from price and promotion to a concerted effort to improve product quality, add product features and models, and develop new distribution channels to gain additional product exposure. The maturity stage, when sales growth has slowed and competition is at its highest, witnesses another shift in the relationship of the variables. In general, the price levels begin to fall into an industry price structure with price leaders and price followers. Promotion dollars are often shifted to the distribution channel to maintain favorable considerations and the advertising emphasis is competitive in nature. A full product line is in place. Finally, the decline stage usually results in a gradual retreat from the marketplace—the number of product offerings is reduced, the promotion budget is reduced and the company withdraws from smaller market segments and marginal distribution channels. An attempt is usually made to maintain price levels while reducing other costs in order to squeeze out as much profitability as possible.

While market niches and brand images set broad pricing parameters, the market mix decisions result in a series of well-defined interdependencies. In fact, one useful example of this was recently born out of the demise of People Express. Another company, one that we have already seen as suffering from high-profile/low-esteem, saw an opportunity to restage a service that was in decline:

> When People Express died, Fred G. Currey was not among the mourners. In fact, the demise of the no-frills, discount airline in December, 1986, was welcome news to the head of the investment group, GLI Holding Company, who had the month before purchased all of Greyhound Corporation's money-losing bus operations. The Greyhound Corporation had spent years managing decline—selling off vehicles, discounting routes and systematically raising prices. In effect, they had been liquidating the business. The new owners went to work within hours after they acquired the bus line. "First, we lowered prices substantially," Currey recalled—about 10% overall and as much as 40% and 50% in many markets. "Then we went to work immediately, simply saying 'We're back in business.' People had lost confidence in the bus as a primary means of transportation."
>
> Research indicated that passengers required a simple formula—clean and safe terminals, a clean and safe ride and a destination reached on time. And they are interested in price. Long-neglected terminals are being cleaned up and moved out of the worst parts of the cities so travelers will feel safer. Added to the $50 million terminal refurbishing is a $30 million 1988 addition of 150 new buses and upgrade of older buses. Also, a new hub-and-spoke system is being installed. The "rural connection" is an effort to restore bus service to many smaller communities by contracting with independent, passenger van operators (using the running Greyhound sym-

bol) to be used as feeders. The Greyhound plan is one that uses service value, and a revolutionary (as far as ground transportation) distribution system to reconnect rural and urban America.[14]

By taking a comprehensive view of the marketing variables, it becomes evident that the pricing decision must be approached from an integrative perspective; that is, its role and relationship are dependent upon a broader set of marketing variables that change over time.

Policy Determination

Pricing policies are rules to be observed under standard conditions. As such they make price setting more structured by minimizing *ad hoc* situations. Also, the policies that are developed tend to further limit or "bracket" the number of price alternatives that a price setter reasonably considers. As one proceeds from the market niche to brand image to the marketing mix, the range of choices continually narrows. And since every company has its own unique mix of customers, competitive forces, product or service strengths, and corporate objectives, it follows that pricing policies should be company specific. Table 1 offers a broad set of pricing policy examples.

While Table 1 is not an exhaustive listing of pricing policies, it does illustrate how policy-making further limits the choice process. A more detailed case example can be used to provide an applied perspective to the notion of pricing policy:

> The president of a fast growing chain of restaurants paid close attention to price. During the late 1970s, when inflation was high, his staff checked prices and costs every week. If margins dropped to a certain level, the president immediately repriced and reprinted the menus. At times he reprinted menus every six weeks. "What about your competitors?" the president had been asked. "Don't they worry you?" His reply: "No, for three reasons. First, no one controls costs better than we do. So

Table 1 Pricing Policies

Alternative Price Level

1. Same as the competition.
2. Lower than the competition.
3. Higher than the competition.

Alternative Price Flexibility

1. Single Price: all buyers pay one price, regardless of the quantity.
2. Quantity Price: the price may vary with quantity, but all buyers of one quantity pay the same price.
3. Flexible Price: different buyers of one quantity may pay different prices.

Alternative Price Changes

1. Frequent cost increases are immediately passed along to buyers.
2. Infrequent smaller cost increases are absorbed with cost increases being passed along in cumulative fashion.

Alternative Discounts and Allowances

1. Trade or Functional Discounts: for buyers who resell the product.
2. Cash Discounts: to buyers who pay within a specified time period.
3. Seasonal Discounts: to buyers who purchase during the off-season.
4. Advertising Allowances: to resellers for advertising the product.

Alternative Transportation Costs

1. FOB Pricing: adjust the price the buyer pays based on distribution costs.
2. Uniform Delivery Pricing: buyers are charged the same price regardless of the location.
3. Zone Pricing: all buyers within a geographic area pay one price.
4. Freight Absorption Pricing: meet competitive prices by absorbing part of the actual transportation costs.[15]

when we see margins slipping, we know that inflation is driving our costs up, not our own inefficiencies. Second, we have so much competition that someone is always raising prices. They've got to. Their costs are probably higher than ours. Third, we raise prices by small amounts frequently. This way, our customers don't seem to mind as much, and we maintain every little bit of margin we can."[16]

While such a pricing policy as "raising prices by small amounts frequently" can be an appropriate and successful rule, the danger in the application of some pricing policies is laziness. The policies should be used to frame the decision-making process. They should not necessarily be applied, as was done by Contextural Designs, as a means to simplify. "Direct labor and raw materials multiplied by two" was a pricing policy that guaranteed trouble. Another example is the widespread rule that is still used in the hotel industry. Room rates calculated on the basis of $1.00 per $1,000 of construction costs have been engraved in stone in spite of the fact that the ratio completely discounts market niche, brand image and marketing mix—It entirely ignores the customer and the competition—but it is simple.

Pricing policies tend to further circumscribe the pricing decision. As such, they are useful devices within the context of a price planning effort. While they cannot and should not be looked upon as an easy way to mechanize a solution to a messy problem, they can improve a firm's competitiveness and profitability when used in conjunction with other planning tools.

Strategic Options

It is not always easy to distinquish between policies and strategies. Perhaps the most basic distinction is that policies are usually formulated to deal with recurring situations—our restauranteur's "price change" policy took effect on a periodic basis (in this case when food costs increased). Strategies, in contrast, tend to be broad-sweeping action steps that are used by management to achieve an objective. But while the list of strategies currently being used by firms is extensive, in all likelihood the firm will be limited in its choices by previous decisions. Market targets, image objectives, convictions regarding the relative emphasis of the marketing mix variables and specific pricing policies tend to further restrict "strategic freedom." It has been noted, for example, that different market segments place different values on the company's products or services, with price sensitivity varying accordingly. Perceived product value depends on what consumers expect to derive from a purchase, as compared to what can be derived by acquiring another product. The degree of strategic pricing freedom, therefore, depends on both the product's perceived value to the consumer (our chosen market niche) and the competitive intensity of the industry. By successfully differentiating their own products from the competitions' products via a strong brand image and unique features, a company is in the position to enable their chosen customer segment to see the value of a particular price. It follows that value and competition, among other variables, can act to further limit the range of pricing options:

- *High value, low competition*—High-value products, such as life saving pharmaceuticals that are initially patent protected, are often so precious that price is independent of sales volume. This high-involvement situation commands the greatest degree of strategic pricing freedom. Premium pricing and image pricing are among the many options available.

- *Low value, high competition*—The strategic freedom in a highly competitive commodity-type industry, such as aluminum or steel, is determined by supply and demand. Strategic choices are greatly limited with price being dependent on sales volume. Second market discounting is one common strategy.

- *High value, high competition*—For products in this category, such as hand-held computers and copier machines, price is competitively oriented. There is an intermediate degree of pricing freedom with some strategic options being limited. Price signaling and experience curve pricing are among the appropriate strategy options.

- *Low value, low competition*—This low-involvement situation containing such items as various food products (e.g., fruits and produce) also has limited price freedom. Periodic discounting is one of the relatively few strategic options available.

While previous choices regarding market segments, brand image, mix variables and pricing policies do further limit the range of pricing options, there are usually several strategies that are compatible with the firm's chosen situation. For example, price bundling is one of a number of product line pricing strategies and can be defined as the practice of marketing two or more products and/or services in a single "package" for a special price. From a managerial perspective, the rationale for bundling is based on one critical factor. The cost structure of many businesses is characterized by a high ratio of fixed to variable costs and by a high level of cost sharing—the same facilities, equipment and personnel are used to provide multiple products and services. As an illustration, many banks currently offer special programs in which customers that maintain large balances can receive free safety deposit boxes, free traveler's checks, no-annual-fee credit cards and other services. Once an individual has established a relationship with the bank on one service (the savings account), the marginal cost associated with marketing or operations associated with the other services are generally low compared to the bank's total costs. An opposing strategy is the notion of unbundling. In this instance a number of component parts to a product or service offering are separated out—the People Express strategy of charging for only those services used such as cold meals ($6) and luggage handling ($3 per bag). IBM set a trend in the computer business years ago when it unbundled hardware and software. Because of their strong ownership of operating systems and the related software, IBM's unbundled software accounted for a greater portion of IBM's profits than sales revenue. Routine, significant price hikes became one of the tools that IBM had used as it began to realize that software was capable of driving hardware sales. The automobile industry is perhaps the best example of how different pricing strategies—in this case, bundling and unbundling—relate to a firm's competitive position within an industry:

> About 20 years ago the president of General Motors boasted that the company offered so many different options for each model that is could go through the entire model year without building the same car twice. The ability to tailor-make a car to each customer's requirement has been a hallmark of the domestic automobile industry and options have been looked upon as providing the bulk of profits. A low base price, for a car with only the barest of essentials, is modified as the customer pays an additional (unbundled) price for a rear window defogger. In contrast, Japanese carmakers use bundling when they present options such as tinted windows as standard equipment. Instead of charging $50 for tinted windows, they increase the base price enough the cover the actual cost—about $3. The payoff is in incremental sales gain coupled with lower production costs—the Honda Accord is available in only 30 variations including color, compared to the tens of thousands of combinations possible for the typical domestic compact model.[17]

Strategic choices, such as price bundling and unbundling, represent a broad array of tools that can be used by management. But strategy, just like the previous stages, does not operate independently. The choice by People Express to unbundle prices closely followed its determination of a market niche and brand image. And in a similar fashion, the conscious choice of other major carriers, such as TWA and Delta, to not follow that strategy, was greatly influenced by the idea that "unbundling" would have been incompatible with its earlier decisions. In these cases, pricing strategy follows structure—the structure of previous managerial choices.

Price Tactics

The essence of the strategic price planning approach is evident in this final stage. Having applied the logic of the previous steps, the price band has been continually narrowed. That narrowing is the result of a series of sequential choices beginning with a market niche and proceeding to a pricing strategy. The final stage is the selection of a specific price. If a planning approach has been followed, the price setter finds the sums that can be charged sharply circumscribed. The result is a constricted zone that has been delimited by the prior stages of the planning process. Again, perhaps the best way to illustrate this process is by using an example of a successful product—in this case, a rather recent arrival in the wine market:

> In late 1980 Michael Benziger persuaded his father, Bruno, to buy the overgrown Glen Ellen property in Sonoma County, California. They were entering the wine industry at a time when California was brimming with more varietal wines than the existing market could consume—"There was an ocean of wi ne out there," as Michael recalled. While the Benziger family may have been new to wine production, they had a long tradition in marketing wines and spirits—the Park-Benzinger company being a New York importer of wines and spirits. By 1981 the Benzigers produced their first wines. The estate-bottled varietals were a critical success winning the top two prizes at the 1982 Sonoma County Harvest Fair. Propelled by the success of its estate wines, the family bought up thousands of gallons of unwanted varietal wine, which was blended, bottled, and retailed under the Glen Ellen Proprietor's Reserve label. The Cabernet Sauvignon and Chardonnay were brought to market at the unheard of price of $3.50 a bottle—about half the price of the cheapest Chardonnay then available.
>
> The payoff for Glen Ellen Wineries was almost instantaneous: From 6,450 cases sold in 1982, sales topped 1.5 million cases in 1987. Other wineries—including Sutter Home, Sebastiani and E & J Gallo—have since entered the market for low-priced premium wines. But Glen Ellen remains the clear leader with the company running ahead of its 1988 projection of 2.2 million cases.[18]

One of the keys to the success of Glen Ellen wine has been its strong positioning in the market. An initial observation is that people don't need to buy wine, and that there's always a price point where they will turn to something else. And the reverse, as the Benzigers knew, is also true. The market segment that they chose to pursue exhibited a great deal of price elasticity. Their image, of course, was fortified early by the success of their estate-bottled wines as they expanded into the low end of the premium market. A policy of not buying additional vineyard acreage to supply the high volume market, but instead relying on long-term leases, has been deliberate. According to Michael, "What we do best is blend, bottle and market wine. We want to stay flexible." This is especially true if one believes the Benziger's formula for setting a final price based upon their years in the importing and retail wine business—you've got to watch the price points in the market. Consumers respond to price points.

Perhaps the most important aspect of good tactical, or day-to-day, pricing is the availability and use of information. The decision maker needs to have current cost and competitive data. The information system should produce reports based on order, customer and segment profitability, not just on sales data. Once such a marketing information system is in place, the setting of a price is driven by the arithmetic of pricing—the testing and comparison of costs and revenues of the price points within the narrowed price band. The growing sophistication of computer technology has provided the means to monitor continuously costs of inputs such as labor and raw materials as well as store, sort and retrieve sales data. Finally, the availability of spreadsheet software for personal computers has made contribution and breakeven analysis standard procedure even for small businesses.

The Price is Right

The usefulness of this suggested approach to price planning is due to two related factors. First, it focuses management attention on a context for decision making. As we have noted, one of the major reasons managers use cost-plus pricing is its relative ease (this is not to minimize costs' important role in pricing). Costs are largely definable and show up in nice neat columns in various financial reports. But we have also argued that being too driven by costs may result in a decision maker overlooking other obvious considerations—e.g., the value that the market segment places on the product or service. The planning framework defines a process for dealing with the major positioning issues of how price relates to the consumer. The narrowing of the price band serves to limit choices and, as such, creates a context within which a final price is determined.

Second, in addition to developing a context for choosing, the planning framework also helps to ensure the effectiveness and correctness of a particular price. This aspect of pricing has not been discussed in this chapter, but it is a natural by-product of our extended price planning efforts. The stages that have been described are the equivalent of a six-sectioned telescope. Looking through the wrong end of the telescope provides a large-to-small view of the world. Such is the context for price planning as it has been described in this chapter—from a market niche to a specific price. When we turn the telescope around, however, we can see how the stages also provide us with a small-to-large view of the world as well. If we have paid attention to the narrowing function as we proceed along in our telescopic exercise, the broadening function will also be effective. The series of steps that provide a logical sequence for choosing a price are also the best assurance we have that the price is correct, that the strategy is appropriate, that the policies are in order and so on. Most importantly, of course, is the assurance that the chosen price will strike a responsive tone with our target market. In this instance, perhaps a final example of poor "telescoping" and an ineffective price-customer link is instructive:

> It was a sound marketing plan but for one tiny oversight: the customer. Since its introduction to the American market in 1985, the Yugo automobile has struggled to gain a foothold. At $4,500 the Yugoslavian econobox was targeted for the entry-level car buyer who could little afford the $10,000 price tag on most of today's new cars. Yugo had its market pegged accurately: 48 percent of its customers are visiting a

showroom for the first time. But sales have been disappointing. When the automobile was introduced three years ago, projections of 200,000 unit sales had been forecasted. The 1987 unit sales, however, were well under 40,000. The Yugo America management believes that two factors have been crucial in the automobile's lack of sales performance. First, a lack of in-house financing has forced shoppers to go shopping for financing and second, a lack of perceived quality has left doubt in the consumer's mind regarding value. In August of 1988, Yugo unveiled a plan for San Diego-based Imperial Savings to provide financing at Yugo dealerships and a $48 million image enhancement campaign was launched.[19]

In the case of Yugo, it is obvious that there was a discontinuity between image, marketing mix and price which may have been avoided by a more planned approach to pricing. In addition, the lack of a financing policy, given the first-time-buyer segment, also seems to have been avoidable under a more careful orientation to the pricing question. Simply, the chosen price point did not have maximum effect in the market. The price may have been right, but the positioning was wrong.

There is an old Russian proverb that suggests that there are two kinds of fools in any market—one doesn't charge enough, the other charges too much. But the seemingly simple problem of charging just the right price is one that continues to puzzle management. It remains a curious mixture of art and science, of guesswork and guile. While the planning framework offered in this chapter can hardly guarantee the elimination of foolishness, it does help us sharpen our judgment in an area of today's market that can easily spell the difference between success and failure.

Endnotes

[1] Udell, Jon G. 1964. "How Important is Pricing in Competitive Strategy?," *Journal of Marketing*; v 28, January, pp.44-48.

[2] Twedt, Dik W. 1973. *Survey of Marketing Research*, Chicago: American Marketing Association.

[3] Twedt, Dik W. 1983. *Survey of Marketing Research*, Chicago: American Marketing Association.

[4] Morton, John and Hugh J. Devine Jr. 1987. "How Prices Really Affect Your Sales," *Business Marketing*, May, pp. 90–100.

[5] Hall, R. L. and C.J. Hitch. 1939. "Price Theory and Business Behavior," *Oxford Economic Papers*, v 2, May, pp. 12–45.

[6] Shipley, David D. 1986. "Dimensions of Flexible Price Management," *The Quarterly Review of Marketing*, Spring, pp. 1–7.

[7] Mamis, Robert A. 1986. "The Price is Wrong," *INC.*, May, pp. 159–164.

[8] Adapted from Kent B. Monroe and Trdib Mazumdar. 1987. "Pricing-Decision Models: Recent Developments and Research Opportunities," in *Issues in Pricing*, pp. 361–388 and Alfred R. Oxenfeldt, 1960. "Multi-Stage Approach to Pricing," *Harvard Business Review*, July-August, pp. 125–133.

[9] Ross, Elliot B. 1984. "Making Money with Proactive Pricing," *Harvard Business Review*, 62, November-December, pp. 145–155

[10] Blair, Ian C. 1986. "A Tale of Two Tiers," *Beverage World*, July, pp. 30–31.

[11] Alsop, Ronald, 1988. "To Know a Brand is not to Love It," *The Wall Street Journal*, June 15, p. 27.

[12] Street, Richard S. 1988. "The El Centro Onion Field War," *California Business*, August, p. 11.

[13] Thomas, Paulette. 1987. "Texas Air to Combine Low-Cost Units, Agrees to Acquire Presidential's Gates," *The Wall Street Journal*, January 13, p.5.

[14] Dallos, Robert E. 1988. "On the Road Again, " *Los Angeles Times*, July 17, p. IV 1.

[15] Adapted from Stephen L. Montgomery. 1988. *Profitable Pricing Strategies*, New York: McGraw-Hill.

[16] Kyd, Charles W. 1987. "Pricing for Profit," *INC.*, April, pp. 120–122.

[17] Keller, Maryann. 1987. "Moving Toward Realistic Pricing," *Automotive Industries*, November, p. 23.

[18] Keppel, Bruce. 1988. "Glen Ellen—A Special Tast for Marketing." *Los Angeles Times*, April 6, p. IV 1.

[19] Salerno, Steve. 1988. "Is Imperial Saving Yugo?" *California Business*, November, p. 9.

Recommended for Additional Reading

Pricing Strategies by Alfred R. Oxenfeldt, New York: AMACOM, 1975.

"Price As Creative Marketing" by Thomas Nagle in *Business Horizons*, July-August, 1983.

"The Pricing Decision" In *Small Business Report*, May (Part 1) and June (Part 2), 1985.

CHAPTER TWO

USING PRICING AS A STRATEGIC WEAPON

ANDREW A. STERN

ANDREW A. STERN

Andrew A. Stern is a Vice President with Booz, Allen & Hamilton, Inc., an international management and technology consulting firm. He leads the firm's strategy practice in Chicago. His assignments focus on developing business and corporate strategies for clients in a wide range of industries, with a particular emphasis on strategic pricing. In addition to his work for clients, Mr. Stern has published articles, conducted seminars, and taught classes on strategic pricing. He is an original advisory board member of The Pricing Institute, and has chaired and made presentations at many of its conferences.

CHAPTER TWO

Pricing should be a critical element of every business' strategy. Pricing is a valuable strategic weapon which helps companies enhance and capitalize on competitive advantage, defend areas of vulnerability, and even cause beneficial changes in competitors' behavior. Carefully designed pricing strategies can have significant bottom line impact, in many instances increasing profitability by 10-20 percent.

Moreover, the benefits of improved pricing are relatively easy to realize. Compared to other strategic actions (such as asset redeployment or new product development), pricing generally requires only limited investment, is straightforward to implement, and generates rapid results. In numerous instances the success or failure of a business has hinged on the strength of its pricing strategy.

Yet, for all their importance to business success, many pricing strategies fall short. They leave money on the table because they do not adequately differentiate between price-sensitive and price-insensitive segments. They leave gaping holes of competitive vulnerability because they average prices across areas of differing competitive advantage. They do not capitalize on opportunities to affect customer and competitor responses. And most critically, they do not adequately support the business' strategy. In fact, many businesses are more tactical than strategic in their pricing. They continue to view pricing exclusively as a revenue-generating mechanism rather than as a key strategic tool.

Successful strategic pricing enables a business to unlock the potential of its resources and competitive position. Strategic pricing can:

- Increase revenue realization without sacrificing volume.
- Alter customer buying behavior to the business' advantage.

35

- Enable a selective response to the competitive environment.
- Increase profitability and long term business value.

The shift from tactical to strategic pricing is not difficult to accomplish. The first step requires an attitude change. Managers must view pricing as a strategic tool and pricing strategy development as an integral part of business strategy development. With that view as a starting point, there are four key steps to realizing the benefits of strategic pricing (see Figure 1).

Figure 1   The Keys to Strategic Pricing

- Link pricing strategy directly to business strategy.
- Develop differentiating price structures to support explicit pricing objectives.
- Establish price levels that take market and competitor responses into account.
- Support pricing with focused implementation programs.

Link Pricing Strategy to Business Strategy

Pricing can support business strategy only if its role is clearly defined. Take for example the case of an industrial products distributor with a strong position in its core product line. The company intended to grow its business by expanding the number of lines it distributed. It believed that it could gain an advantage over competing distributors by combining shipments of multiple products to individual customers. Combined shipments would enable the company to improve service levels (smaller volumes of individual products shipped more frequently) at lower cost than competitors who could not baseload shipments with the core product volume. A key objective of the new strategy was, thus, to cross-sell product lines for simultaneous shipment to individual customer locations.

Strategic pricing had a role to play in supporting this objective. Traditional industry pricing would have provided a discount on increasing volumes of individual products. Instead, the company developed a pricing schedule that discounted against total volume of all products in an order. The discount created an incentive for customers to order multiple products for simultaneous shipment (see Figure 2). The company could afford this new discount because of the associated reduction in its costs. However, because it was also providing a higher level of service, the company found it could set its list prices at a slight premium to its competitors. By viewing pricing strategically, this company used pricing to help achieve its key strategic objective.

In contrast, far too many businesses go no further than saying "increase profitability" when establishing pricing objectives. Strategic pricing requires a clear understanding of business strategy objectives and an articulation of how pricing can support fulfillment of those objectives. Pricing can support business strategies because it can be used to:

- Segment markets
- Define products
- Create customer incentives
- Send signals to competitors

Let's look at each of these uses for pricing and how they can support fulfillment of business strategies.

Segmenting Markets

Frequently businesses have different strategic objectives in different market segments. Pricing can be used to help delineate those segments and support the differential objectives.

For example, the leading manufacturer of a high-technology capital good supported its product with a strong, nationwide service network. Its primary competitor, because it was smaller, could only afford to locate service personnel in major markets that supported a large installed base of the equipment. This situation led to

Figure 2 Traditional and Revised Discount Schedules

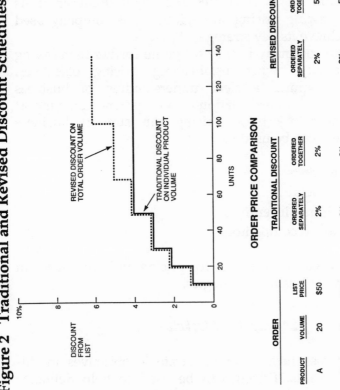

segment specific objectives for the leading manufacturer: compete aggressively in major markets and realize higher prices in less concentrated markets where the competitor could supply equipment but delivered less timely service. (Equipment downtime was very costly for most customers.)

To support this dual objective, the manufacturer separated its service pricing from its equipment pricing and varied the price of service contracts by market. The equipment pricing was highly competitive in all markets, but in markets where the competitor delivered less service value, the manufacturer priced service contracts at a premium. By pricing in this manner, it distinguished the two market segments and supported its differentiated objectives.

For similar reasons, most major newspapers have different prices for full-coverage advertisements (ads that are printed in all copies of their paper) and for zoned editions (ads that run in only a portion of the newspaper's geographic market). Advertisers whose customers are clustered in only one part of the city (such as smaller retailers, local banks, or real estate agents) do not benefit from the newspaper's broader coverage. In addition, these advertisers have lower-cost advertising alternatives such as direct mail, billboards, and community newspapers.

To compete with more localized media, major newspapers set lower prices for ads that will be run in zoned editions and higher rates for full-coverage ads that appeal to mass advertisers without the lower-cost competitive alternatives. The newspaper benefits because the price per reader is higher in the zoned editions; the advertiser benefits because the smaller number of readers lowers the absolute price, (see Table 1). Here, too, the pricing strategy differentiates between two advertiser segments and enables the newspaper to achieve different objectives in each.

Defining Products

In some businesses, prices can actually define the product. This is particularly useful when strategic objectives vary across segments but there is no way, *a priori*, to identify into which segment a particular customer falls. In these cases, appropriate pricing can cause

Table 1 Newspaper Pricing

	Full Coverage	Zoned Edition
Number of Readers	250,000	50,000
Price per Thousand Readers	$20.00	$30.00
Total Price of Advertisement	$5,000	$1,5000
Revenue to Newspaper if All Zones Sold	$5,000	$7,500

customers to select the product (defined by price) that fulfills the desired objective.

Banks face this problem with retail checking accounts. A recent survey found that 70 percent of retail checking account customers maintain average balances of under $1,000. For many banks, the interest earned on balances of this size is insufficient to cover the costs of providing service. Instituting an across-the-board service charge would cover these costs, but could cause the loss of profitable high-balance customers. Strategically, the bank would like to assess a service charge on low-balance customers while encouraging purchase by high-balance customers. Unfortunately, there is no direct means to distinguish these customers at the time they open their accounts.

To support these differentiated objectives, many banks have used price to define multiple checking products. In all cases, the underlying product is the same; only differences in pricing create the "different" products. (The payment of interest on account balances can be considered an offset to the price charged.) In the example in Figure 3, the bank has used price to define three checking products.

- Product 1—a $4.00 monthly fee plus $.40 per check
- Product 2—a $10.00 monthly fee if the account balance falls below $1,000
- Product 3—a $12.00 monthly fee if the account balance falls below $2,000, offset by interest paid on all balances

Customers can generally estimate what their average balances will be. Accordingly, they will choose products that minimize the price they pay. As Figure 3 shows, customers who expect to maintain balances under $1,000 will choose Product 1, customers who expect to maintain balances over $2,000 will choose Product 3, and customers in between will choose Product 2. By using price to define its checking products, the bank causes customers to self-select in a manner that fulfills its strategic objectives: assessing a charge on low-balance customers while encouraging purchase (through net positive interest payments) by high-balance customers.

Creating Customer Incentives

Because prices create incentives for customers, pricing can be used to encourage customers to behave in ways that fulfill strategic objectives. Automobile manufacturers have pursued this strategy in their pricing of optional equipment.

The provision of individually chosen options for each customer can be very expensive for automobile manufacturers. The different combinations of options multiply rapidly, and when combined with other variables (such as color, drive train, and body style) can yield thousands of variations of the same basic car. These variations cause complexity and, thus, cost in manufacturing and inventory.

Cost control is a key strategic objective for most vehicle manufacturers. Achievement of the objective would be supported if customers bought only standard groupings of options. Accordingly, many manufacturers use price to create an incentive for customers to purchase cars with standard options packages. Table 2 illustrates this incentive for the 1988 Mercury Sable. A customer purchasing the options individually pays almost $750 more than a customer who buys the standard package. One could actually pay less for a Sable with more optional equipment than for the same car with only a subset of those features. By pricing to create appropriate customer incentives, the manufacturer encourages customers to behave in a manner that supports the business' strategic objective.

Figure 3 Checking Account Pricing

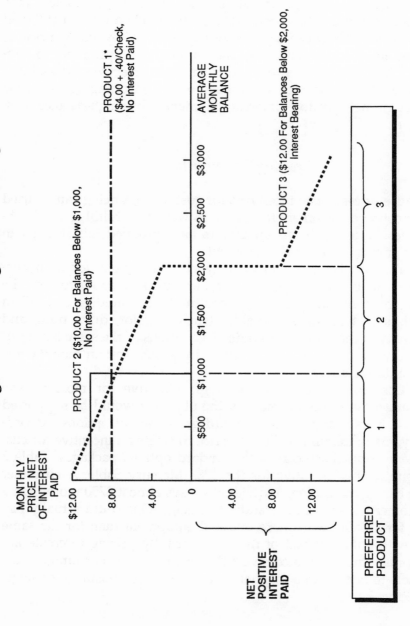

*Assumes 10 Checks/Month

Table 2 1988 Mercury Sable LS Sedan

	Packaged Options With Preferred Equipment Package	Options Priced Separately Without Preferred Equipment Package
Base (List) Price	$15,138	$15,138
Preferred Equipment Package Includes:	$749	
Automatic OD Transmission		Standard
P205/65R15 BSW Tires		$ 56
Tilt Steering Wheel		124
Leather Wrapped Steering Wheel		59
Finger-Tip Speed Control		176
6-Way Power Drive Seat		251
Electric Rear Window Defroster		145
Electronic AM/FM Stereo Cassette Radio		137
15" Aluminum Wheels		172
Premium Sound System		168
Power Lock Group		195
Total Cost	$15,887	$16,621

$734 Incentive to Buy Standard Package

Source: Edmund's 1988 Car Prices Buyer's Guide

Signalling Competitors

In addition to creating incentives for customers, pricing sends signals to, and creates incentives for, competitors. Used strategically, prices can thus encourage competitors to behave in a manner that benefits the business.

For example, a commodity raw material supplier participated in an industry with seasonal overcapacity. Each year in the "down season" industry margins collapsed as competitors fought for volume to fill their plants. Strategically, the supplier wanted to lead the industry to behave more rationally. It chose to use pricing as a signalling mechanism.

The manufacturer recognized that a customer's distance from its plant affected profitability, a fact that was also true for competitors. Therefore, the supplier priced less aggressively to customers located relatively near its competitor's plants but decided to maintain prices to its own "most profitable customers", those located near its plant. When these customers were under attack, the supplier competed aggressively. Competitors responded to this supplier's pricing signals even though it was not the industry's volume leader. Over time this strategy improved market discipline. As a result, the supplier was able to realize higher margins with only a slight decline in volume and, on net, improve profitability. Even in this commodity industry, a pricing strategy developed to support an explicit strategic objective led to improved business performance.

Develop Differentiating Price Structures

With clear strategic objectives for pricing defined, appropriate price structures can enable the fulfillment of those pricing objectives. Price structures are the set of product, customer, and purchase characteristics along which price levels will vary—the specific attributes of the product/service or its purchase for which price levels will be established. For example, most taxicabs have a three-part price structure: a price to get into the cab, a price per mile, and a price per minute. Within this structure, prices can be set independently at any level desired. While familiarity has made this structure seem normal, taxicab price structures could easily include other elements. (For example: a price per passenger, a flat rate by zones, a premium for radio calls, or a premium for peak hours.) Most businesses develop their price structures implicitly, but explicit attention to price structure can expand the set of strategic alternatives.

Price structures enable differentiated pricing to segments defined by customer price sensitivity, differences in cost to serve, or differences in competitive position. As a result, businesses can achieve varied and sometimes conflicting objectives in different segments. For example, if the pricing objective is to optimize the trade-off between revenue and volume, a price structure that differentiates based on customer price sensitivity is appropriate. Price levels can be set relatively high to price insensitive customer segments and low to segments of customers who would not purchase the product at the higher price. The desired basis of differentiation depends on the pricing objective(s) to be achieved, (see Figure 4).

Figure 4   Frequently Some Degree of Price Differentiation is Needed to Fulfill Objectives

Differentiate Based On

Price Objective	Customer's Price Sensitivity	Cost Behavior	Competitive Position
Optimize tradeoff between revenue and volume	X		
Alter customer buying behavior	X	X	
Reflect differences in cost-to-serve		X	
Selectively respond to competitive environment			X

Differentiating Based on Customer Price Sensitivity

Many airlines have successfully used price structure to differentiate based on customer price sensitivity. Business travelers are relatively price insensitive, while tourists are very sensitive to price. In order to increase the volume of tourist traffic without foregoing revenue from bread-and-butter business customers, airlines have developed a price structure based on characteristics that differentiate the two customer segments. For example, tourists generally spend a weekend at their destination, while business travelers do not. By changing the price structure from pricing flights to pricing itineraries, the airlines can discount itineraries that include a Saturday night. Most business customers cannot take advantage of the discount without incurring substantial inconvenience, so the new structure enables the airline to increase tourist volume while maintaining high business customer prices. This, and similar elements of airline price structure, have led to as much as a fivefold difference in fares paid for the same seat.

Rarely is a single price appropriate for all customers. As Goldilocks discovered with the bears' porridge, some customers will find prices too high (they won't buy), others too low (they would have paid more), and only a few just right. Using price structure to differentiate based on customer price sensitivity enables businesses to have their porridge and eat it too, realizing high prices from customers who are willing to pay them without sacrificing volume from customers who are not.

Differentiating Based on Cost Behavior

Similarly, price structures that differentiate based on cost-to-serve can create incentives for customers to purchase in ways that are most cost efficient from the supplier's point of view. Figure 5 shows such a price structure for telecommunications services. The cost of providing switched (standard) service rises as the number of the customer's calls increases. The cost of providing private line service (a dedicated link between two points) is insensitive to calling volumes over a wide range. Most customers are indifferent between the two products and choose the one with the lowest price. By structuring prices for the two products so that the customer decision point occurs at the call volume where the product cost lines cross, the telecommunications supplier can create an incentive for customers to choose the most cost effective service. If the cross-over points were not aligned, the supplier would incur higher costs to realize equivalent revenue (see Figure 6).

Figure 5 Differentiating Based on Cost Behavior

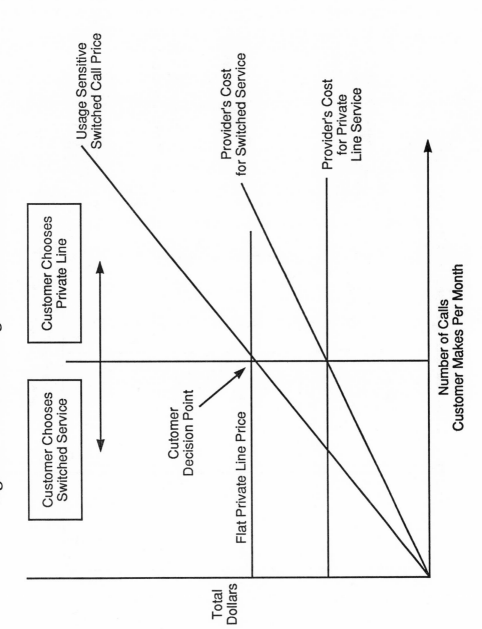

Figure 6 Differentiating Based on Cost Behavior

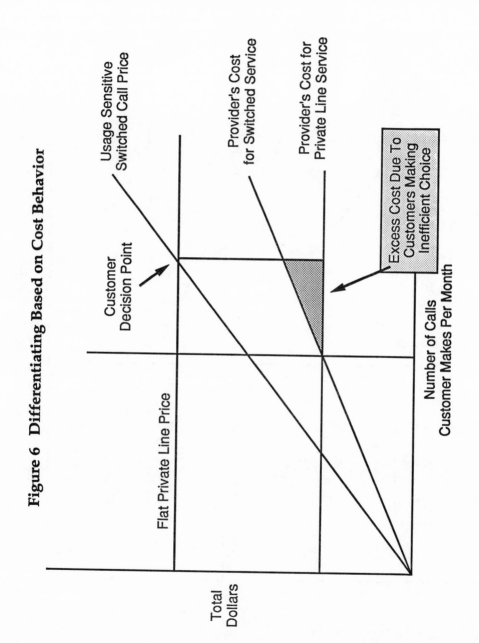

Differentiating Based on Competitive Position

Price structures can also be used to differentiate based on relative competitive position. The key is to choose dimensions of price structure to reflect the product or purchase characteristics that determine differences in competitive advantage: for example, processor speed and service capabilities in a computer product line; target audience reach and penetration in advertising media; order size and relative shipping distance in commodity manufactured products. Prices can then be varied to respond to specific opportunities and threats in the competitive environment.

Figure 7 shows how one company accomplished this. The company sold a product that incorporated two features, A and B. While the mix of these features varied from purchase to purchase, both features were always purchased from the same supplier. This situation is characteristic of any business that sells a semi-customized product (e.g., computer systems, process control equipment, many service businesses). Competitive advantage was determined by purchase volume (due to scale effects) and product feature mix (due to technology differences). The company was increasingly disadvantaged as purchase volume rose and as the percent of a particular product feature (Feature B) increased.

The company developed a price structure that directly reflected these characteristics. Prices declined with increasing total volume (reflecting scale effects) and varied depending on the percentage of Feature B in the mix (reflecting its technology disadvantage in providing Feature B). The structure enabled the company to increase prices where it was most advantaged, reduce prices where it was slightly advantaged but losing volume, and cede unprofitable volume where it was inherently disadvantaged The result was a 20 percent increase in contribution.

Price structures that differentiate competitive positions allow a business to respond to its competitive environment in a dexterous, fine-tuned manner. Lacking such a price structure, pricing responses are constrained and ham-handed—generally resulting in either an overreaction or an underreaction to competitive threats and opportunities.

Figure 7 Differentiating Based on Competitive Position

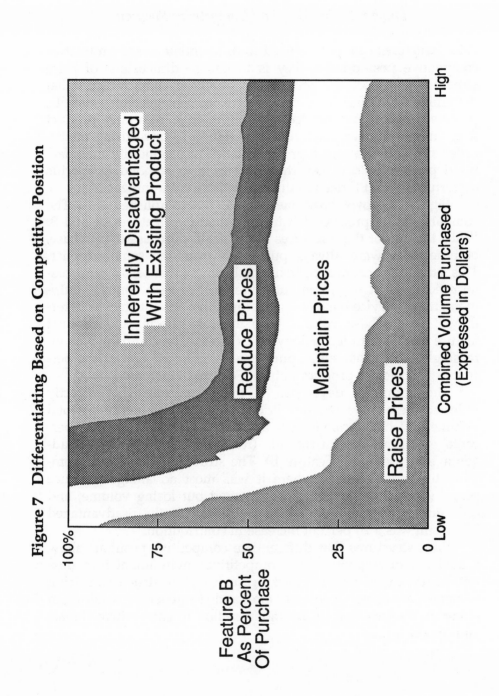

Establish Price Levels that Take Market and Competitive Responses into Account

Within the appropriate structure, price levels should be established to reflect:

- Customer response to prices
- The business' own cost behavior
- Competitor response to prices

Some businesses thoroughly analyze customer response to price and their own cost behavior in setting price levels. Most businesses at least consider these effects. But relatively few business make a serious attempt to project competitive responses to their pricing actions.

Yet competitors' pricing responses are often the key determinant of a pricing strategy's success. For example, consider a business which reduces its prices in order to increase market share. It may be possible to increase its revenue while realizing a volume-driven reduction in its costs. The scenario is a happy one if key competitors maintain their prices. However, if competitors match the price reduction, no share will shift, volume will not rise substantially, costs will not decline, and margin will be lost.

While it may not always be possible to forecast short-term competitive responses, appropriate analysis can project long-term response fairly predictably. It is simply a matter of the business' managers putting themselves in their competitors' shoes and asking, "How would I respond?" "What strategic objectives are competitors attempting to achieve?" "What pricing response is optimal from a strategic and profit perspective?" "How will their customers respond and their costs behave?" Most of these questions can be answered analytically, allowing price levels to be tested for competitive response as well as for customer response and cost behavior.

Armed with a projection of competitive response, managers may be willing to pursue pricing strategies that would otherwise seem too risky. A market leader whose share had been steadily eroding dropped its prices by 15 percent after projecting that competitive response would be minimal and short-lived. As a result, it regained its lost share and almost doubled the value of the business.

Support Pricing with Focused Implementation Programs

A well-conceived pricing strategy can be undercut if programs are not in place to ensure its implementation. The specifics of implementation, of course, depend on the business and the strategy; but in almost all cases at least three areas are key.

- *Salesforce training and incentives*: Has the strategy been explained to the salesforce and do they understand how to make it work? If the sales force retains pricing flexibility, have the members been given guidelines for making pricing decisions? Do sales incentives support or undercut the strategy?
- *Price monitoring and evaluation program:* If prices have been set in expectation of specific customer and competitive responses, is there a mechanism in place to assess actual responses? How will business managers know if their expectations are being met, or if a change in strategy is required? Will they know in a timely fashion?
- *Flexible and responsive decision making*: Price changes have rapid effects in the market. In the airline industry, with its sophisticated computer systems that rapidly disseminate price information, share shifts in response to price changes can occur overnight. Has the business developed a pricing process that can respond in real time to unexpected customer behavior and unpredicted competitive actions? Lengthy decision making often results in an inability to capitalize on short-term opportunities and sometimes leads to an irreversible loss of position.

Summary

Developing strategic pricing is a creative process. Almost any business can find ways to improve its pricing strategy. However, a number of symptoms indicate that a substantial improvement opportunity exists.

- Pricing strategy development is not an integral part of the firm's strategic planning process.
- Management's pricing objective can best be expressed as "raise them."
- Prices to all customers are based on only one dimension.
- Competitors without a product or service advantage are rapidly gaining share in some segments.
- Prices are generally set in response to competition.
- Pricing is *ad hoc*: everyone is making pricing decisions

Managers in businesses displaying these symptoms may want to rethink their approach to pricing. All managers should consider whether they are adequately strategic in their use of pricing. They should ask themselves if they:

- Integrate pricing and strategy—view pricing as a strategic tool, not an afterthought?
- Use price structure to differentiate pricing and achieve multiple objectives?
- Price in light of customer and competitor incentives and likely responses?... Project rather than presume?... Lead rather than follow industry pricing?
- Build implementation systems to specifically support our pricing strategy?

Strategic pricing should be one of a business' most potent competitive weapons. If that weapon remains sheathed, substantial business potential may well be lost.

Recommended for Additional Reading

The Strategy and Tactics of Pricing: A Guide to Profitable Decision Making, by Thomas Nagle, Englewood Cliffs, NJ: Prentice-Hall, 1987.

"The Strategic Value of Price Structure," by Andrew A. Stern in *Journal of Business Strategy*, Fall, 1986.

"Manage Customers For Profits (Not Just Sales)," by Benson Shapiro et al. in *Harvard Business Review*, September-October, 1987.

CHAPTER THREE

THE ECONOMICS OF PRICE: MEASURING ELASTICITIES

JOHN MORTON

JOHN MORTON

John Morton is Vice President, Director of Advanced Statistical Research, for Total Research Corporation. Total Research is a publicly held company which has been documented by Ad Age as the fastest-growing major provider of advanced strategic market research. Mr. Morton has been designing, conducting, and interpreting strategic market research studies for over 20 years. He has been previously employed as a member of the Planning and Analysis group at Prudential, as a member of the Strategy Research Group at General Foods, as Vice President of Aulino/Baen, as Executive Vice President of Robinson Associates, Inc., and as President of John L. Morton, Inc. His articles have appeared in numerous professional and trade publications, most recently Business Marketing, Marketing Communications Magazine, and AMA Marketing News. He is the creator of Total Research Corporation's Price Elasticity Measurement System (PEMS), which has been used in approximately 60 U.S. and international markets and is widely recognized as the most powerful available system for assessing price elasticity.

CHAPTER THREE

The phrase "price elasticity measurement" may evoke images of musty college text books, and academic economists discussing aspects of a theoretical world that seems to bear little resemblance to the one in which we live, or in which our businesses compete. But to scores of "Fortune 500" and smaller U.S. manufacturers/marketers, as well as a growing number of international firms, this concept has recently taken on an exciting new relevance, promising near-immediate bottom line payoffs. Price elasticity measurement *can* be successfully done. Suppose the following:

- You raise the price of your premium Product A by 12%;
- You raise the price of your economy Product B by a more modest 4%; and
- You lower the price of your ailing, middle-of-the-line Product C by 7%.

Simultaneously:

- Competitor X raises his prices by 8%;
- Competitor Y raises his prices by 4%; and
- Competitor Z holds the line.

What will happen in the real world to you and your competitors' sales and shares within this complex scenario?

New techniques are providing answers to these kinds of questions in ways never seen before. For instance, a major U.S. pharmaceutical company developed a new surgical product that it felt offered a unique and highly desirable set of features. The company decided it needed to investigate the price elasticity of this new product—how would it fare at different price levels? Using technology to be described in this chapter, it tested prices across a broad range: plus and minus 20% around its anticipated price. The study showed that the new product was considerably less price elastic than its competitors, and in fact would surpass its unit sales goals at the highest price tested. Emboldened by this information, the company entered the market at a price 35% higher than anticipated, and reaped millions of dollars in extra rewards for doing their price elasticity homework.

Information Objectives

As business executives interested in price elasticity, we might begin by listing the information we would like to have. Assume that we have a line of products (or services—for simplicity, we'll refer to "products" throughout the rest of this chapter), and want to improve performance versus financial goals via pricing strategy. Our ideal system would achieve a number of objectives as next described.

1. Measure Self-Elasticity

How will the sales of each of our products change as their prices increase or decrease? Does a 10% price increase for our brand result in an equivalent 10% loss of revenue? A 5% loss? A 15% loss? Or even a gain? Are there *threshold points* on our price curve, levels where price sensitivity abruptly increases or decreases?

Figure 1, from a recent study of a highly competitive, billion dollar packaged goods market, shows how the unit sales of each major brand will vary as its price varies. The average brand (see "All Nine Brands" graph) loses slightly less than 1% of its sales for each 1% increase in price. Some brands are considerably more price sensitive than average. Brand D loses 17% in sales with a 10% price increase, and gains an even greater 23% in sales with a 10% price decrease. Other products, such as Brand W, must beware of critical threshold points on their price curve. Some brands are less price elastic. Due to chronic underpricing which has created doubts about product quality, Client Brand A was actually predicted to gain share as its price is increased!

Incidentally, Client Brand A raised their price 20%. The price elasticity model shown here was accurate within a fraction of a share point in predicting the outcome of this action. The result: better image for Client Brand and millions of dollars more on the bottom line than would have occurred with a more conservative pricing strategy.

2. Measure Competitive Cross-Elasticities

How do the pricing strategies of each of our key competitors affect the sales of our product line? Which competitors can really hurt us with price decreases? Which can help with price increases? Which competitive pricing actions can be ignored? Table 1 shows the effect of various price strategies on Client Brand A. For instance, if Brand F lowers its price by 10%, it costs Client Brand A 0.4% of its business. Client Brand A has to keep a "weather eye" on the price strategies of competitors Brand D and Brand W, with which it is most cross-elastic. Also, these effects are additive so if all competitors (D,F,T,W,M,P) decreased their prices by 10%, the net effect on Client Brand A will be an 8.4% loss in unit sales.

3. Measure Our Cross Elasticities

How will the prices of our product line affect the sales of our competitors? How can we best contain the growth of a threatening competitor by pricing action? Is price competition in our market symmetrical (the competitors that affect us most are the ones on which we have the strongest effect) or asymmetrical?

Table 2 shows the extent to which our prices for Client Brand B can control the shares of other brands. It demonstrates how the pricing of Client Brand B can strongly influence the success of Brands D and M, while having almost no effect on Brand P.

Figure 1 Brand Self-Elasticities

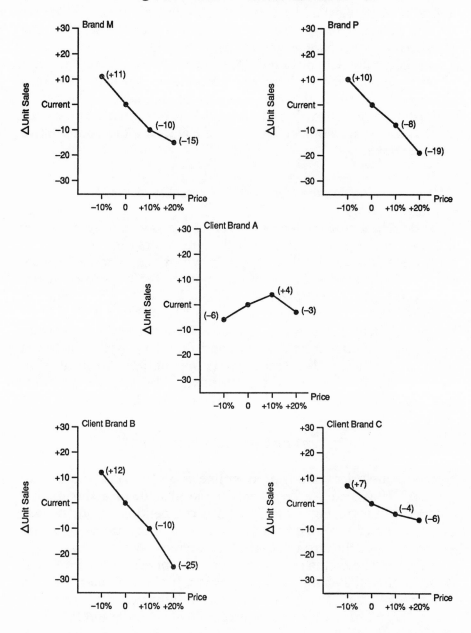

Figure 1 (Continued)

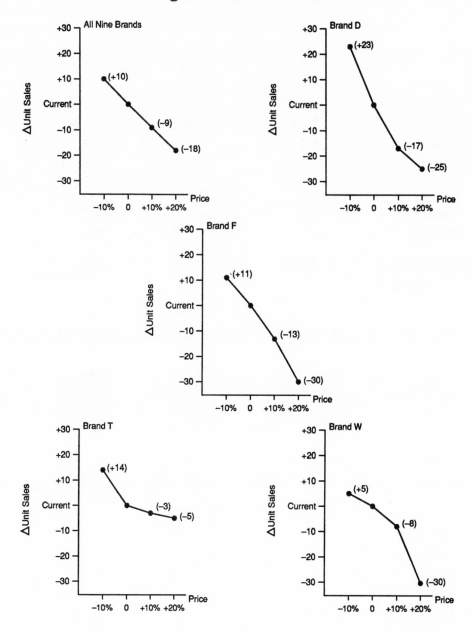

Table 1   Effect of Various Price Strategies on Unit Sales of Client Brand A

	10% Price Decrease	10% Price Increase	20% Price Increase
Brand D	-3.5%	+2.5%	+3.6%
Brand F	-0.4	+0.2	+1.1
Brand T	-1.8	+0.4	+0.7
Brand W	-1.5	+2.3	+8.6
Brand M	-0.9	+0.8	+1.2
Brand P	-0.3	+0.2	+0.5
Client Brand B	-2.1	+1.7	+2.6
Client Brand C	-1.3	+0.7	+1.1

Table 2   Effect of Various Price Strategies on Competitors

	10% Price Decrease By Client Brand B	10% Price Increase By Client Brand B	10% Price Increase By Client Brand B
Brand D	-2.4%	+2.0%	+4.8%
Brand F	-0.9	+0.8	+2.0
Brand T	-1.1	+0.9	+2.3
Brand W	-1.5	+1.2	+3.2
Brand M	-2.8	+2.4	+5.9
Brand P	-0.1	+0.1	+0.3
Client Brand A	-3.0	+2.4	+6.3
Client Brand C	-0.2	+0.3	+0.7

4. Measure Intra-line Elasticities

How do we quantify the price competition that exists within our own product line? How does the price of our Product A affect the sales of our Product B and vice versa? Which of our products tend to cannibalize which when we make prices more attractive to buyers? When we raise the price of part of our product line, how much business is lost to competition, and how much simply shifts to the rest of our product line?

Tables 1 and 2 contain for intra-line information. Generally, Client Brands A and B tend to price compete and share a more common base of customers than A and C or B and C.

5. Simulate the Market

Have we the capability to easily simulate the sales of our and our competitors' products under any possible future pricing scenario? What happens if we raise prices by 8% on half of our product line, 4% on the other half, and competitor X follows with a 6% increase while competitor Y lowers its prices 3%? We might want to test hundreds or possibly thousands of alternatives.

6. Optimize Our Pricing Strategy

Once we have the simulation capability, why not let the computer locate our best possible strategy? We will need to specify likely competitive actions and counter-actions, as well as provide information on our product marketing and manufacturing costs. Then the model can show which of the pricing strategies in our command has the best impact on our financial goals.

Traditional Approaches

Over the years, several approaches to price elasticity measurement have been advocated and used. Each has its merits and demerits.

Table 3 Quarterly Sales* and Prices

	Price of A	Sales of A	Price of B	Sales of B	Price of C	Sales of C	Price of D	Sales of D
First quarter 1986	$5.45	292	$4.60	74	$5.15	144	$4.95	108
Second quarter 1986	$5.45	290	$4.60	82	$5.25	156	$4.95	102
Third quarter 1986	$5.75	278	$4.60	76	$5.25	146	$5.15	112
Fourth quarter 1986	$5.75	284	$4.60	80	$5.35	134	$5.15	114
First quarter 1987	$5.75	294	$4.60	72	$5.35	142	$5.15	106
Second quarter 1987	$5.75	290	$4.60	78	$5.50	128	$5.15	104
Third quarter 1987	$6.05	272	$4.60	90	$5.50	144	$5.45	94
Fourth quarter 1987	$6.05	276	$4.60	96	$5.75	126	$5.45	98

*In 1,000s of units.

Econometric Analysis

Econometric analysis for price elasticity takes the point of view that all we need is to understand and quantify what has happened in the past. It usually takes the form of time series analysis, trying to answer questions such as: "When I have increased or cut price for my product in the past, what happened to my sales?" The primary advantage of econometric analysis is that it is based upon the real world; we pin our analysis on the same phenomena we wish to predict.

Price effects, however, may account for only a small portion of all the changes that occur in brand sales. The sales of a brand may be constantly in flux, buffeted by the large and small effects of everything that is happening in the market, including new product introductions, product improvements, advertising programs, changes in product availability, and other marketing actions. It may be difficult to isolate the role of price amid the clamor of the real world.

Still, we can observe a market over time and track price and sales changes for the major brands, hoping to deduce the relationships that exist between price and sales levels. Table 3, for instance, shows two years of quarterly price and sales data for four brands in a product category.

Some of problems of econometric analysis may surface in an actual implementation, such as:

- The ability to estimate price elasticity is dependent upon price variation. In Table 3, Brand B's price did not change over the two-year period, so it will be difficult to estimate how *changes* in the price of B will affect sales.
- Elasticity estimates also depend on the independence of price variations. Brands A and D have changed their prices simultaneously (each third quarter) within the time period under study. When shares change subsequent to a Brand A/Brand D price increase, how much of the change is due to the action of Brand A? Of Brand D? It may be impossible to disentangle their separate effects.
- Because many factors other than price affect sales, price/sales relationships as shown in Exhibit 4 may appear inconsistent. For instance, Brand D experienced 10% growth in sales from second quarter 1986 to third quarter 1986 despite a coincident price increase. But a later price increase in 1987 seems to produce a 10% drop in sales. In general, much of the sales variation in Exhibit 4 seems unrelated to price changes.
- An implicit assumption of econometric analysis is that *price elasticities do not change over time.* Historical data that represent the market and the world at a different point in time and under different circumstances are regarded as applicable to the present and the future. Other approaches indicate that the price elasticity of a product does in fact change over time, particularly when new products enter the market.

A new and perhaps more promising approach to econometric price elasticity measurement uses scanner data and a cross-sectional approach. This methodology takes advantage of the fact that in certain markets (e.g., consumer packaged goods), actual store prices for identical products can vary widely by outlet and region. The Acme at 5th and Broad may be selling a jar of Hellmann's Mayonnaise at $1.29 while the Acme at Walnut and Locust may be selling the same product for $1.69. How much higher is the share of Hellmann's at the first store? This technique quantifies the relationship that exists between a product's varying price levels and its sales.

Test Market

Test markets deal with some of the problems inherent in econometric analysis. As noted above, real-world measurement of price effects is problematic since reality is unwieldy and rarely conforms to the neat rules and assumptions required by statistical models. Test markets are an attempt to deal with some of these vicissitudes. We take charge and create a series of real-world situations that better conform to our information needs by introducing different price changes into separate, but presumably very similar, markets and seeing what happens to sales.

If the markets are well-matched and have stable, consistent competitive actions during the length of our test, this technique can provide excellent and realistic information on our product's self-elasticity. Frequently, though, results emerge as shown here:

Market	Price Strategy	Change in Sales
A	-10%	+ 3%
B	- 5%	+ 8%
C	+ 5%	- 8%
D	+10%	+ 2%

Price and sales changes seem to be unrelated, although we know that this can't be true. In short, the test may not show any systematic relationship. How can this happen?

Usually, these kind of inconclusive results are due to differential competitive action in these markets. For instance, during our test Competitor X may himself use Market A as a test market for a new line extension. Or two key regional sales executives may leave Competitor Y in Market D, improving our performance there.

Unlike the econometric approach, the test market method permits estimation of only the self-elasticity of one brand, our test brand. Thus we have met just one of our six information objectives, and only partially at that since our intent is to measure the price elasticities of our competitors as well as our own.

Under ideal circumstances, test markets may show us how the market will react to unilateral price actions taken by our brand. Suppose the test market study shows that a 10% price reduction will lead to a 15% increase in sales. We like this scenario and take the 10% price decrease. Then our competitors notice and retaliate, dropping their prices sharply. Suddenly we find we have dropped our price and lost sales, a lose/lose situation by any definition: a short-lived success and a long-term disaster. For that reason, comprehensive price elasticity knowledge also must estimate cross-elasticities. We must know the effects which our competitors' price changes will have on our products' sales.

Market Research

Market research has been playing a growing role in price elasticity measurement. Due to the failure of reality-based techniques to provide consistently good answers—and the tremendous financial risks involved in acting on uncertain or possibly fallacious information—various forms of market research have been increasingly called into play. Market research has one tremendous advantage over reality. If it uses a laboratory-type approach, situations can be set up wherein *prices are the only variables.* Thus results aren't muddied or muddled by historical trends, regional differences, unpredictable competitive actions, advertising efforts, new product introductions, or other vagaries. Of course, these techniques must overcome the skepticism inherent in any approach that measures reactions in a test tube and then applies them to the real world.

Direct questioning methodologies attempt to address price elasticity issues with market research surveys rather than observation of behavior. Respondents are asked questions such as: "How likely would you be to renew your relationship with (Vendor A) if the annual cost were $75? $65?" For example, the following results are from an actual market research study of a service currently priced at $50:

Reported Likelihood of Continuing Participation

	$75	$65
Very Likely	28%	34%
Somewhat Likely	32%	32%
Unlikely	40%	34%

The direct-questioning approach would lead one to believe that a large proportion of customers—perhaps as many as 50% or more—would discontinue the service if it cost $75 rather than $50. But a more indirect questioning technique described below predicted customer loss at $75 to be only 6%. This is a huge difference (50% versus 6%): which method was right? Actual loss of business was closely in line with the results of the indirect approach.

The primary problem with direct questioning is that it grossly overestimates customer price sensitivity. Results of such studies can be dangerously misleading unless the researcher has somehow developed a reliable way to deflate his or her projections based upon past experience.

Conjoint Scaling

Indirect questioning techniques, most notably *conjoint analysis*, overcome many of the crippling problems of the direct-questioning approach. Probably no technique has ever revolutionized the market research field, and demanded the interests of so many practitioners and academics, as has conjoint scaling (otherwise known as trade-off analysis). Estimates of the number of conjoint scaling studies conducted by major corporations run in the several thousands, with a total cost probably in the hundreds of millions of dollars. On the Fortune 500 list, only the most conservatively run companies have avoided dabbling with conjoint, and many of the conjoint-using companies have made some of their most crucial marketing and manufacturing decisions based upon conjoint studies. Conjoint and related indirect questioning approaches may work because:

- They place people in a series of complex product-selection scenarios that in many ways reflect the shopping behavior and decisions of the real world.
- The interviewee cannot fathom the specific purpose of the task (e.g., for company X to learn about its price elasticity), and thus is not subject to demand biases (i.e., the tendency respondents have to try to provide answers that fulfill the hypotheses that they think the researcher has.)

In pricing research, these questioning procedures avoid unrealistic focus on one product and its price. In most real-life choice situations, there are many products to choose from, each with its own characteristics, advantages and disadvantages. Price is just one of many elements in the consumer's decision.

Full-profile conjoint scaling measures the value or utility of each component of a product in the buyer's decision process. The researcher provides customers with sets of complete descriptions of hypothetical products. Each hypothetical product varies from the next on factors such as performance, safety/consistency, convenience—and price. Customers evaluate the products based upon their likelihood of using, leasing, or buying them. The researcher derives utilities for different product features as well as price. Utilizing the inherent modeling capability of conjoint, information such as the price/sales plots shown earlier in Figure 1 become possible.

Conjoint can also be used to understand the effects of economic incentives such as premiums and giveaways. For instance, for many years a major service provider had been using trading stamps as an incentive for their customers. But as the popularity of trading stamps began to wane, they started to question this long-standing strategy.

A conjoint scaling study was carried out which measured the utilities that customers had for the components of their business—

courtesy of employees, quality of equipment provided, transaction speed, frequency of service problems, type and breadth of available equipment—as well as the trading stamps. The conjoint research then provided a prediction of what would happen to the service provider's market share if they discontinued the stamp program. This research was accurate within one tenth of a share point.

Commonly Observed Price Curves for New Products

Since conjoint scaling works best when the hypothetical products are unbranded and unidentified, its primary value in price elasticity research is to identify the expected price elasticity patterns for a typical new product offering in a market. Established brands have idiosyncratic price curves that are best measured by related indirect questioning technologies. Conjoint scaling provides the capability of estimating new product price elasticities for each individual customer in a research sample. There is a great deal of variation in the way people react to the price of a new product.

Five of the most commonly observed new product price elasticity curves are shown in Figure 2. Each illustrates how a particular segment of people will react to price for a new product by plotting its overall utility against different price levels. All other factors (e.g. product or service quality) are held constant in the analysis.

Type A, "Rational Economic Man," shows the price elasticity curve that the economist or pragmatist might expect. For Type A people, the lower the price, the better. At every step, increased price decreases new product utility, and therefore sales. This is the way people "should" respond to price.

Yet it is not unusual for half of all customers or even more to *not* respond to price in a purely rational economic way. For example, a recent conjoint study conducted in an industrial equipment market found only 41% of customers responding to price in a "rational" way. Despite a desire to economize, many people feel that some prices are too cheap—and despite all guarantees to the contrary, that the low-priced imitator or knock-off brand is lacking in some fundamental if undefinable quality.

Figure 2 Commonly Observed Price Curves

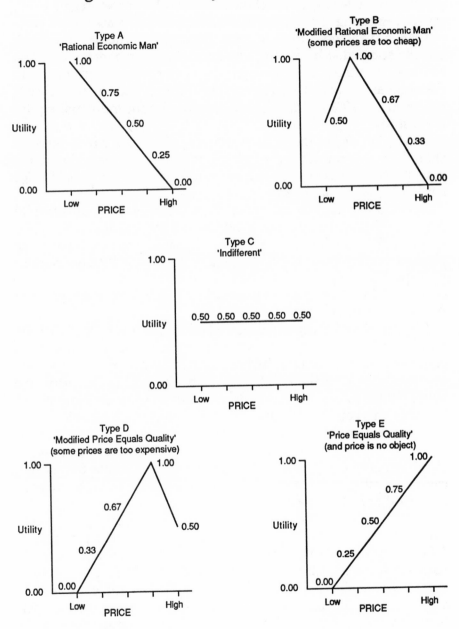

Type B of Figure 2 shows the most commonly observed new product price elasticity function when results are aggregated into groups. Entering the market at a lower price increases one's competitive advantage—up to a point. Beyond a particular threshold, usually somewhat below the current price for an average offering, the overall utility (and market share) for a new product will decrease as its prices decreases. The Type B pattern was clearly observed for 29% of the customers in the recent industrial equipment study.

Whether or not the same patterns apply to one's own markets should be determined by empirical investigation. But if it is the case, *we must be careful to price our new product at a respectably high level even if we could provide it more cheaply.*

Still other customers, as in Type C, may be indifferent to price, at least within the range tested. In a typical study, the price range tested may be 20% above or below the price of the average product current price levels. Price may not be totally unimportant to Type C's, only so within the range tested. About 11% of the customers from the recent industrial equipment study appeared to follow the indifference pattern.

Types D and E represent new product price functions that are more frequently observed in consumer than industrial markets. In certain consumer markets, half or more of all customers may react as those shown in the charts. To them, the higher the price, the better. What causes customers to respond to price so irrationally? In many markets, higher price is associated with desirable status. A more expensive product, whether or not it is superior, is presumed to make a statement about the buyer, one that is especially important if it is a visible purchase. But status purchasing can occur even with personal, less visible products, an expression of reward and self esteem.

Risk is another factor. Despite all guarantees and proof to the contrary, some customers find it hard to believe that products at different prices can be exactly the same. For instance, it may be hard for some to believe that New Product X at $5 per pound is exactly identical to New Product Y at $6. The reason: somehow, in a way that is not revealed by specifications, appearance, or perhaps any form of rational observation, New Product Y *has* to be superior to New Product X. Of course, New Product Y will supply plenty of folklore to customers to convince them that this is exactly the case, while New Product X reps shake their heads in disbelief. Such gullibility is especially pronounced when:

- Product knowledge is sketchy. Such lack of knowledge is more likely with products with a long purchase cycle.
- Great personal risk is entailed. If the stakes are really high, the natural inclination is to go with the best possible product, even if it is the best only in terms of expensiveness.
- It's a low-cost product category. The small extra price is a cheap way to gain security.

Sophisticated marketers increasingly recognize the psychological dimensions of business and consumer buying decisions.

Certainly, conjoint analysis of price elasticities is an enlightening way of researching buyers' reactions to cost. For instance, a major marketer of women's lingerie conducted a conjoint scaling study and found that their average customer had a Type C price response—indifference to new product pricing. This meant that whether they priced their high-quality new product at $3 or $4 would make no substantial difference in sales. Naturally, a high price strategy was preferable from a revenue and profitability standpoint.

Further analysis of the database did not change this conclusion, but revealed that in fact the average purchaser was *not* a Type C. Rather, the market was about evenly split between Type A's and Type E's, and averaging these two groups together gave the appearance of a Type C reaction.

Price Elasticities of Existing Brands

When it comes to measuring price elasticity for existing products, conjoint scaling is faced with major problems:

- If the hypothetical products used in conjoint scaling are branded, many if not most of them will not make sense. The integrity of the task will be threatened. For instance, you will show respondents a Ford Escort type car with a Mercedes brand name; a Mercedes type car with a Ford Escort brand name.
- If the products are left unbranded, then in essence price will be treated as a piece of information about the tangible or intangible qualities of the product beyond those specifically defined, and sensitivity to price will be deadened (as in the new lingerie product example).

With a known, existing product, people tend to have much more of a Type A rational response to pricing than unbranded conjoint scaling would indicate. This has led to a new breed of brand/price experimental design models. To date, Total Research Corporation has applied one such price elasticity measurement system (PEMS) to approximately 60 U.S. and domestic markets. Corporate users have had consistently high levels of satisfaction with the results and have found it very accurate in predicting actual market behavior.

The Price Elasticity Measurement System

The PEMS system supplies the information described earlier in this chapter:

- The price elasticity of each brand in the market.
- The cross-elasticities among all brands.
- Intra-line price elasticities and cross-elasticities.
- The ability to simulate market shares for any conceivable pricing situation.
- Identification of a single optimal pricing strategy.

We have recently experienced how advanced computer technology in the form of program trading has altered the very nature of the stock market. Picture then a market wherein each marketer has a computer model which enables him to predict accurately the outcome of any pricing action, either by him or his competitors. Rather than the current syndrome of relatively orderly price increases by the market leader, followed by similar action on the part of competitors, we may see a much more volatile and chaotic pattern in market pricing. A giant multidimensional chess game may ensue as each marketer continuously tries to optimize, versus the current or anticipated near-future pricing configuration.

As of now, only one, or at most two, of the competitors in any given market have applied these kinds of models; typically, they are the dominant brands. And as long as they keep this informational advantage, they have virtually guaranteed themselves higher levels of profit at the expense of their competition. However, once these pricing models become more widely held, the scramble for profits will be on. While having the capability will no longer promise pre-emptive advantage, *not* having it will virtually guarantee subpar financial performance. A whole new secondary science may develop—that of predicting what your competitors' strategic response will be, given that both you and they have access to such complete market knowledge. Then you can develop a pricing plan that will be optimal versus their anticipated behavior, and if you're lucky, you'll be ahead of the game until the next round of pricing changes.

Like it or not, we are entering a "Brave New World" on most marketing issues, including pricing. More complete and accurate market simulation capabilities will be at our fingertips, and the marketer who sticks to guesswork and historical analyses will be left in the dust. The number of major corporations involved in this kind of venture is rapidly growing—from photographic film to herbicides to frozen dinners to amusement parks to dishwashers to savings accounts to beta blockers. And as the number of available databases grows, the opportunity to even further refine and augment the predictive power of the technology also increases. By the year 2000, the problem may not be predicting how the consumer will react to your strategies—that will be known—but predicting how your competitor will.

Recommended for Additional Reading

"Optimal Product Line Pricing: The Influence of Elasticities and Cross-Elasticities" by David J. Reibstein and Hubert Gatignon in *Journal of Marketing Research*, August, 1984.

"'Trade-off' Pricing Research: A Discussion of Historical and Innovatory Applications," by Chris Blamires in *Journal of the Market Research Society*, April, 1987.

CHAPTER FOUR

THE POWER
OF FUNCTIONAL
COSTING IN THE
PRICING DECISION

J. STANTON MCGROARTY

J. STANTON MCGROARTY

Stan McGroarty is a Partner in the manufacturing consulting firm of Ingersoll Engineers, Rockford, IL. Mr. Mc-
Groarty has spent over 20 years in industry with responsibilities in the areas of tooling and production start-ups
of new products and processes, as well as in the development of equipment and methods improvement for existing operations. He has a B.S. in Mechanical Engineering
from the Detroit Institute of Technology, an M.A. in
Management from Central Michigan University, and is a
Certified Manufacturing Engineer.

CHAPTER FOUR

Pricing decisions have a unique power—the ability to determine profits. They can multiply the value of everyone's contribution to the company, or eliminate it. Thus, pricing is a strategic issue of the highest importance. Unfortunately, most organizations fail to treat pricing as a strategic issue at all. They rarely bring their collective corporate knowledge to bear on it. Instead, the typical corporation lets marketing people, or some other faction, make pricing decisions.

The resulting decisions are usually based on two bodies of information: the parochial wisdom of whatever corporate faction is the most influential, and the output of a traditional cost accounting system. The first is limited by the perspective of the faction in question. The second, cost information, is usually so riddled with assumptions, and so difficult to read, as to be useless. The shortcomings of traditional systems will be discussed in a later section of this chapter.

The use of two better costing systems—Contribution Margin Costing and Functional Costing—along with some pointed questions, can help to reveal the information obscured by traditional systems, and can support a more strategic approach to pricing decisions.

Determinants of Pricing Strategy

Cost-plus pricing is dead. This primitive approach thrived in the Nineteenth and early Twentieth centuries, when markets were unsophisticated and products scarce. Today, only the low cost producer in a market can afford cost-plus pricing, and he will probably not maximize profits by using it.

This does not mean, however, that knowledge of true cost has become unimportant in pricing decisions—far from it. Production cost, along with pricing decisions, determines profit, the *raison d'etre* of any business. A very simple relationship makes this point:

Selling Price – Cost = Profit

This relationship is not news to anyone in business, but it has implications which are usually missed in pricing decisions.

Since typical corporate profit margins hover somewhere under ten percent, a ten percent increase in price, as long as it doesn't reduce market share, can often double profits. This has the effect of doubling the value of everything done by everyone in the organization! In modern markets, a ten percent price increase is probably too aggressive, but how about two percent? This would increase profits, and therefore ROI, ROA, and all the other ratios which determine stock prices and bonus plans, by twenty percent! Conversely, underpricing a product by ten percent can rob employees and stockholders of their just returns even when selling a viable product in a healthy market.

Pricing, then, is a key strategic issue, worthy of the attention of the entire organization. But again, most organizations do not treat it this way. In the typical American corporation, most decisions are made by adversarial processes. Pricing is no exception. This phenomenon is the result of how we build our organizations, making them up of functional units which do not communicate, except at staff levels. Each of these functional groups has a different understanding of strategic issues, since each has only *part* of the organizational picture. Typically, these views on pricing are something like this:

- Accountants usually feel that costs are always too high and prices too low.
- Sales people feel, as a rule, that pricing expectations of the rest of the organization are unrealistically high.

- Operations people generally feel that cost control expectations are unreasonably tight, and that underpricing is making life very difficult.
- Top management knows what accounting systems tell it about costs, and what market reports tell it about pricing opportunity, and that any of these groups, if left to its own devices, is *quite capable of suboptimizing the organization to death.*

Most companies develop individual identities such as market driven, quality or technology driven, or as financial entities. This is a reflection of the relative strength of the various factions within each firm. The ruling factions tend to make the decisions on most issues, pricing included.

The problem with this approach is that no one faction has all of the information needed to make strategic decisions. Pricing, as a case in point, requires knowledge of markets, manufacturing costs and technology, distribution costs and approaches, and a thorough understanding of how these and other factors interrelate to give the organization its particular personality.

Of all the incomplete and inaccurate information used in pricing decisions, product cost is often the worst. In order to know whether a given market element is even worth pursuing, it is essential to know the true cost of products, as well as the prices the market will pay for them. Most cost systems, however, fail miserably in providing this information. This failure is compounded by the fact that most accounting people feel that they do a good job of providing and interpreting cost information, and so feel comfortable measuring other functions by these numbers.

The Problems with Traditional Cost Systems

Traditional cost accounting is built upon a figure called "direct labor," which is the straight hourly wages paid to workers who add value to the product. All other costs, with the exception of raw material, are lumped together as "burden" or "overhead," and are averaged over direct labor dollars. This puts tooling, training, vacation pay, oil, material handling, and the plant manager's bonus all in the same pot. The resulting stew does little to identify the cost impact of any change in the business, pricing included.

In a bicycle repair shop, where the labor cost is 80 or 90 percent of the total operating expense, this system works fine. In a modern factory, where direct labor is usually five percent to 15 percent of total cost, the system breaks down. This breakdown should not come as a surprise to anyone. After all, how many jobs allow us to actually perform only ten or fifteen percent of the work, and then average the rest over it? Sales, teaching, manufacturing and engineering certainly don't provide this kind of luxury. Why would accounting?

Table 1 is a traditional cost statement for a manufacturing plant—in this example, a high-volume producer of automotive components. If we look at the line items and ask ourselves what the impact would be on each of a change in production volume, as we might in pricing an additional product, what answer do we get?

Table 1 Generic Plant Traditional Costing
(Generic Product)

Cost Area	Annual Cost ($000s)	Cost per Unit (Dollars)
Direct Labor		
Direct labor wages	$3,675	$14.70
Direct Material		
Raw material	$6,100	24.40
Purchased components	1,250	5.00
Subtotal	$7,350	$29.40
Burden		
Plant Charges		
Fringe benefits	$4,000	$16.00
Indirect labor wages	2,385	9.54
Production supplies	1,275	5.10

Cost Area	Annual Cost ($000s)	Cost per Unit (Dollars)
Materials management	725	2.90
Utilities	575	2.30
Overtime premium	565	2.26
Administrative and accounting	400	1.60
Depreciation	325	1.30
Shift Premium	325	1.30
Data processing	300	1.20
Manufacturing engineering	300	1.20
Plant supervision and management	275	1.10
Personnel	230	.92
Scrap material	175	.70
Taxes and insurance	150	.60
Rework labor	125	.50
Quality assurance	100	.40
Miscellaneous	60	.24
Sale of scrap	-80	-.32
Corporate Charges		
Research and development	650	2.60
Marketing	475	1.90
Miscellaneous corporate charges	125	.50
Capital carrying cost	25	.10
Other income	-10	.04
Subtotal	$13,475	$53.90
Total Cost	$24,500	$98.00
Profit	1,750	7.00
Sales Dollars	$26,250	$105.00

Units sold: 250,000

Clearly, the decision support we need is not here. Even with a sound understanding of the operation itself, we are unable to adjust such major items as "Fringe Benefits," "Indirect Labor," and "Taxes and Insurance," since they combine hourly, salaried, factory and office costs. This is not a useful model of the way costs are generated in the factory.

There are really two problems evident here. The first is the accountants' pretense that modelling the organization's cost flows is too big a job to be done exhaustively. This may have been true in Henry Ford's day, but today all that is needed is some well designed data gathering and data processing support. The second problem is the refusal of engineering and operations people to learn enough about cost accounting systems to point out their inadequacies and change them. Engineers built the factories and determined how they would run. Manufacturing people spend their days there. It follows that engineers and manufacturing people should be involved in the financial modelling of factories. They seldom are.

The solution to this two-pronged problem requires the cooperation of the same groups that caused it. The first step in the solution must be the joint development of a new cost model—one that is accurate and useable. To be accurate, a cost system must be a model of the business it serves. This means that it must be tailored to that business. No single model can cover every business. No one person knows the business well enough to model all of it. A team effort is absolutely essential.

To be useful, a cost system must use and generate data in forms that correspond to real entities. This is another area where traditional systems fail miserably. Line items like "production supplies variance" or "general factory costs" are useless, even to those who understand them. They don't represent real-world entities, so they can't be attacked in the real world. Line items like "tooling" or "material handling" are real; we can find them on the shop floor and identify the impact which new business or other changes would have on them.

What we need, then, is an approach to cost modelling, rather than a standard model. Our approach must be flexible enough to address the specifics of any business. We must also insist that the information we generate be intelligible to everyone in the organization. Only then can it help us understand the way we do business and the way that business generates cost.

New Cost Accounting Tools

Dissatisfaction with traditional cost systems began in the late 1960s. This dissatisfaction spawned contribution margin costing, which is in wide use today. Contribution margin costing consists mainly of separating fixed and variable costs and developing a factory level profit figure which is used to offset the fixed costs generated in the parts of the organization not directly connected with manufacturing. This was a decided improvement over traditional costing, but it still failed to group costs in a way that made them a useful model of the factory and the organization.

Functional costing is a more recent development. It divides costs into real-world items which can be compared with a factory layout, an organizational chart and a manufacturing plan, to ascertain the impact of changes on the cost of doing business. When applied through a well-organized team effort, it can provide the models and the kinds of output we need.

Functional costing has only three firm guidelines—they permit the generation of a wide variety of formats and the use of local terminology for most items. This enhances the acceptance and intelligibility of the results. Here are the guidelines, beginning with the official cost breakdown for the business unit being studied:

Rule 1. Group costs into four categories: operator labor, factory overhead, production material, and non-factory cost. When done over an entire factory or product line, this yields bottom-line figures that can be tied back to the official profit and loss (P&L) statement for the business unit. Making this tie-back is the only way that you can be sure you've covered all costs.

Rule 2. Group things together if they are spent as a result of a single decision. This may mean that a line item like "factory supervision" will include both fixed and variable costs, but that presents no problem in our analysis. In fact, the fixed/variable cost distinction is, to some extent, fictitious. Every cost is variable until we decide to incur it; then it becomes fixed.

Rule 3. Assign names that mean something to the new line items. "Incidental costs, other" doesn't conjure up a picture; "oils and cleaners" does. Break up line items that now include unrelated costs.

It will probably take two or three passes at cost grouping before a clear picture emerges of where your business unit stands. Each pass will raise questions that you will resolve in the next pass. Arranging the line items of each major cost group in order of total annual cost will help make your picture clearer. Beginning each cost group with its biggest constituent helps to characterize the group and to focus attention on the most significant costs.

Another technique that can bring the cost picture home is dividing the annual expense in each line by the number of units produced in a year. This enables us to say things like, "The cost of each unit produced includes an average of $7.00 worth of tooling." This only works, of course, if you are dealing with a reasonably homogeneous product mix.

By developing a functional cost statement, the manufacturing/engineering/accounting team is actually generating a proforma P&L statement for the business unit. This format can be used very effectively to compare the "before" and "after" scenarios in a new product introduction. Since the line items in the functional cost statement are real-world entities, the format makes it easy to answer questions like, "What does a machine operator really cost us?" This will make the financial impact of some decisions easier to evaluate, and it will help in the determination of the "after" part of the P&L comparison. For instance, if manufacturing tells us it must hire x additional direct labor people and y supervision and control people to support new business, we are able to tell almost on inspection what the cost impact of this change would be.

The functional cost statement that follows (Table 2) can serve as a hypothetical example of the reporting that can be produced from a functional costing effort. This business unit is the same high-volume machining and assembly operation for automotive parts that was modeled in the traditional cost statement above (Table 1). A costing team can review these line items one by one and deliver a timely, accurate estimate of the impact of any change on the cost of doing business.

The line items in a functional cost statement for the reader's business would probably differ from this example in both name and importance, but, as in the functional costing example, they would be real-world entities. Comparison of Table 2 and Table 1 will provide a clear idea of their relative usefulness.

The bottom line of a functional cost statement is identical to the bottom line of a traditional P&L. Only the cost assignments in the body of the statement change. This assures us that we haven't missed any significant costs within our business unit.

Table 2 Functional Costing (Generic Product)

Cost Area	Annual Cost ($000s)	Cost per Unit (Dollars)
Production Labor		
Production wages and fringes	$ 4,500	$ 18.00
Setup	625	2.50
Rework	325	1.30
Overtime premium	275	1.10
Training	150	.60
Night premium	125	.50
Workmen's compensation	75	.30
Miscellaneous	50	.20
Subtotal	$ 6,125	$ 24.50
Production Material		
Raw material	$ 6,100	$ 24.40
Purchased components	2,125	8.50
Production utilities	225	.90
Paint and process chemicals	125	.50
Subtotal	$ 8,575	$ 34.30

Cost Area	Annual Cost ($000s)	Cost per Unit (Dollars)
Factory Overhead		
Tooling material and labor	$ 1,750	$ 7.00
Maintenance material and labor	1,100	4.40
Quality assurance	575	2.30
Plant supervision and management	550	2.20
Material handling	525	2.10
Building utilities	350	1.40
Depreciation on equipment	250	1.00
Manufacturing engineering	250	1.00
Scrap material	175	.70
Current product engineering	150	.60
Plant security	125	.50
Data processing	125	.50
Building taxes and insurance	75	.30
Depreciation on real estate	75	.30
Miscellaneous supplies	75	.30
Purchasing and scheduling	30	.12
Capital carrying cost	25	.10
Other	10	.04
Sales of scrap	-80	-.32
Subtotal	$ 6,135	$ 24.54
Factory Total	$20,835	$ 83.34
Non-Factory Costs		
Research and development	$ 750	$ 3.00
Administrative	675	2.70
Marketing	650	2.60
Divisional personnel	450	1.80
Other allocations	400	1.60
Divisional data processing	375	1.50
Divisional mfg. development	275	1.10
Miscellaneous corporate charges	250	1.00
Divisional accounting	225	.90
Divisional purchasing	200	.80
Divisional quality assurance	175	.70
Other income	-10	-.04

Cost Area	Annual Cost ($000s)	Cost per Unit (Dollars)
Non-factory Total	$ 3,665	$ 14.66
Total Cost	$24,500	$ 98.00
Profit	$ 1,750	7.00
Sales Dollars	$26,250	$105.00

Units Sold: 250,000

Using The New Tool

Let us suppose that a manufacturer of road resurfacing equipment is contemplating the addition of some snow moving equipment to his product line. Though they do not appear anywhere in normal cost statements, the benefits of this new product line would be obvious to some members of the organizational team:

- The new products are countercyclical to the road equipment products, that is, they will provide the most business during the fall and winter, slack periods for the older product lines.
- The new products use exactly the same kinds of manufacturing facilities as the road equipment. Almost no capital investment will be needed to tool the factory for the production of snow blades, augers, or chains.
- Snow moving equipment is purchased by the same groups as is road resurfacing equipment, and the sales people continue to call on these people all winter, just to keep their contacts warm.
- Most of the winter activity in the factory is busy work anyway. In low-tech product lines, it is common practice to provide work just to "keep the team together," since inadequate production documentation and informal factory procedures usually mean that product information is housed in the heads of the factory people. In this environment, seasonal layoffs would be fatal to the organization.

Someone else would hire the factory workers, leaving the company without a staff or a product line!

The normal accounting system would determine the number of direct labor hours required to make the new products, then multiply it by the existing overhead rate for each department. The result would be a cost which greatly overstates the cost of broadening the line. Using this cost to support pricing discussions might well cause the new line to be priced out of the market. The true cost would be something like material cost plus direct labor (with fringes) plus a few percent for additional technical staff, a much lower number. Team pricing would bring the above information out. In a team environment, the interaction between the marketing people and the manufacturing organization would soon convince the accountants that pricing the snow moving equipment at whatever the market will pay, as long as it exceeds the costs above, would be sound business practice.

This is a trivial example, since countercyclical products are well understood by most managers. At this level of analysis, the Contribution Margin cost model will probably prove adequate. When a higher resolution tool is needed, Functional Costing will pay dividends. It provides data to answer the hard questions like:

- If a new product requires special inspection (as in military versions of existing vehicles) what will that do to the cost picture?
- What happens to cost if we have to add a shift to produce the new product?
- What happens to the cost picture if we purchase most of the components for a new product, rather than make them?

No P&L statement will provide all the answers needed to support pricing decisions. The functional cost statement will, however, supply the cost impact of a change in the organization. It must be left to the same team who drew up the functional costing model to determine the impact on headcount, material cost, operating hours, floorspace, etc., of a new product, or a change in mix and volume of any products. This group can identify the non-financial components of the decision as well. These include the fit of the new business with existing products, the impact upon the existing business cycle, and the time involved to implement the necessary changes in the plant and workforce. They can also help to review the manufacturability of a new product under consideration. For custom made products in particular, design changes are often easier to achieve before a price is set than after.

In short, there is no substitute for teamwork. When pricing is treated as a team decision, profit potential increases, due to the tailoring of the business and the new product to one another. (We haven't stressed tailoring of the product to existing manufacturing facilities, but this is a very effective way to increase profit.) When we operate this way, competitive position becomes a determinant of plant policy, instead of its victim. The parochial concerns of the functional groups within the organization take second place to the proper overriding concern of the business—profit.

Recommended for Additional Reading

On Contribution Margin Costing:

Charles T. Horngren, *Introduction to Management Accounting*, Prentice-Hall, Inc., Englewood Cliffs, NJ.

On Functional Costing:

J. Stanton McGroarty, "Functional Costing: Understanding Where the Money Goes," *Manufacturing Engineering*, January, 1987 issue, Society of Manufacturing Engineers, PO Box 930, Dearborn, MI 48121.

J. Stanton McGroarty, "Cost Accounting: Bringing It into the Real World," *Industry Week*, November 2, 1987, Penton Publishing, 1100 Superior Avenue, Cleveland, OH 44114.

CHAPTER FIVE

CONSUMER BEHAVIOR FOUNDATIONS FOR PRICING

JERRY N. CONOVER

JERRY N. CONOVER

Jerry N. Conover is Associate Professor of Marketing and Coordinator of the Marketing Area at Northern Arizona University. He previously served on the marketing faculty at the University of Arizona after earning Ph.D.'s in both psychology and marketing at the University of Missouri. Dr. Conover's research focuses on consumer information processing, particularly the processing of product and price information. He is also Director of Market Insight, a Flagstaff, Arizona, consulting firm specializing in marketing research, analysis, and planning with organizations in both consumer and business markets.

CHAPTER FIVE

W hat is the role of price in consumer behavior? This question seems so simple anyone could answer it—even those who didn't take Economics 101 in school. But the apparent simplicity of the question is deceptive, for price influences consumers in varying, and often unpredictable, ways. Those with a grasp of the findings of consumer research will have a decided advantage in using price as a strategic component of their marketing mixes. In this chapter, some key lessons from that research are revealed.

The Consumer As Economist

As common experience indicates, the higher the price of an item, the less likely it is to be bought. This is illustrated by the classic demand curve showing the quantity of a product demanded at various prices (Figure 1).

The economic theory of buyer behavior views the consumer as a rational decision maker who seeks to maximize the utility he or she receives from a purchase. Having a limited budget for buying, the consumer will buy a product if he or she cannot gain more satisfaction by spending the same amount on another product. Thus, all else being equal, a lower price will increase the unit sales of a product, as shown in Figure 1.

This view of the consumer as deliberate and rational implies predictable, consistent purchase patterns that we know are not always in accord with reality. For example:

A wine retailer offered Cabernet Sauvignon wines from two different California wineries. Though one sold for $6.99 and

Figure 1 Quantity Demanded at Various Prices

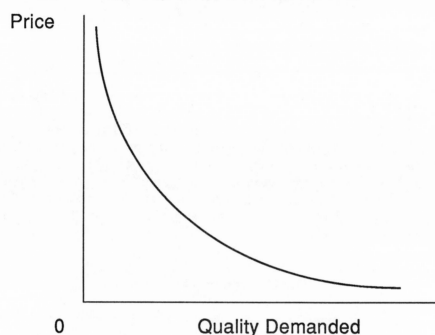

Price

0   Quality Demanded

the other for $9.99, the more expensive wine regularly outsold the cheaper one. Since the retailer's margins were about the same on each wine, he thought he'd do his customers a favor by posting a review that stated the two Cabernets were of comparable quality. Even with this information available on the shelf, however, the more expensive wine continued to be the better seller.

Why would a consumer choose the more expensive of two products of similar quality? As it turns out, consumer behavior is not always rational and predictable as assumed in the economic theory of buyer behavior. The consumer is not simply a "black box" that responds in a set fashion upon exposure to a particular price; many factors mediate response to price. We must look inside the black box to see how it works if we are to understand how price affects consumers.

The Consumer As Information Processor

In recent years there has emerged a large body of research based on the notion that consumers are processors of information (as depicted in Figure 2). They are constantly exposed to a variety of informational inputs such as advertisements, product labels, sales pitches, word-of-mouth, magazine articles, and so on, that provide direct information concerning product performance, quality, price, and features. Consumers also receive less overt information through using products and observing others use them.

For such information to play a role in purchase behavior, the consumer must first *pay attention* to it. Attention serves a selecting function, focusing awareness on one or more of the many stimuli to which the consumer is exposed. Attention may be involved and deliberate, as when the consumer is intent on making a smart purchase choice and seeks out information to aid the decision. Or attention might occur more passively, as when a television viewer sits through a commercial without closely monitoring its content. Chances are some information from that commercial gets through to the viewer, but without any great involvement on the viewer's part. Designers of advertising are well acquainted with techniques (such as employing unusual visual, verbal, or symbolic elements; using bright or contrasting colors; and so forth) for grabbing the attention of consumers who are not intent on noticing a message.

Attention to product information simply means it is noticed to one degree or another, but just noticing it is not enough to influence behavior. If the information is to have any further impact, the consumer must also *encode* that information into an internal, psychological representation that may be stored in memory for future reference or that may influence behavior on the spot.

The encoded version may be an accurate, objective representation of the external product information on which it is based. However, the encoding process frequently is biased by the consumer's expectations, other related information, past experiences with the product, social pressures, and a host of other factors. For example:

Figure 2   Consumer Processing of Price Information

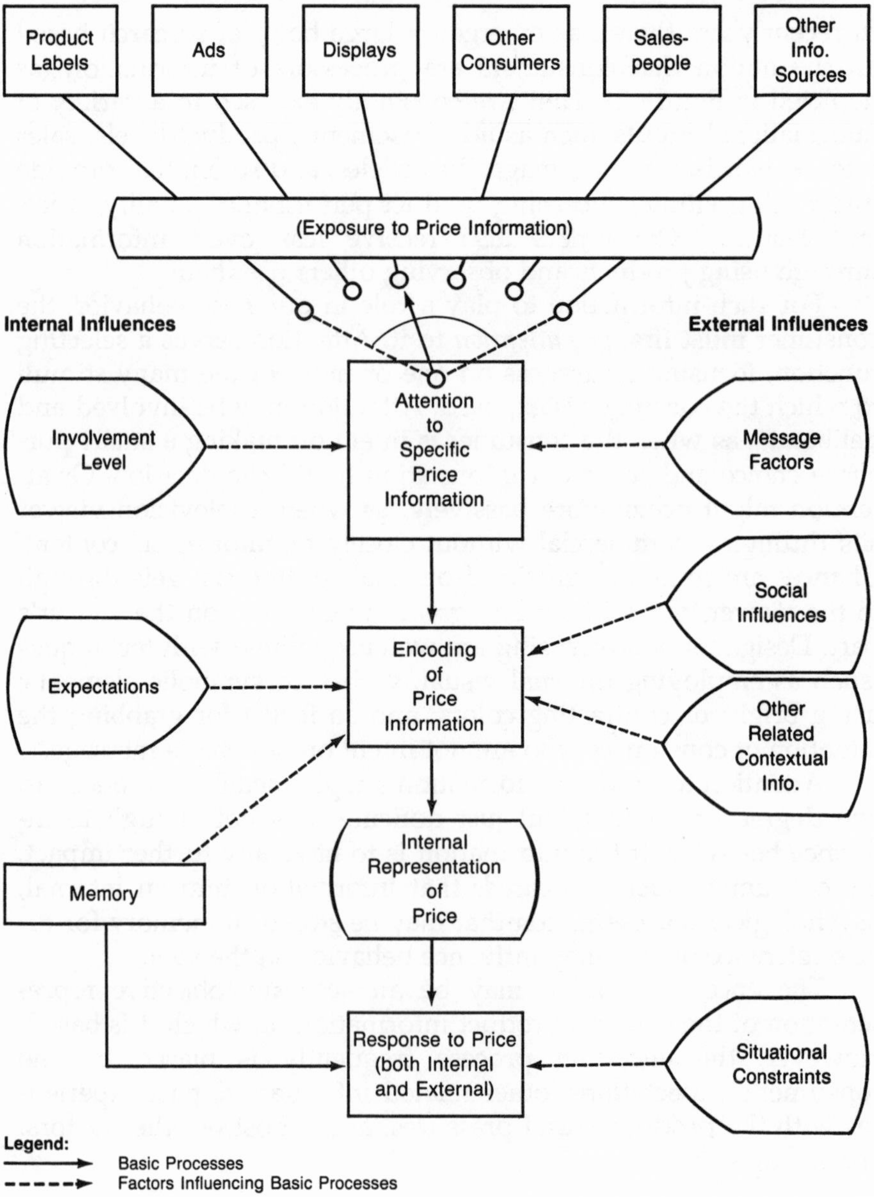

Legend:

⟶ Basic Processes

- - - - -▸ Factors Influencing Basic Processes

The honors for the best national TV ad campaign at the 29th annual Clio Awards went to North American Philips Lighting Corporation's humorous efforts to boost awareness of its light bulbs. While many viewers found the commercials amusing, a survey revealed that 20% of those who'd seen them thought they were for market leader General Electric, while only 17% correctly identified (encoded) them as Philips ads.

The important point for the marketer to remember is that, however the product information is encoded, it is this internal representation, not the objective external information itself, that influences the consumer's actions.

The process of stimulus (i.e., external information) encoding leads to various *responses* by the consumer. Upon reading the signs in a new-product display in the store, for example, a consumer may ask a salesperson for more information, or he may buy the product on the spot. Such overt responses are mediated by situational factors active at the moment. For instance, the shopper may decide to buy the new product on display, only to realize he doesn't have enough money with him to do so.

In addition to, or perhaps instead of, these overt responses, the consumer may generate internal responses such as forming a favorable attitude toward the new item, or simply making a mental note of the information, storing it in memory for later retrieval as needed.

Processing Price Information

How does price enter into this very abbreviated overview of consumer information processing? Price is treated simply as another piece of product information available to consumers—a stimulus from which attention, encoding, and response processes may result.

If the marketer seeks to elicit a particular response to price, such as purchase of the product, then consumers must pass through this sequence of information-processing events in a manner appropriate to that response. Thus, the consumer must attend to the price and then encode it appropriately to lead to the desired response. Impediments may occur at any stage of information processing, however, to lessen the likelihood of the desired response occurring.

Attention to Price

Marketers often seek to direct shoppers' attention to price when their product is attractively priced compared to competitors. However, the mere presence of an attractive price does not guarantee attention:

> One coffee marketer planned a major price promotion in the form of a $1.00 mail-in rebate to purchasers of its instant coffee. Having budgeted several hundred thousand dollars for rebate payments, the marketing manager was surprised when she had to pay out only one-fifth the anticipated amount. And she was disappointed that unit sales did not show the big increase she expected. A consultant, called in to find out why the promotion bombed, discovered from consumer interviews that those who sent in the rebate coupons were regular users who would have bought the brand anyway, while users of competing brands had not noticed there was a rebate available. The consultant suggested a simple shelf talker to draw shoppers' attention to the deal, coupled with a larger flag on the package highlighting it. Upon implementing these simple changes, redemptions picked up considerably, increasing unit volume and taking substantial market share away from competitors.

There are many similar overt ways to elicit consumers' attention to price. For instance, an ad or a display might graphically depict the savings a low price offers by portraying a pile of money before a smiling consumer. Or a retailer might post signs explicitly comparing specific prices of store brands with national brands. As research suggests that such efforts do lead to increased awareness of price, marketers whose prices are favorable in comparison to competitors would be wise to take steps to ensure attention to price at the point of purchase and in advertising.

Price Encoding

A consumer's mental representation of a particular price may take various forms. In some situations it may be encoded in literal, numeric terms paralleling the dollars-and-cents figure on the product. In other cases the consumer may encode a given price in more abstract, semantic terms, such as "ridiculously high," "on sale today," or "within my budget." It is also possible that multiple encodings, both literal and semantic, might result from a consumer's attention to a price.

Unfortunately, there is no solid basis for predicting how a given price will be perceived by consumers. Indeed, different consumers probably use diverse encodings in response to the same price. There is some evidence, however, that both absolute, literal price representations and more abstract interpretations are commonly employed, and also that situational factors may influence the nature of price encoding.

In the absence of clear data on price encoding, marketers might attempt intuitively to shape the way consumers perceive prices. Careful construction of promotional messages, for example, should help influence the interpretation of price information contained in those messages. Many advertisements compare, either implicitly or explicitly, a product's price with prices of its competitors: for instance, "...the most expensive television set in America—and darn well worth it," or, "if you can see the difference, you must be looking at the price."

Of course, price is rarely the sole criterion for a purchase decision, so its presentation in communications should take into account its impact on perception of other product attributes. An effective ad with a comparative-savings theme will somehow—through illustration, copy, imagery, etc.—communicate the satisfaction the buyer will obtain for the lower price. For example:

K-Mart promotes itself as "The Savings Place" with a strong discount orientation. To offset the negative image of discount stores held by many middle-class consumers, K-Mart advertises that it carries well-respected name brands, and it blesses its own line of clothing with the name and endorsement of celebrity Jacqueline Smith. Through such communications,

America's second largest retailer seeks to stimulate in consumers an encoding of low price that means "good value" rather than "poor quality."

Thus, it is important for marketers to consider the impact on price encoding of all aspects of the marketing mix—product and packaging characteristics, promotional messages and media, distribution outlets, and so on.

Responses to Price

The most obvious consumer response to price information marketers seek is, of course, its use in deciding to purchase the product. There also are often other desired overt price responses, such as telling a friend about a good deal, saving up to buy an expensive item, and applying for a credit account.

Perhaps more interesting for their variety are the wide range of covert, or internal, responses consumers have to price. As suggested earlier, perceptions of other product attributes are involved in shaping the consumer's response to any given attribute. Depending on how congruent a product's price is with its other characteristics, consumers may respond variously with impressions of real economy and value or of outrageous overcharging; with incredulity about the product's attributes (e.g., "it can't have all those features for so little cost!"); and with a host of other subjective reactions, many of which are in the realm of feelings, more than thoughts, about the product. In addition to possibly shaping immediate purchase decisions, these subjective reactions to price may influence later purchase decisions, even if price itself is not considered at that time.

Given the potential importance of subjective responses to price for purchase decisions, the remainder of this chapter will address in some detail three aspects of consumer behavior involving such responses.

Price and Perceived Quality

The economic theory of buyer behavior assumes that consumers have perfect information about all alternatives under consideration as they contemplate a purchase. In the real world, however, this is often not the case, as our ability to evaluate products is constrained by limited information on product composition and features, uncertainty as to appropriate evaluative criteria, technological complexity, and other factors.

Since price is one piece of product information almost always available, consumers sometimes rely on price as an indicator of product quality. If higher-priced products are perceived to be of higher quality, and thus are more desirable, then the demand curve may have a positive slope, as in Figure 3. Of course, demand could not increase indefinitely with price, or marketers would all get rich by charging enormously high prices. Thus, demand must eventually decrease as price continues to rise.

Economists have long acknowledged that certain special types of goods could have a positive relationship between price and quantity demanded. For example, when Toni home permanents were first introduced at a price around a dollar, sales were disappointingly low. An astute marketing manager decided to more than double the price, to a level closer to that of beauty-shop perms, and sales took off. Apparently, women who were interested in the product doubted its quality at such a low price—it was seen as an "inferior good"—but the higher price conveyed an impression of quality.

Other cases in which a positive link between price and perceived quality is expected are goods with "snob" appeal—Rolex watches, Glenfiddich Scotch, Rolls-Royce automobiles—bought by people with substantial means, for whom a high price may itself be a desirable attribute.

But what about more "ordinary" situations? Do consumers generally infer higher quality from a higher price? There is reason to believe they do, at least in some situations. As price is but one of many available cues for judging most products, its impact on quality perceptions depends in part on what other information is available. Several studies have reported a price-perceived quality relationship when price was the only information available for choosing between two hypothetical brands—clearly not a very common situation.

Figure 3   A Positive Price-Perceived Quality Relationship

Price

Quality Demanded

0

Research comparing quality judgments at various prices when brand names were available to the subjects has reported a stronger positive impact of price on perceived quality than when brand names were not present. That is, consumers' impressions of quality increase more rapidly as price is raised for brand-name products than for products that don't bear a respected brand name. This suggests that brand reputation and high prices work together to shape impressions of high quality.

Viewing collectively the results from several studies, it appears that price is often used by consumers in forming impressions of product quality, and more so to the extent that other product information is not available or cannot be assessed knowledgeably. Thus, in evaluating technologically complex items (e.g., state-of-the-art home electronic equipment) or items about which the buyer has little detailed knowledge (e.g., oriental rugs or premium imported wines), many consumers may infer higher quality from a higher price.

It is important to note that a consumer who perceives a high-priced brand to be of higher quality than others will not necessarily choose that brand. A product whose high quality comes only at a very high price may not be viewed as a good value. The perception of *value* (the amount of quality received relative to the price paid), not just quality *per se*, influences one's willingness to buy a product. Thus, high prices both positively influence perceived quality and negatively influence perceived value; it is the tradeoff between these two forces that determines whether the consumer buys.

Odd-Pricing Effects

For many decades merchants have widely practiced "odd pricing," which entails pricing products a little below a round-number price (e.g., $3.98 instead of $4.00). While retail price surveys have demonstrated the widespread use of odd pricing, there has been little consensus as to whether it enhances sales, and, if so, why it might work. Several field studies have been conducted on odd pricing, variously reporting negative, positive, and neutral effects of odd prices on sales.

Some supporters of odd pricing have argued that consumers pay more attention to the left-most digits of a price figure than to the last digits, leading to the perception that an odd price is lower than it actually is (and, therefore, more of a savings compared to the corresponding even price than is really the case). For example, a price of $3.98 might be encoded as "three dollars and something", rather than as "about four dollars." There is some evidence that odd prices are later recalled as lower than they actually were, more so than is the case with even prices. But increases in consumers' willingness to buy has not been linked reliably to odd prices.

Odd prices may also influence the consumer's perception of product quality and savings. One study reported that odd prices lead to the impression that the product is on sale. But, potentially offsetting this effect, there is also some evidence that odd-priced products are viewed as being of poorer quality than their even-priced counterparts. Though these two image effects are not typically large, the marketer contemplating use of odd prices in a particular case would be well advised to assess their relative impacts on overall willingness to buy. The scarcity of solid findings about the effects of odd pricing calls for a cautious approach in its use by marketing managers.

Deal Proneness

A final topic of substantial interest to consumer goods marketers is *deal proneness*—the greater likelihood of some consumers to buy when a brand is "on deal" (i.e., offered with some sort of price promotion) than when it is at the regular price. Given the rapidly growing use of coupons, rebates, and other consumer price promotions, it would be useful to identify how those most prone to take advantage of such deals differ from other consumers.

Several studies have explored characteristics of deal-prone consumers. Most of this work has tracked purchases of individual consumer-panel households over time, comparing occurrences of buying on deal to buying at the regular price.

The most deal-prone households consistently have been characterized as non-loyal buyers of the brand on deal. This is not surprising, as the more brand-loyal consumers may have strong reasons for preferring their regular brands other than its price. This finding has significant implications for marketing managers, since those buying on deal are likelier than those buying at the regular price to switch to a different brand once the deal is over.

In fact, the rapidly increasing use of both trade and consumer price promotions may help account for the results of a recent study on brand loyalty. This survey found that the percentage of people who try to stick with well-known brands dropped in just eight years from 77% to 59%—and it's probably still falling. Many manufacturers feel that the heavy use of price promotions has eroded consumers' reliance on brand names in their shopping decisions. Thus, such promotions may undermine the heavy investments marketers have made in building brand franchises.

Other characteristics reported among deal-prone households include: older, non-working wives; few children; light usage of the product category; relatively high exposure to media; and personality characteristics such as venturesomeness and gregariousness. Not all of these characteristics, however, will likely apply in any given case.

The incredibly rapid growth of couponing as a key tool of price promotion has led recently to several studies of consumers' usage of coupons. A common finding is that the likelihood of coupon usage increases with household size and income. One recent study of "coupon-proneness" reported that households using coupons regularly in multiple product categories tend to have high levels of education and to be in urban locations.

Of particular interest to marketers may be the observation that the likelihood of using a coupon for a particular brand increases with the number of prior purchases a consumer has made of that brand. Consequently, a large proportion of the sales increase that often follows a coupon drop may be attributable to regular users of a brand, leading to reduced profits. However, the common observation that coupon redemption increases with face value has been found to result mainly from incremental purchases by non-regular users of the brand. Thus, higher-value coupons may be especially useful in attracting new customers.

One final note concerns *why* some shoppers seem to be coupon-prone. As noted above, these consumers tend not to have greater economic constraints than others, since coupon usage increases with income. But some recent evidence suggests that coupon-prone shoppers may gain feelings of pleasure and pride in getting deals, achieving savings, and generally "smart shopping." The marketer who relies heavily on couponing may be appealing especially to a limited segment of the market which seeks out the deals. Other types of promotions may be called for to influence the larger numbers of less deal- and coupon-prone consumers in order to build a brand's consumer franchise.

Key Lessons from Consumer Research

This overview of consumer behavior ideas related to pricing has presented a framework for understanding price responses, and has summarized research findings in three key aspects of such responses: the impact of price on perceived quality; response to odd prices; and deal- and coupon-proneness.

In summary, the following propositions are offered to help marketing managers make pricing decisions that are consistent with what is known about consumer behavior:

1. *Pricing should not be done in a vacuum.* Other marketing mix variables help determine the impression a consumer forms of a product, and thus his willingness to buy. A product whose price is incongruent with brand or store image, packaging, advertising, and the like will not be viewed as favorably by consumers as it should.

2. *Price competition is not for everyone.* Following from the previous point, some products are well-suited to a low-price strategy because the remaining components of their marketing strategy help create a sense of value compatible with the low price. But other products can suc-

cessfully employ a high-price strategy if their companies enjoy, or can create, a market perception of high enough quality to justify the price.

3. *If price is to play a key role in the marketing strategy, make sure consumers notice it.* Too many marketers have assumed that consumers will respond to their attractive prices, only to find out that the price wasn't gaining consumers' attention.

4. *Use odd prices cautiously.* Despite their popularity in certain industries, evidence that odd prices boost sales is very equivocal. The few cents' sacrifice in unit profits that odd prices imply could add up quickly for high-volume products. Simple field studies comparing odd- and even-price strategies can quickly reveal whether they'll pay off.

5. *Consider whether the deal-prone segment is a desirable target for your product.* Deal-proneness has grown at the expense of brand loyalty. Can your product survive in the long run engaged in heavy price-dealing competition? Or does it make more sense to build an image of quality and value that will attract a loyal consumer franchise? A non-dealing strategy may yield fewer sales, but higher profits, than heavy dealing.

Consumer response to price is an important topic for all marketing managers to understand. The present state of knowledge in this area, however, leaves many questions to be resolved. Fortunately, there is currently much activity in research centers directed at finding those answers. The marketer who wishes to make the most of this knowledge will pay close attention in the years to come to the results of these efforts.

Recommended for Additional Reading

Bawa, Kapil, and Robert W. Shoemaker, "The 'Coupon-Prone' Consumer: Some Findings based on Purchase Behavior across

Product Classes," *Journal of Marketing,* Volume 51, No. 4 (October 1987), pp. 99-110.

Conover, Jerry N. "Shoppers' Recall of Grocery Product Prices," *Proceedings of the 1988 Summer Educators' Conference.* Chicago: American Marketing Association, pp. 62-67.

Monroe, Kent B., *Pricing: Making Profitable Decisions.* New York: McGraw-Hill, 1979, pp. 23-25.

Monroe, Kent B. and R. Krishnan, "The Effect of Price on Subjective Product Evaluations," in Jacob Jacoby and Jerry C. Olson (eds.), *The Perception of Merchandise and Store Quality.* Lexington, MA: Lexington Books, 1985, pp. 209-232.

Monroe, Kent B. and Susan M. Petroshius, "Buyers' Subjective Perceptions of Price: An Update of the Evidence," in Harold Kassarjian and Thomas Robertson (eds.), *Perspectives in Consumer Behavior.* Glenview, IL: Scott, Foresman and Company, pp. 43-55.

Price, Linda L., Lawrence F. Feick, and Audrey Guskey-Federouch, "Couponing Behaviors of the Market Maven: Profile of a Super Couponer" *Advances in Consumer Research,* Volume 15, Ed. Michael J. Houston, 1988, pp. 354-359.

Webster, Frederick E., Jr., "The 'Deal-Prone' Consumer," *Journal of Marketing Research,* Volume 2 (May 1965), pp. 186-189.

Zeithaml, Valarie A., "Issues in Conceptualizing and Measuring Consumer Response to Price," in Thomas Kinnear (ed.), *Advances in Consumer Research,* Volume 11. Provo, UT: Association for Consumer Research, pp. 612-616.

CHAPTER SIX

LEGAL CONSIDERATIONS IN PRICING DECISIONS:

"Predatory" Pricing

KEVIN J. O'CONNOR

KEVIN J. O'CONNOR

Kevin J. O'Connor is an Assistant Attorney General in charge of antitrust enforcement at the Wisconsin Department of Justice and an occasional lecturer at the University of Wisconsin-Madison. He received his J.D. from Harvard University and Ph.D. in Economics from the University of Wisconsin-Madison. Dr. O'Connor's research interests include the legal and economic analyses of predatory business strategies and a variety of antitrust and trade regulation issues.

CHAPTER SIX

A firm's pricing decision can have profound legal consequences. As is well known, an agreement by a firm with its
competitors to fix prices, to rig bids, to standardize promotional discounts, or to limit competition in almost any manner is
clearly unlawful and likely to subject the offending firms to substantial criminal and civil penalties. Less clear are the limits under
the antitrust laws on pricing decisions by firms *acting alone*. To
what extent can a firm legally cut price and adopt related promotional tactics with the purpose or effect of increasing or maintaining market share or eliminating a rival or potential rival from a
market? This chapter first examines various tests for predatory
pricing which have been offered in recent years. It discusses in
depth litigated cases which have implemented some of these tests.
Finally, it suggests some general guideposts to be followed when
making that rock-bottom pricing decision and related promotional
campaign.

Predatory Pricing Defined

"Predation" or "predatory business conduct" has been the focus of
much attention in the law and economics literature. Despite this,
these terms have no universally accepted definition. Although virtually every aspect of business behavior (e.g., decisions concerning
output, promotional spending, plant location and plant size) can
be considered "predatory" in some contexts, the literature has
focused primarily on predatory pricing. The focus on pricing is
undoubtedly due to the relative ease with which pricing decisions

can be analyzed, at least superficially, using the standard neo-classical theory of the firm. For example, predatory pricing has been defined loosely as the adoption of a pricing policy which involves a reduction of price in the short-run so as to drive competing firms out of the market or to discourage new entry in order to gain higher profits in the lon-run than would have been earned had there been no short-run price reduction.[1] Others have attempted to bring to bear on this problem much more sophisticated theoretical and empirical tools developed in the industrial organization literature.[2] Such tools are usually ill-suited to analyze nonprice business phenomena. Whether more sophisticated tools necessarily lead to a better rule or a better constellation of rules and institutions is, of course, open to question.

Although the legal standards applied to such conduct by the courts have been rather amorphous, evidence of such strategies under certain conditions can establish violations of Section 2 of the Sherman Act[3] (for monopolization and attempts to monopolize) and Section 1(a) of the Robinson-Patman Act[4] (for price discrimination), as well as comparable provisions of state law.[5]

Judicial Analysis Confused

Unfortunately, the judicial analysis of predatory behavior under these very general standards has been plagued by chaotic decisional law, usually informed by little or confused economic analysis. The courts simply have not had an intellectual apparatus which would allow them to distinguish consistently between predation and vigorous, but legal, competition. Indeed, despite the economic character of the problem, the role of economic and accounting data in most aspects of the analysis has been very unclear. Even when the United States Supreme Court made its most recent (1967) attempt in the landmark *Utah Pie* case[6] to set a costfloor, for allegedly predatory pricing, the standard was widely criticized as being very unclear and as creating inhibitions upon vigorous price competition.

The Areeda-Turner "Solution"

In 1975, two Harvard Law School professors, Philip Areeda and Donald Turner, used an essentially static neoclassical economic framework to prescribe a set of "rules of thumb" for courts to follow in dealing with predatory pricing cases.[7] This article has led to the formulation of the "Areeda-Turner" test.[8] Briefly, this cost-based test presumed the prices charged by a monopolist that were above "reasonably anticipated average variable cost" were lawful but that prices below that level were unlawful. Areeda and Turner reasoned that such below-cost pricing could only be for predatory motives since it would be less unprofitable for the monopolist to shut down than to continue suffering out-of-pocket losses. Where a non-monopolist was concerned, the test required a plaintiff to show that the alleged predator had greater "staying ability" in the marketplace. This requirement gave the alleged predator an opportunity to show indirectly that low barriers to entry in the market would preclude the later enjoyment of monopoly profits even if the pricing practices led to the exclusion of current rivals.

The Areeda-Turner article not only generated an intense controversy among industrial organization economists, but also has led courts to apply and, in some instances, to misapply the Areeda-Turner test in predatory pricing cases which have come before them.[9] Despite this controversy, a trend towards acceptance of the Areeda-Turner analysis developed. Often, however, the distinction between monopolists and non-monopolists was blurred and the courts applied varying degrees of conclusiveness to the price-average variable cost comparison. Numerous federal judges have rejected the straightforward test and have jerry-rigged much more complex tests which are intended to remedy some of the more obvious defects in the Areeda-Turner test.[10]

Beyond Areeda-Turner: Full Cost Standards and Complex Approaches

Despite the intensive analysis of predation over the past fifteen years, no consensus has developed on the appropriate methodology with which to approach the subject, much less on the appropriate rule or set of rules decisionmakers should adopt. The policy prescriptions have varied widely. Several authors have proposed simple cost-based rules similar to the Areeda-Turner rules for distinguishing between non-predatory and predatory pricing behavior.[11]

Alternatively, several authors have proposed predation rules which explicitly incorporate an element of "intent" to exclude a competitor from a market. These rules usually couple intent with the requirement that the plaintiff bear the burden of showing that prices are below long-run marginal costs or a surrogate of long-run marginal costs, such as average total costs. For example, Greer proposes a rule that presumptively defines predatory pricing as (1) pricing below average total cost and (2) substantial evidence of predatory intent.[12] Greer would allow anyone accused of predatory pricing to rebut a *prima facie* case based on average total cost with proof that long-run marginal costs were significantly below his average total cost and price.

Similarly, Posner proposes a presumptive rule that defines predation as selling at a price below average total cost with intent to exclude a competitor.[13] Posner like Greer also allows the defendant to rebut this presumption by demonstrating circumstances which indicate that either long-run or short-run marginal cost was the appropriate standard. Both Greer and Posner place the burden of proof and persuasion on the plaintiff for showing intent and price below average total cost. Greer in particular suggests that the plaintiff's burden with regard to intent is somewhat above the usual preponderance of the evidence standard by using such adjectives as "substantial," "ample," "explicit," and "strong" to describe the requisite evidence of intent for a predation violation. Apparently, because he deems it "extraordinarily difficult to ascertain the intent of a large corporation by methods of litigation," Posner does not require a similar "clear and convincing" showing of intent to exclude a competitor.

Both Greer and Posner view the Areeda-Turner rule as, in effect, a special case of their broader rule. That is, Posner views selling below short-run marginal cost as a sufficient (but not a necessary) grounds for establishing predation, even in the absence of predatory intent.[14] Greer, similarly, provides that a price below short-run variable cost "certainly indicates predatory intent, given that such deep cutting is not consistent with short-run profit maximization or loss minimization."[15]

Others have argued that cost-based rules can be useful only in specific contexts,[16] in conjunction with other non-economic indicia of predation,[17] or as part of a multi-tier analysis of alleged predatory pricing.[18] Other authors have rejected explicit reliance on cost-based rules and have opted for rules emphasizing, at least in part, the timing of price changes[19] or the timing of changes in the quantity sold.[20] Some economists have rejected appeals to such interindustry rules of thumb as described above and have proposed a case-by-case *ex post facto* analysis of alleged predation cases.[21] Finally, some commentators have suggested that there is no need at all for rules governing predation.[22]

All of these recommendations are designed, in one fashion or another, to specify which conduct ought to be allowed as "vigorous competition" and which ought to be prohibited as likely to harm competition or the competitive process. Determining which category a specific pattern of conduct falls into is the essence of the difficult problem of articulationg meaningful predation rules and, indeed, defining the word "predation" itself.

Judicial Reaction to Economics-Based Predation Tests

For the past decade, the federal courts have been grappling with the legacy of the Areeda and Turner test for predatory pricing. Several conclusions can be drawn from these cases. First, a pervasive problem in virtually every predatory pricing case which implemented the Areeda-Turner test is the plaintiff's difficulty in obtaining adequate cost records from the defendant to determine whether any of the alternative cost-price tests had been met. This problem was particularly acute where the defendant was a large, dominant firm with a complex product, where regulation was a factor in the manner in which the defendant conducted business (*e.g.*, AT&T), or where the defendant operated in a variety of geographic and product markets and kept cost accounting records accordingly (*e.g.*, Inglis, IBM, Martin Marietta). Even in situations where the markets were relatively simple, discovery problems plagued plaintiffs attempting to establish the most rudimentary economic cost measures (*e.g.*, Adjusters Replace-A-Car).

In general, plaintiffs encountered extreme difficulty obtaining cost information in usable form, much less shaping that information in a manner consistent with the Areeda-Turner test. For example, in litigation involving AT&T, a succession of courts were faced with the Hobson's choice of two AT&T cost measures: fully distributed cost accounting or long-run incremental analysis. Both measures had serious deficiencies; neither was an accurate analogue for any economic measure of cost. Because of the great emphasis on the cost measures in these price-cost tests and because the plaintiff bore the burden of establishing cost, plaintiffs in every single case analyzed were put at a severe disadvantage meeting their burden on the cost issue. Plainly stated, the plaintiffs lost many cases on the ground that they had not carried their burden of showing an appropriate cost measure using the defendant's records. In other words, the court did not make an affirmative finding in many cases that price was *above* the appropriate cost measure; only that the plaintiff had not borne its burden of showing that price was *below* an appropriate cost measure.

Second, several striking disparities between the plaintiffs and defendants in these actions suggest why the defendants might rationally have decided to engage in this price-cutting activity and why it might objectively be considered a rational strategy. For example, in virtually every case, the defendant operated in broader geographical and product markets than the plaintiff. This enhanced the defendant's ability to cut prices selectively and avoid the attendant across-the-board losses of the sort contemplated by Areeda-Turner. Also, in some cases, the defendants stood in a vertical, supplier relationship with the plaintiff which enhanced the effectiveness of the pricing strategies on the plaintiffs.

Finally, in virtually every case, price-cutting tactics were only part of an overall strategy adopted by the defendant in the market in question. That is, although the records of these cases were often deficient because the Areeda-Turner rule limited the admissible evidence to price and "reasonably anticipated" cost measures, the records indicated that price-cutting was adopted, usually in conjunction with a panoply of other related actions. In other words, the litgated cases suggest that aggressive price-cutting activity occures most often where there are absolute size disparities, product range disparities, regulatory disparities, significant barriers to entry, and the persistence of these factors over time.

Two cases involving wholly opposite market structures exemplify the deficiencies in the Areeda-Turner and related cost-based tests. One case involves the highly regulated, highly concentrated, technologically dynamic telecommunications industry. The other involves the virtually unregulated, virtually atomistically competitive car replacement rental market.

Northeastern Telephone Co. v. American Telephone and Telegraph, Et Al.[23]

In 1972, Northeastern Telephone Company entered the market for business terminal equipment provided to business customers in Connecticut in competition with Southern New England Telephone Company (SNET), a partially owned subsidiary of AT&T. In 1975, Northeastern sued SNET, AT&T and Western Electric Company, a division of AT&T, alleging that the defendants had monopolized, attempted and conspired to monopolize, and restrained trade in the business terminal equipment market in the State of Connecticut in violation of sections 1 and 2 of the Sherman Act. Northeastern alleged that SNET had maintained its monopoly power in the market for business terminal equipment provided to business customers in those areas of Connecticut where SNET provided local telephone exchange service through a variety of predatory and anti-competitive tactics falling into several general categories: (a) pricing; (b) misuse of protective coupler arrangements ("PCA"); (c) advertising practices; (d) marketing practices; (e) misuse of utility functions; and (f) the introduction of new products. Northeastern won at a trial to a jury on all counts. The jury's decision was reversed by the Second Circuit Court of Appeals which entered judgment for the defendants on all grounds except for their alleged misuse of the protective coupler device which was remanded for retrial at the district court level.

Central to Northeastern's case were its pricing claims. These claims included: first, that SNET's rates for terminal equipment ("PBXs" or private branch equipment and "KTS" or key telephone systems) were predatory (*i.e.*, below fully distributed cost) and second, that a two-tier pricing system adopted by SNET to encourage current customers to stay with SNET in the face of competition was anti-competitive. In response, SNET argued for the adoption of a long-run "marginal" or incremental cost standard for determining whether their pricing was predatory. The defendants denominated their incremental cost standard "long-run incremental cost" ("LRIC"). LRIC purportedly included only the incremental costs of supplying a particular good or service and did not include any portion of the joint costs incurred in providing those goods or services along with other goods an services SNET provided.

Market Characteristics

By stipulation of the parties, the relevant product and geographic market was defined as the market for business terminal equipment (PBXs and KTSs) provided to business customers in those areas of Connecticut in which SNET provided local telephone exchange service. Prior to 1969, SNET was the only seller permitted by federal and state tariffs to attach terminal equipment to the local telephone network. Entry into this market was effectively blockaded by regulatory restrictions. In 1968, the Federal Communications Commission ruled that such tariffs were unreasonable and unlawful under federal law and that AT&T and its local operating subsidiaries (*e.g.*, SNET) must provide alternative equipment suppliers with direct electrical interconnection with terminal equipment to the Bell System lines. The Bell System responded to this ruling by permitting interconnection of competitive business telephone equipment, provided a PCA was used allegedly to protect the Bell System from damage caused by improperly designed equipment.

SNET's market share declined from 100 percent in 1968 to somewhat over 90 percent in 1978, whether measured by the number of systems installed or by revenue. New entrants into the market after the 1968 ruling included large conglomerates such as International Telephone and Telegraph and Nippon Electronics, as well as smaller firms such as the plaintiff, Northeastern Telephone Company. In its best year, Northeastern's annual revenue was less than five percent of the revenues SNET earned in the terminal equipment market alone.

SNET was a large, diversified, regulated, utility operating not only in the business equipment markets but also providing local telephone service. SNET bought its KTS's from Western Electric Company, a division of the integrated telecommunications system of AT&T. SNET purchased much of its private branch exchange equipment from Nippon, as did Northeastern. In 1977, SNET began purchasing some PBX equipment from Western Electric. SNET's position as part of a vertically integrated system allowed costs to be shifted from one enterprise to another within the AT&T family of corporations.

Subsequent to the *Carterfone* decision, entry was possible but was impeded by the requirement of SNET that competitors obtain a PCA which required a power source external from the power generated over SNET's telephone lines. These couplers were for the most part incompatible with the PBXs provided by Northeastern. Moreover, in the event of a general power outage, the competitor's equipment would be put out of commission, whereas SNET's equipment would not be. Hence, in addition to the cost disadvantage of having to include a PCA, new entrants were faced with a significant product disadvantage. AT&T's electrical engineers admitted on cross-examination that the coupler could have been designed to operate using the power available in SNET's telephone lines, thus eliminating the disadvantage to SNET's competitors. Thus, the substantial barriers to entry which existed after the Carterfone decision in 1968 were erected by the Bell System.

Evidence Relating to PBX Rates

The plaintiff submitted four categories of evidence to the jury concerning SNET's pricing of its PBX systems called Dimension 100 and Dimension 400. Each type of evidence indicated that SNET was not covering all of its costs when setting prices on its PBX systems. First, SNET conceded that its rates were based on LRIC and not FDC. Hence, SNET admitted not attributing any portion of its direct or common costs to Dimension PBX rates. Second, a tracking study (based on LRIA) prepared by SNET in October 1978, designed to measure Dimension's performance over the previous year, showed a small loss ($2,000 on total revenue of $232,000) for 1977, the first year of Dimension offering. Third, prior to the introduction of the Dimension PBX systems, SNET had been told by AT&T that it should reduce prices on the Dimension system. SNET in so doing also revised its forecasts of Dimension sales and costs which in effect reduced the additional cost that SNET assumed would be incurred by the introduction of Dimension. In other words, there was evidence indicating that SNET had altered its cost estimates for the introduction of Dimension to the extent that those costs were not attributable to Dimension directly, so as to permit a lower offering price yet allow the projection of a profit. Fourth, there was general testimony of the plaintiff's expert that the Dimension 100 system was underpriced by 46.73 percent and Dimension 400 by 9.65 percent.

Nowhere in the plaintiff's case was a direct comparison made between the rates for Dimension 100 and 400 PBXs and the fully distributed costs. The District Court held that even in the absence of such a direct comparison, the evidence outlined above was sufficient to support the jury's verdict. However, because the Second Circuit Court of Appeals adopted the defendants' surrogate for marginal cost, LRIC, and because the plaintiff could not or did not offer any comparisons between the price for the Dimension systems and LRIC, the Second Court reversed this portion of the district court's judgment.

Areeda-Turner Rule

As indicated above, the Areeda-Turner price-cost test, as modified, provides that a price is predatory when it is below the appropriate cost floor. The cost floor applicable in a given situation, however, depends upon the relationship between various measures of cost. For example:

> Where average variable cost ("AVC") is greater than or not substantially below marginal cost ("MC"), average variable cost is the floor; where marginal cost rises significantly above average variable cost at moderate output levels, marginal cost is the floor; and where marginal cost is significantly above both average total cost and average variable cost, marginal cost is the floor.

Both the district court and the Second Circuit Court of Appeals paid lip service to the Areeda-Turner analysis. However, the district court ultimately rejected strict adherence to the Areeda-Turner standards arguing that such a rule was inappropriate for a multi-product firm which obtained a large portion of its revenues from regulated monopoly services. Instead, the district court adopted fully distributed cost (FDC) as its cost floor. FDC combined the marginal or incremental cost of supplying a particular good or service with some portion of the unattributable costs or joint costs of providing the product.

The Second Circuit Court of Appeals rejected the FDC standard. In an extensive exegesis relying heavily on Areeda-Turner's analysis, the Second Circuit did not find that price was greater than the MC/AVC floor. It simply cited the plaintiff's failure of proof that price was below the MC/AVC standard.

Neither court discussed how Northeastern could have obtained a measure of marginal or average variable cost given the accounting systems adopted by the defendants. The Second Circuit seems to imply that the long-run incremental analysis (LRIA) used by the defendants to evaluate the contribution they could expect new products to provide to "non-allocable" overhead expenses was a loose surrogate for short-run marginal cost or average variable cost. In essence, LRIA is the manner in which AT&T and its related corporations estimate costs expected to be incurred as a result of the introduction of a new product on the market. Typically, sales volumes and revenue for particular price levels are projected. Obviously, this calculation is dependent to a large extent on the price cross-elasticity of the SNET product versus the products of competitors. Then, to determine the new products' profitability, the revenue generated is compared to the sum of five general cost categories: operating expenses, captial costs, cross-elastic cost, start-up costs and inflation factors. Operating costs are those costs associated with the installation and sale of particular PBX systems and payments to Western Electric for the equipment provided, specific direct expenses, and installation costs. The cost of capital assumes a fourteen and one-half percent return on equity and a nine percent cost of debt which when properly weighted approximates a twelve percent cost of capital.

"Cross-elastic cost is simply a fancy phrase for indicating what the cost impact of this new product (i.e., PBXs) might be on some pre-existing product that the company offers."[24] That is, if setting the price of a PBX system at a certain level causes current SNET customers to switch to the new system from an existing SNET system, the lost revenue is calculated as a "cost" under the LRIA methodology. Start-up costs are those costs which are unique to the particular service involved but are incurred only when the service is first introduced. An example would be the cost of setting up a special billing system for the PBX system in question. Finally, LRIA would include an "inflation factor" which would simply be an estimate of the expected increases in material and labor costs through the duration of the projection.

As should be apparent from this discussion, LRIA bears virtually no discernible relationship to an economist's definition of short-run marginal cost or average variable costs. LRIA includes certain costs (e.g., captial costs, cross-eslastic costs, and start-up costs) which should be excluded from any measure of short-run measures. Excluded from the LRIA are administrative costs associated with the white collar offices of SNET, white collar salaries, institutional informative advertising, insurance, franchise requirements, and a general category of costs referred to by the Bell System as carrying charges on facilities or related equipment. Because the Bell System considered these expenses as joint costs, they are simply not allocated to new services under the LRIA analysis even though some of the costs (*e.g.,* institutional advertising) could logically be considered part of the variable costs of the introduction of a new system. Moreover, the prices paid by SNET to Western Electric for PBX systems did not reflect the true cost of those systems to Western Electric in that certain expenses, such as licensing fees for the technology involved in the systems, had been billed directly by Western Electric to SNET and recovered by SNET in the rate regulation process. In addition, SNET's research and development costs are spread over their entire operation whether regulated or unregulated, regardless of whether they are incurred specifically with respect to a new product such as a new PBX system.

Because of these inclusions and exclusions, it is virtually impossible to obtain any meaningful numbers from the data provided in the case record regarding the actual marginal or average variable costs of the PBX systems at issue. Moreover, given the manner in which SNET accounted for its costs, it was virtually impossible for the plaintiff to have met the burden of the Areeda-Turner test. However, given that the costs included in LRIA (*e.g.,* cost of capital equal to twelve percent) seemed to be in excess of the costs improperly excluded from a variable cost measure (*e.g.,* licensing fees paid by AT&T equal to roughly 1.5 percent), it is probable that the short-run average variable cost floor would have been somewhat lower than the numbers yielded by LRIA. Because there was no indication that price was below the long-run incremental unit cost of particular PBX systems, it is unlikely that the plaintiff in this case would have met the Areeda-Turner standard.

126 • KEVIN J. O'CONNOR

Full Cost Standards

As noted above, several authors have proposed rules which incorporate as necessary elements of a predation claim (1) pricing below average total cost; and (2) evidence of predatory intent. The first prong of Greer and Posner's tests is pricing below average total cost, whereas Shimer proposes a comparison of price to accountant's average total cost. Greer would allow anyone accused of predatory pricing to rebut a *prima facie* case based on average total cost with proof that long-run marginal cost was significantly below average total cost and price.

The fully distributed cost standard urged by the plaintiff is a better surrogate for average total cost although deficient in some respects. For example, fully distributed cost simply adds a uniform proportion of joint costs or overhead costs to LRIC. Hence, those elements of LRIC which are not correctly part of a "cost" standard, such as the cross-elastic effect, should not be included in the fully distributed cost standard. The plaintiff's expert witness testified that SNET had underpriced the Dimension 400 PBX by 9.65% and the Dimension 100 by 46.73% below fully distributed cost. This should not be terribly surprising. Even SNET's rate expert admitted that the LRIA formula used to price dimension PBXs completely excluded common overhead cost. The SNET projections indicate that SNET *expected* to achieve a minus .7% rate of return on capital investment over a five-year period given the pricing level it chose for the Dimension systems. It also expected to lose 34% of the market for PBX systems at this price level. When the common overhead costs are factored in it is apparent that the pricing level chosen by SNET did not come close to covering their average total cost, and SNET knew this.

Other evidence of SNET's predatory intent is mixed. First, SNET conceded that it was not pricing the Dimension systems to cover FDC or ATC. Second, a tracking study prepared by SNET in October 1978 indicated that SNET had not even covered its own measure of long-run incremental cost for a particular year. Third, there was evidence indicating that SNET had altered its cost estimates for the introduction of Dimension by asking AT&T to reduce the price of the Dimension products to SNET and permitting the recovery of AT&T's lower price through other amounts paid to AT&T. Fourth, SNET explicitly accounted for the loss of market share it would realize if it raised prices. Fifth, both the trial court and the appellate court agreed that the plaintiff had submitted substantial evidence indicating that AT&T had intentionally designed the protective couplers so as to impede competition in the terminal equipment market. The Bell System's own experts indicated that the protective couplers were over-designed, making them more expensive than necessary, and were designed in a way to require modification of non-Bell equipment or to require additional equipment and an external power source on the customer's premises. In short, it is apparent that SNET was attempting to maintain as much of its market share as it could in the area of PBXs and key telephones in the aftermath of the *Carterfone* decision.

Nonetheless, there did not appear to be any evidence in the record indicating that SNET had singled out Northeastern Telephone Company as a target for forceable exit from the market, although the conduct described did have a clear impact on Northeastern. Indeed, the use of the PCA is probably one of the clearest examples available of conduct which has the "effect of significantly impairing the ability of rivals to compete."[25]

Whether the evidence of intent described above meets the various tests is problematical. Greer in particular suggests that the plaintiff's burden with regard to intent is somewhat above the usual preponderance of the evidence. Posner on the other hand does not require "clear and convincing" evidence of intent to exclude a competitor apparently because he believes it is extraordinarily difficult to ascertain the intent of a large corporation by methods of litigation. Yet, given the history of this market, SNET had been the only provider of these systems prior to the regulatory changes in the late 60's and early 70's the evidence is fairly convincing that SNET intended to exclude all of its competitors from this market to the fullest possible extent. The fact that none of the potential entrants into this market was targeted by SNET relates more to the fact that entry was being attempted into this market simultaneously by several SNET competitors.

Shimer would have shifted the burden of production to the defendant after the plaintiff had demonstrated that price was below average total cost. Although Shimer would not permit the introduction of direct evidence on intent, he would permit the defendant to rebut the presumption of predatory "intent" established by the pricing below average total cost using one of four justifications. Because this rule was not applied at the trial of this matter, none of the defendants attempted to meet Shimer's criteria. However, a review of the appellate record indicates that it is unlikely that any one of Shimer's four categories applied. SNET was not liquidating excess merchandise, the industry did not have severe excess capacity, there was no evidence that SNET was matching a competitor's price, and there was no evidence that planned increases in SNET's sales of the Dimension systems would lower average total costs.

The contrast between the Shimer test and the Greer and Posner approach is instructive. Greer and Posner would apparently put the burden of persuasion on the plaintiff on the intent issue. Northeastern made a concerted effort to meet this burden by examining voluminous evidence from SNET's files and by attempting to reconstruct the business rationale for many of SNET's actions. Despite Northeastern's aggressiveness, meeting the burden of showing predatory intent, especially if it is defined as intent to exclude a particular rival as opposed to all rivals, is difficult. Operationally, Shimer's test would seem to have been more suited to the *Northeastern v. AT&T* case. If AT&T and SNET had been forced to answer the question as to its prices being below fully allocated average total cost, it is doubtful they could have offered a rationale that would be convincing other than that they were attempting to forestall loss of significant market share in the face of new entry by competitors such as Northeastern. None of the non-predatory explanations for such pricing behavior makes sense in this sort of a market.

Summary

This case is significant to the business practitioner because it represents a market situation where predatory pricing is likely to occur and likely to be successful. Because of this, it is the type of predation case defendants are most likely to lose or, at a minimum, the type of case courts will force defendants to litigate exhaustively. Hence, even though the defendants ultimately won most issues on appeal, they were forced to endure years of discovery, the loss of a jury trial, and a very expensive, time-consuming appeal.

A court is likely to find this market conducive to predatory pricing because SNET (AT&T) had a dominant position in this market best represented by the fact that its market share was over 90 percent in the late 1970's despite persistent attempts at entry. SNET's control of the local telephone grid made entry by SNET's rivals difficult. Moreover, although entry into this market did not require a significant amount of capital, it did require significant management and marketing skills as well as an ability to counter SNET's "image" advertising emphasizing its position as the sole provider of local exchange service.

This case is also significant because it demonstrates the link between pricing tactics and other exclusionary tactics which a dominant firm can adopt to maintain or increase its market position. For example, SNET's requirement for the protective coupler attachment, their active opposition to any entry in the 1960's and early 1970's, their explicit calculation of the trade-off of market share for profitability, and the adoption of an accounting scheme which failed to allocate joint costs on even a long-run basis, would be viewed by a court as supporting the inference of predatory intent. This would be the case especially where the entrenched, dominant firm was facing prospective entry by technologically innovative rivals. Also, because the defendant operated in broader geographical and product markets than its smaller rivals, a court and jury would tend to take a dimmer view of selective, targeted price cutting by the dominant firm. Targeted, selective price cutting in specific geographical or product markets could be characterized before a jury as a means by which such a dominant firm could avoid the heavy losses associated with across-the-board price cuts of the kind contemplated by Areeda and Turner.

Finally, this case is significant in that it demonstrates the difficulty of defining economic "cost" using real-world business accounting records. Even though the defendants ultimately prevailed on the pricing claims in this case, they were forced to endure years of intensive litigation centering upon their cost accounting methods.

Adjusters Replace-A-Car, Inc. v. Agency Rent-A-Car, Inc. [26]

The *AT&T* case illustrates the problems courts face when attempting to apply various predatory pricing rules to the conduct of a firm with market power. In stark contrast to the *AT&T* case is the *Adjusters* case. As is apparent from the discussion of the facts of the case which follow, it is probable that no firm could achieve substantial market power in the replacement car rental market given the low barriers to entry in the market and the price sensitivity of the principal buyers (i.e., insurance companies) of these car rental services. Moreover, the defendant in the case was in fact the *new entrant* who drove the other competitors from the relevant geographic markets. Nevertheless, the Fifth Circuit Court of Appeals analyzed this case as an attempt to monopolize the replacement car rental market, in much the same way the court in the *AT&T* case attempted to analyze a much different set of facts. Indeed, the court in the *Adjusters* case seemed to ignore the lack of any market structure characteristics which would suggest that predatory pricing could possibly be effective in monopolizing this market, much less be grounds for a violation of the Sherman Act.

Two firms operating in the insurance replacement car rental business, Adjusters Replace-A-Car ("Adjusters") and Wakley & Associates ("Wakley") sued their chief rival, Agency Rent-A-Car ("Agency"), alleging that Agency had employed predatory pricing as part of an attempt to monopolize, in violation of Section Two of the Sherman Act, two geographic markets in Texas: San Antonio and Austin. Adjuster also charged that Agency had attempted to monopolize the Corpus Christi market by hiring away a key employee of Adjusters. At trial, the jury found that Agency had attempted to monopolize the relevant market in San Antonio and Austin by means of pricing in 1975 and 1976, and again in Austin by means of pricing in 1978 and 1979 when Wakley was forced to leave the market, and in Corpus Christi by the hiring of a key employee. The jury awarded total damages, without trebling, of $800,000.00. Subsequent to the jury verdict, the district court awarded judgment for the defendant notwithstanding the verdict of the jury on the grounds that the evidence presented by the plaintiffs failed to present a jury question. The Fifth Circuit affirmed the action of the district court.

The relevant product or service market was the provision of cars on a long-term rental basis to people whose cars had been stolen or were being repaired. The principal "buyers" that the parties to the litigation dealt with were insurance adjusters. Because the universe of potential buyers was small and advertising was not important, replacement car rental firms were able to offer cars at a substantial discount from car rental fees charged by more traditional car rental firms such as Hertz and Avis.

The essence of the plaintiff's claims against Agency was that Agency drove plaintiffs from the San Antonio and Austin markets through an exceptionally aggressive pricing strategy. After Adjusters entered the San Antonio market in September 1973, Wakley and Agency entered in October 1974 charging $9.50 daily rental versus Adjusters' existing rate of $8.50. Agency then cut its daily rate to $8.00 in March 1975 and to $7.00 in November 1975. The latter price cut, unlike the former price cut, markedly increased Agency's market share. In March 1976, Agency began gradually raising its price, first to $7.50 then to $8.00 and by July 1976 to $8.50. In pretrial discovery, Agency admitted that at $7.00 per day and at $8.00 per day Agency's "San Antonio rental office experienced a net loss from operations."[27] At trial, Agency's expert testified that notwithstanding the income statements cited in response to plaintiffs' pretrial discovery request, the average variable cost of Agency's San Antonio and Austin operations fluctuated during the relevant time periods between $3.65 and approximately $5.00 per day.

In December 1974 Adjusters entered Austin, with Agency following in November 1975. Again, Agency lowered its price to $7.00 and was able to attract a substantial share of the market, resulting in Adjuster's departure from the market in December 1977. At that point, Wakley entered the Austin market charging first $10.00 and then $11.00 per day. Upon Wakley's entry, Agency dropped its price from $10.45 to $9.00 in January 1979. Although Wakley attempted to respond to Agency's price cut, it eventually closed its Austin office after April 1979. As in the case of the San Antonio market, Agency responded to plaintiffs request for admissions by stating simply that at both $7.00 and $8.00 per day "its Austin rental office experienced a net loss from operations."[28] As in the San Antonio case, this evidence of net operating loss was seemingly contradicted by a defendant's expert, who testified that average variable cost per day ranged from $3.65 to $5.00.

The plaintiffs attempted to prevent the admission of exhibits which underlay the testimony of the defendant's expert relating to the breakdown of Agency's income statement. The plaintiffs argued that Agency had not fully and completely answered their request for admissions regarding net losses from operations, and hence should not be permitted to introduce evidence contradictory to their responses to the request for admission. The trial judge denied the plaintiffs' motion, finding that the admissions of the defendant and the exhibits offered by the defendant to support its expert cost testimony were not inconsistent. In effect, the trial judge interpreted Agency's income statement as statements relating to total cost and total revenue which, for example, allocated a portion of Agency's headquarters overhead to the various agency offices.

The plaintiffs apparently concluded that because the defendant had admitted to net operating losses, they did not need to break down the defendant's income statements so as to distinguish the fixed and variable costs making up the expense side of the income statement. The defendant, on the other hand, surprised the plaintiffs at trial with evidence that almost 40% of the expense items related to fixed costs. In effect, because the plaintiffs failed to break down the defendant's income statement, they failed to carry their burden of proving even a *prima facie* case of below-AVC pricing, and therefore the trial court granted judgment notwithstanding the verdict.

The pretrial discovery problems of plaintiffs in this case were consistent with problems encountered in other cases where the plaintiff has failed to bear its burden of proving even a *prima facie* case of below-cost pricing. The case is instructive for two reasons.

First, in order for plaintiffs to anticipate adequately the types of defenses defendants may raise related to cost allocation issues, plaintiffs must aggressively pursue discovery so as to ascertain all possible avenues defendant may use at trial to justify pricing tactics. Second, the Fifth Circuit made it very clear that a defendant has no obligation to correct plaintiffs' misapprehensions concerning defendant's cost data. The Fifth Circuit noted that "…nothing in our adversary system prevents Agency from exploiting plaintiffs' error by watching silently as plaintiffs failed to carry their burden of proof."[29]

The Fifth Circuit adhered to the rule promulgated in the *American Excelsior Case* decided in 1975.[30] Quoting from that decision, the Fifth Circuit stated that:

[I]n order to prevail as a matter of law, a plaintiff must at least show that either (1) a competitor is charging a price below his average variable cost in the competitive market or (2) the competitor is charging a price below his short-run profit-maximizing price and barriers to entry are great enough to enable the discriminator to reap the benefits of predation before new entry is possible.[31]

Having made this categorical statement, the Fifth Circuit seemed to express doubt about the *per se* presumptions inherent in the Areeda and Turner test stating that "we are unwilling in an attempted monopolization case to relegate the intent element to the status of an automatic and irrebuttable inference."[32]

Areeda and Turner Test

Plaintiffs were unable to demonstrate that the price in either the San Antonio or Austin markets was below average variable cost. The top end of the range for average variable cost given by defendant's expert (i.e., $5.00 per day) was still 40% below the lowest price charged by defendant (i.e., $7.00 per day). Hence, even if one were to quibble with the details of the defendant expert's characterization of cost as fixed and variable it is unlikely that prices ever dropped below an accurate accounting of average variable costs.

Posner, Greer and Shimer

It seems equally clear that at $7.00 and $8.00 per day, Agency was pricing below accountants average total cost. The income statements of defendant Agency included allocations for overhead expenses and most fixed costs. Although not including a normal rate of return, the $7.00 and $8.00 per day prices were clearly below average total cost.

However, because the Fifth Circuit test for predation did not include an intent element, little evidence of intent was adduced at trial. However, the timing of the price cuts and subsequent price increases by Agency suggest that Agency's intent was to obtain substantial market share at the expense of Adjusters and Wakley if not to drive them out of business entirely. Also, Agency's successful attempt to lure away Adjusters' Corpus Christi sales manager, who brought with her many of Adjuster's clients, supports an inference that Agency's intent was to not only increase its own market share but to harm Adjusters as well.

Undercutting the claim of intent to monopolize is the fact that barriers to entry appear to be moderate to low in this industry. Indeed, even plaintiffs' expert admitted that "I think it would be easy for me to get in it [the automobile replacement market]. I guess it obviously would be easy for them [Hertz and Avis]."[33] Other witnesses for the plaintiffs indicated that it would be a relatively easy matter for public car rental places and even new car dealers to enter this market. Indeed, the incremental cost for an established car dealer or car rental firm to enter this market might be substantially below the average variable cost of a firm that was solely devoted to this type of market. Hence, to the extent that barriers to entry are relatively low, the inference that defendant intended to realize monopoly profits after driving out plaintiffs is weakened. The fact is that this defendant was able to drive out plaintiffs and reap high profit margins for a period of time subsequent to plaintiffs' exit. Hence, using a preponderance test it would seem on balance that the requisite intent was present for these tests. However, it is extremely doubtful Greer's "clear and convincing" burden could be met.

Summary

This case is significant because it represents a market situation where predatory pricing was unlikely to be successful and hence unlikely to have occurred. Despite this situation, a Texas jury awarded the plaintiff substantial damages although the trial judge subsequently threw out the jury's verdict. Successful predatory pricing was unlikely to occur in this market because barriers to entry were low to moderate. Entry at minimum efficient scale required only moderate management and marketing skills and a moderate amount of capital to purchase or lease cars. Moreover, the insurance industry customers for car replacement rental services were very price sensitive. Hence, it would be unlikely that a firm cutting prices now to garner market share could hope to recoup much profit later by raising prices. The likelihood of this is underscored by the fact that the defendant in this case was a new entrant!

Notwithstanding these facts, this case exemplifies a situation where aggressive price-cutting, even by a firm without any market power when it first entered the market, can subject itself to extensive litigation, including an adverse jury verdict.

Conclusion—Beyond Areeda-Turner

Fortunately, the courts seemed to have learned much in deciding cases such as those discussed above. In some cases the courts are relying on the extensive literature that has developed concerning approaches to predatory pricing, which emphasize market structure characteristics more heavily than the Areeda- Turner test and similar cost-based tests.[34] This literature suggests that the structure of the market ought to be analyzed carefully before a court engages in time-consuming and expensive litigation relating to the specific pricing and related promotional practices of the defendant firms.

The two cases discussed above highlight the principal issues surrounding the legality of unilateral pricing decisions by firms seeking to expand their market share. The legality of these pricing decisions are covered by several legal doctrines under the Sherman Act and related antitrust laws. However, the question of legality has in recent years boiled down to comparisons of the price charged with some measure of the cost incurred. As is obvious from the two cases discussed, the courts have had great difficulty reconciling available accounting records with theoretical economic cost measures. Rarely does an accountant's measure of cost resemble a true economic definitions of cost.

But more importantly, the legal literature and the courts seem to be shying away from simplistic cost-price comparisons which ignore the market structure backdrop of the pricing and promotional conduct involved. For example, in the *Adjusters* case, the appellate court ultimately concluded that the pricing conduct ought not subject the defendant to treble damages because the market in question was unlikely to be monopolized through low prices. In other words, because the barriers to entry in the market were very low, it is unlikely that a firm could offset the foregone profits and out-of-pocket losses caused by the low prices by charging a higher price later.

Given this trend in the law, tests for Section Two Sherman Act violations will rely more heavily on market structure factors to screen out those cases in which predatory behavior is unlikely to be profitable and, hence, unlikely to occur. If, and only if, the structure of a market indicates that unilateral pricing conduct by a firm would be likely to lead to an anti-competitive result, would the pricing and other promotional activity of the defendant firm then be subjected to intensive judicial scrutiny. The philosophy underlying such a two-tier approach is the direct linkage, inherent in the Section Two prohibitions on monopolization and attempts to monopolize,[35] between pricing conduct allegedly "predatory" and the market power present.

Ways to Avoid a Successful "Predatory Pricing" Lawsuit

1. Firms seeking to judge the legality of their unilateral pricing and related promotional activities ought to analyze the structural characteristics of the market involved and

their firm's relationship to it by asking the following questions:

a. Is your firm the dominant firm in the particular product and geographical market at issue?

b. Are barriers to entry moderate to high or, in other words, have other firms experienced difficulty entering this market?

c. Has your firm done anything to make entry by others more difficult (such as the introduction of the protective coupler arrangement by SNET)?

d. Are there large disparities between your firm and rival firms relating to absolute size and product and geographical market diversity?

2. If the answer to any of the questions above is "yes," the firm ought to incorporate the following precautions in its pricing and promotional strategies:

a. Avoid targeted, selective action against a smaller rival. To the extent price-cutting is part of the promotional mix, it should be broadened across product and geographical markets so that it is less likely a plaintiff or prosecutor could make the argument that the price-cutting is part of a strategy by a dominant firm to beat up on a smaller rival.

b. Avoid targeted, excessive promotional spending for the same reason.

c. Avoid targeted, selective product changes, especially where competition revolves around new technology rather than pricing strategies.

d. Avoid creating documents which indicate that rationale for pricing and promotional activity was to target a particular competitor or market through any of the above-mentioned tactics, or which permit the inference that another firm has been targeted by the adoption of differential profit rates in various markets.

e. Avoid across-the-board price cutting which is below some meaningful and articulable measure of accountants' cost customarily used by the firm or its accountants in measuring costs for business purposes, absent some extraordinary justifications such as the need to liquidate excess inventory, severe excess capacity in the industry, matching a competitor's price, and so forth.

3. If the answers to the market structure questions above are "no," a firm can proceed to make its pricing and promotional plans as aggressively as possible without much fear of being on the receiving end of a successful predatory pricing lawsuit. On the other hand, the mere fact that a lawsuit is unlikely to succeed, may not deter a wounded rival from bringing a lawsuit which has little merit. It is small consolation to a firm without much (if any) market power to win a relatively meritless lawsuit only after being confronted with time-consuming, expensive litigation. Hence, even in those cases where there does not appear to be a market structure conducive to predatory pricing, it is advisable for firms to abide by the prescriptions set forth above in Section Two, especially the last two items concerning the creation of documents and the consistent, articulable use of defensible cost measures to guide pricing decisions.

Endnotes

[1] Joskow and Klevorick, "A Framework for Analyzing Predatory Pricing Policy," 89 Yale L.J. 213, 219–20 (1979).

[2] *See, e.g.,* Scherer, "Predatory Pricing and the Sherman Act: A Comment, " 89 Harv. L. Rev. 868 (1976); Williamson, "Predatory Pricing: A Strategic and Welfare Analysis," 87 Yale L. J. 284 (1977).

[3] 15 U.S.C. §2 (1981).

[4] 15 U.S.C. 13 (a) (1982). *See, generally*, Attorney General's National Committee to Study the Antitrust Laws, 165 (1955); Rowe, Price Discrimination Under the Robinson Patman Act, 145, 149 (1962).

[5] Specific state statutes prohibiting sales below cost may also be violated. *See, e.g.*, California Business & Professional Code, Sections 2703.6 and 1702.9; Section 100.30(3), Wis. Stats.

[6] *Utah Pie CO. v. Continental Baking Co.*, 386 U.S. 685 (1967).

[7] Areeda and Turner, "Predatory Pricing and Related Practices Under Section 2 of the Sherman Act," 88 Harv. L. Rev. 697 (1975).

[8] P. Areeda and D. Turner, Antitrust Law, ¶711 *et seq.* (Little, Brown and Co., 1978; 1988 Supp.) (contains statement of the most recent formulation of the Areeda- Turner test).

[9] *See, e.g., Janich Bros. Inc. v. American Distilling Co.*, 570 F.2d 848 (9th Cir. 1977), *cert. denied*, 436 U.S. 921 (1978); *Pacific Engineering and Prod. Shell Oil Co.*, 551 F.2d 700 (10th Cir.), *cert. denied*, 434 U.S. 879 (1977); *International Air Industry Inc. v. American Excelisor Co.*, 517 F.2d 714 (5th Cir. 1975), *cer. denied*, 424 U.S. 943 (1976); *Webber v. Wynne*, 431 F. Supp. 1048 (D.N.J. 1977). *See also Chillicothe Sand and Gravel Co. v. Martin Marietta Co.*, 615 F.2d 427 (7th Cir. 1980) (holding average variable cost figure to be relevant, but not necessarily determinative in all situations).

[10] *See, e.g., Wm. Ingliss & Sons Baking Co. v. Ill. Continental Banking Co., Inc.*, 688 F.2d 1014 (9th Cir.), *cert. denied,*103 S. Ct. 58 (1982).

[11] Compare Areeda & Turner, note 7, *supra*, to Posner, "Predatory Pricing," from R. Posner, *Antitrust Law: An Economic Perspective*, 184-96 (Chicago: University of Chicago Press, 1976).

[12] Greer, "A Critique of Areeda and Turner's Standard for Predatory Practices," 24 Antitrust Bull. 233, 245 (1979).

[13] Posner, *supra* note 11, at 188-91. *See* also R. H. Koller, "On the Definition of Predatory Pricing," 20 Antitrust Bulletin 329 (Summer, 1975); A.E. MacIntyre and J.J. Volhard, "Predatory Pricing Legislation—Is It Necessary?," 14 Boston College Industrial and Commercial Law Review 1 (November, 1972).

[14] Posner, note 11, *supra*, at 188. The National Commission on the Antitrust Laws recommended that the Areeda- Turner test in its strict sense be applied only where there is no other evidence of specific intent and that the fact that the defendant's prices were above average variable cost or marginal cost should not be controlling but may be considered in assessing the defendant's intent and the conduct at issue. *See* Handler & Steuer, 129 U. Penn. L. Rev. 125, 145-46 (1980).

[15] Greer, note 12, *supra*, at 235.

[16] *See, e.g.*, Williamson, note 2, *supra*, at 336-37 wherein Williamson proposes cost-based rules regarding price rivalry among established oligopolists.

[17] *See, e.g.*, Greer, note 12, *supra*, at 235, 247-50, 259, wherein Greer defines predatory pricing as (1) pricing below average total cost (as a surrogate for long-run marginal cost) plus (2) substantial economic and non-economic evidence of predatory intent. The Areeda-Turner rule is considered by Greer to be a special case of his own rule.

[18] Joskow and Klevorick, note 1, *supra*, at 249-55.

[19] *See, e.g.*, Joskow and Klevorick, note 1, *supra*, at 254- 255.

[20] *See, e.g.*, Williamson, note 2, *supra*, at 331-36.

[21] *See, e.g.*, Scherer, note 2, *supra*.

[22] *See, e.g.*, R. Bork, *The Antitrust Paradox* 149-55 (1978); Easterbrook, Predatory Strategies and Counter-Strategies, 48 U. Chicago L. Rev. 263, 264, 265-74, 336-37 (1981); MaGee, Predatory Pricing Revisited, 23 J.L. & Econ. 289 (1980).

[23] *Northeastern Telephone Co. v. American, Telephone and Telegraph Co.,* 651 F.2d 76 (2d Cir. 1981), *rev'g*, 497 F. Supp. 230 (D.C. Conn. 1980), *cert. denied*, 455 U.S. 943 (1981). The record on appeal in this case consists of 5,000 microfiched pages which are numbered sequentially with an "A" prefix. Hence, A2470 is the 2,470th microfiched page or combination of pages.

[24] Testimony of Frank Alessio, at A1484.

[25] P. Areeda and D. Turner, note 8, *supra,* at ¶626, at 80 (1978).

[26] 1984-2 Trade Cases ¶66,097at 66,115 (5th Cir. 1984).

[27] *Id.* at 66,118.

[28] *Id.*

[29] *Id.*

[30] *International Air Industries, Inc. v. American Excelsior Co.,* 517 F.2d 714 (5th Cir. 1975), *cert denied,* 424 U.S. 943 (1976).

[31] 1984-2 Trade Cases ¶66,097 at 66,117, *citing* 517 F.2d at 724.

[32] *Id.* at 66,117.

[33] *Id.* at 66,120, n. 10.

[34] *See, e.g.,* Joskow and Klevorick, "A Framework for Analyzing Predatory Pricing Policy," 89 Yale L. J. 213 (1979); Castensen, "Predatory Pricing in the Courts: Reflection on Two Decisions," 61 Notre Dame L. Rev. 928 (1986); K. O'Connor, *A Legal and Economic Analysis of Predation,* Ph.D. Dissertation, Economics, University of Wisconsin- Madison (1986).

[35] *E.g., United States v. Grinnell Corp.,* 384 U.S. 563 (1966). Under *Grinnell,* a plaintiff in a monopolization suit was required to show that the defendant had: "(1) the possession of monopoly power in the relevant market and (2) the willful acquisition or maintenance of that power as distinguished from growth or development as a consequence of a superior product, business acumen, or historic accident." *Id.* at 570-71. In effect, the Supreme Court held that a firm possessing monopoly power would be deemed to have monopolized illegally only if its actions were illegal or exclusionary, in and of themselves. Subsequent to the *Grinnell* decision, the types of conduct labeled exclusionary and hence sufficient to impose liability under Section Two were narrowed substantially. For example, the simple cost-based test for predation can be viewed as an extreme example of the narrowing of the types of exclusionary conduct deemed sufficient to support such a claim.

Recommended for Additional Reading

Areeda and Turner, "Predatory Pricing and Related practices under Section 2 of the Sherman Act," 88 *Harv. L. Rev.* 697 (1975).

Carstensen, "Predatory Pricing in the Courts," 61 *Notre Dame L. Rev.* 928 (1986).

Joskow and Klevorick, "A Framework for Analyzing Predatory Pricing Policy," 89 *Yale L. J.* 213 (1979).

ANALYZING AN INDUSTRY:

Price Levels, Price Structures, and Price Changes

WILLIAM H. REDMOND

WILLIAM H. REDMOND

William H. Redmond is Visiting Assistant Professor of Marketing at Bowling Green State University, Bowling Green, Ohio. Prior to entering the academic field, Dr. Redmond held positions involving markets analysis and marketing planning with several energy-related firms, and received consulting assignments from a variety of firms and industries. Dr. Redmond's research interests are centered upon marketing strategy and, in particular, the strategy/structure interface.

CHAPTER SEVEN

Price levels, price structures and price changes—these constitute the basic pricing environment from a competitive standpoint. This chapter examines critical aspects of the pricing environment from a distinctly competitive perspective and with a view to understanding both current conditions and future prospects.

To achieve the goal of better pricing strategies and tactics requires a complete understanding of what's happening now and what's likely to happen in the future. The means to this goal are a systematic evaluation of competitive prices, along with some guidelines for understanding why the competitors do what they do.

As the first and most important step, we focus on price structures. These describe fundamental relationships within the industry and delineate the overall competitive arena.

Understanding Your Industry's Price Structure

The price structure of an industry is the most basic reference point for pricing decision making, and therefore the first step in industry analysis. We use the term "structure," simply to signify the relationships among the various products' prices: are some priced higher than others? If so, are there distinct groupings or is there a continuous spectrum from low to high? The answers to these and a number of related questions constitute an industry price structure analysis.

From the outset, it is important to note the *relative* nature of price structures. There is no such thing as a high price or a low price in absolute terms; prices are only higher or lower relative to some other product in the industry. The issue of absolute price levels is relegated to abstract discussions among savants from the realms of econometrics and public policy. In addition to the relative aspect of prices, the notion of a price structure also implies a certain degree of stability in the relationships. That is, the relationship among prices generally persists over a considerable time frame, sometimes over many decades. Of course, restructuring can and does occur: events such as technological innovation, over- or under-capacity and price wars for market share can suddenly and drastically alter an existing price structure. But in general, pricing relationships are characterized by stability, and thus price structure is a key subject of analysis.

The following four methods constitute a systematic approach to evaluating the price structure of an industry and have been found to be useful for a broad range of consumer and industrial business environments.

Commodity versus Differentiated Pricing

Here the most fundamental question of all is asked: can I charge a higher price than my competitor? For the Illinois corn farmer the answer is usually no; for the Illinois construction machinery manufacturer the answer is usually yes. However, the issue is by no means as simple as the distinction between agricultural and manufactured goods.

The key point is whether or not one product or service can be distinguished from another along one or more dimensions of that elusive concept known as quality. If so, the offerings are seen as different (hence differentiated) and can carry different prices. If not, the offerings must all carry the same price because anyone attempting to change a higher price will sell nothing.

An equally key point is that differentiation is in the eye of the buyer, not the seller. Many industries have several producers claiming to offer the "Cadillac" of the industry, but only one can have the highest price. For their part, buyers respond positively only to those elements of quality which hold value for them, and rightly ignore elements of quality which do not. This point cannot be overemphasized, especially as it is quite common for sellers to get so wrapped up in the technical merits of their products that they are blinded to the fact that the customers either don't understand the features or that they don't care. This situation sometimes leads to bewildering results. Some quite basic and pedestrian products, such as laundry detergents or spark plugs, are highly differentiated and considerable attention is paid by producers to price differentials. On the other hand, highly sophisticated electronic chips are commonly sold in commodity fashion with little or no difference in price.

Two factors seem to mediate the distinction between commodity and differentiated markets. The first is that people have varying perceptions of the salience of the product or service in question. Some people attach considerable importance to the brightest wash or the best engine performance and will readily pay more for a superior product; others aren't so interested and will tend to buy the lower-priced product. The second factor is final demand versus intermediate use (i.e., raw materials, component parts, and so on). The same firm that is price-conscious when purchasing electronic components may be quite insensitive to price when buying a corporate jet.

Lastly, it is important to note the relationship between differentiation and segmentation—you really can't have one without the other. Essentially, segmentation is the identification of differentiated demand; and the only economic utility for a differentiated offering is in the presence of differentiated demand. This, of course, leads to a classic chicken-and-egg conundrum: which comes first, differentiated demand or differentiated offerings?

A good deal of markets research is predicated on the notion that demand does indeed pre-exist for new and improved products and that potential buyers have sufficiently concrete ideas about them so as to articulate both product attributes and target prices. On the other hand, many buyers don't know that they want something different until they see it. How many East Coast supermarket shoppers knew they wanted upscale chicken until Perdue introduced it?

Price/Quality Tiers

As set forth more fully in other chapters, there exists a pervasive association between the price of a product or service and its perceived quality. Similarly, "You get what you pay for" is an expression of the concept of value expressed as the ratio of quality to price. For this reason, the fundamental structure in differentiated industries is roughly linear: from low price/low quality to high price/high quality. (Please note that "quality" here denotes *perceived quality*. This means different things to different people—e.g., durability or style or extra features). Thus, off-diagonal combinations such as low price/high quality or high price/low quality are either confusing or unacceptable to buyers and are therefore encountered only infrequently.

The structural issue involved here is the distribution of price/quality points along the main diagonal. In general, there may be a relatively continuous spread of offerings or there may be clusters of products at distinct points along the diagonal. In the former case, it is presumed that demand is finely differentiated and that buyers are both capable of and willing to investigate the distinctions among products which are nearly similar in price/quality characteristics. Automobiles are an excellent example: from the $4800 Yugo to the $35,000 Mercedes there is scarcely a $100 increment which escapes the notice of sellers and the interest of buyers.

Many other industries are characterized by distinct levels or tiers of price/quality offerings, much like the old Sears scheme of good, better and best. Beers offer a current illustration of this approach: the industry recognizes four tiers of brew. Popular (e.g., Busch), premium (e.g., Budweiser), super-premium (e.g., Michelob) and special import (e.g., Corona) represent four distinct levels in which quality, according to some observers, can *only* be distinguished by price. In any event, the four tiers are widely recognized by both sellers and buyers of beer and there is considerably more brand switching within levels than across levels.

Still other industries exhibit a dichotomous structure. These have a low level and a high level which are widely separated on the price/quality diagonal. The market for aspirin is broadly divided into national brands and house brands, with national brands commonly selling for triple the price of house brands or more. For the consumer who prefers Excedrin, Revco brand may be completely unacceptable as a substitute, while the Revco brand buyer may consider it foolish to pay Excedrin's asking price.

In summary, the evaluation of price structures is in reality an investigation of price/quality relationships within an industry. Much more than just a listing of competitors' prices, industry price structure analysis yields crucial information about product positioning. That is, careful structural analysis both indicates segmentation objectives of competitors and delimits the areas of potential substitution.

Discounts, Deals, Coupons

Discounts, rebates, deals and coupons represent a pricing substructure that is found in most industries. This substructure should be considered a separate entity from the main price/quality structure for the good reason that it is different in both purpose and effect. While the basic price/quality structure serves to position products or services broadly against other *competitors*, the discounting substructure has a distinct *customer* orientation. In particular, the substructure serves to recognize differences among customers, to recognize the importance of individual transactions, and to recognize subsegments of buyers.

Discount schedules are meant to recognize different classes of customers, based on volume of purchases, geographic location, type of business or other classification scheme. Here, differences in the final price are meant to reflect differences in cost of doing business with lower prices going to lower cost transactions. So a discount chain pays less for its toothpaste than a mom-and-pop shop and a fabricator in Pittsburgh pays less for its steel than another in Moosejaw.

Nobody dickers with his grocer over the price of a loaf of bread, but few would step up and pay the sticker price on a new Buick. When an individual transaction is important for the buyer and the seller, negotiations are undertaken and deals on price are made. Unlike discounts, however, price deals are not established on a regular basis and the price paid by similar types of customers may vary according to the bargaining skill of the parties, the urgency of getting the order, the options available to the buyer and so on.

Same product, same store, same day; two set prices. The intended effect of coupons and rebates is to subsegment the potential buyers of consumer products and services into two groups: a price-sensitive group and a convenience oriented group. Coupons and rebates simply allow sellers to retain the business of price-sensitive buyers who might otherwise be attracted to competitors, while at the same time maintaining full margins on customers who don't take the extra bother.

In general, the discount/deal/coupon substructure represents a fine tuning of the basic price/quality structure. Discounts reflect differences in transaction costs among different classes of customers; deals reflect the importance of individual transactions; coupons reflect a subsegmentation strategy. In this sense the substructure enables effective price competition plus high average margins while preserving basic price/quality relationships.

Accessories, Parts, Services

A final note in the analysis of price structures is the role of so-called "extras." Accessories, peripherals, spare parts, installation and training services seldom have an important part in package goods markets but can play a crucial role in profit performance in certain industrial and commercial businesses. Particularly in situations involving a formal bidding process, such as government contracts or public utility projects, margins on the basic equipment may be cut to the bone in order to secure the order. Add-ons to the original bid list frequently amount to between 15% to 30% or more of the value of the original quote and are a well recognized way to "get well" on the overall profitability of the order.

Similarly, repair parts prices are generally not scrutinized as closely as the basic equipment and are a long-term means of recovering profit on the original order. An old rule of thumb in several manufacturing industries specified that the assembly of a piece of equipment entirely from spare parts should cost about three times the catalog price of that same piece of equipment.

In summary, the basic price structure along with substructures and extras constitute a means of organizing knowledge and focusing thinking about prices.

The objective is to provide a systematic and informative order to an otherwise voluminous and tangled mass of industry price data. In other words, the structural *approach* is similar to a learning heuristic and, as such, must be activated by industry-specific information. The following section explores ways of obtaining this information.

Keeping an Eye on the Competitors

Effective price monitoring is a crucial part of pricing decision making. Good monitoring not only involves an evaluation of the current price situation but also plays a key role in the assessment of and reaction to competitive price moves. Indeed the need for pricing information seems to be widely appreciated: a recent volume of the *Survey of Marketing Research* reports that 83% of companies surveyed conducted some form of price research.

A useful perspective on price monitoring is to view it as a part of the overall market research effort. In this sense, price monitoring is seen to have the same goal as other forms of market research: information. And information is understood as not merely a collection of data but in terms of its goal, which is a reduction in uncertainty about current market conditions and probable future conditions. Therefore, the goodness or badness of a price monitoring effort is not to be judged by volume of output but rather by effectiveness in reducing critical areas of uncertainty so that decisions can be made with a clear understanding of actual business conditions.

Although the following discussion is organized into informal and formal monitoring methods, it should be clear that there is really no sharp dividing line between the two. The degree of formality of a monitoring system is determined by its degree of consistency and conformity. That is, the extent to which the same people (or positions) gather the same data on the same products and competitors at regular time periods. The goal is to avoid the sort of confusion that results when the price of competitor's product X is gathered from a mom-and-pop store in January, from a discount store in February and from a convenience store in July. Clearly very little useful information can be gained from such an exercise.

Informal Monitoring Approaches

There are two typical approaches to informal price monitoring: salesforce reports and published price data. Note that salesforce reporting will also be discussed under formal methods of monitoring; the difference being that informal salesforce reporting is done on an irregular basis and is mainly aimed at reporting only price changes or other exceptional activities.

The salesforce, including agents and distributors, have a natural and keen sense of interest in pricing as relative prices have an impact on their success or failure to obtain an order. In addition, the salesforce is in daily contact with customers who are a good source of competitors' price data. The salesforce is therefore in a position to obtain data and generally well-motivated to report back to their managers.

On the other hand, the human factor tends to produce some rather predictable consequences at the expense of accuracy. Failure to obtain an order must result in some assessment of the cause, and most of us would rather attribute a failure to something outside of our own control. Price is frequently the scapegoat. This tendency is sometimes reinforced by buyers who, for motives of their own, would rather not disclose the true reason for awarding the order to a competitor and cite price as the critical factor. In any event, informal salesforce reports are not a reliable way to find out if your prices are on the low side.

The other informal approach—analysis of published prices—is a form of secondary market research using data that has been compiled by another party. There is an enormous variety of such sources but the availability and accuracy of these sources tends to fluctuate widely among industries. Some typical sources include competitors' price lists, industry trade publications, industry or company profiles in business news magazines, business report publications such as *Standard and Poor's Industry Surveys*, reports of important transactions in business press such as the *Wall Street Journal* and the results of public bidding at governmental agencies or public utilities. The United States government collects an enormous amount of price data, but is generally required to protect the confidentiality of individual firms. However, valuable information on average prices can be obtained from a number of government reports such as the *Census of Manufactures* or *Industry and Trade Statistics* (see Table 1).

Table 1   Sources and Examples of Price Data

Type of Data Needed	Specific Transactions	Competitor's Price Levels	Industry-wide Prices	Industry Average Prices
Source	Business Press	Trade Journals/ Price Lists	Industry Reports	Government Reports
Example	Wall Street Journal	Quick Frozen Foods/ Sears catalog	S & P's Industry Surveys	Census of Manufactures

Guides to specific articles and trade journal reports for a wide range of industries and products can be found in two excellent reference sources, *Business Periodicals Index* and *Predicast F&S Index*. Guides to United States government reports on prices can be found in the *American Statistics Index*. These three sources are found in most large libraries and all college libraries with business departments.

For the more computer-minded, a huge number of databases are available, some of which are industry-specific and some of which are oriented to general business items. In fact, there are so many of these databases that services are available which provide single-point access to groups of them. For example, the DIALOG service links to over 250 databases ranging from Agribusiness USA to Zoological Record. The use of key words (such as Price) along with a product name provides a quick way of scanning an enormous amount of data.

As usual with secondary research sources, two caveats are worth noting. First, there are frequently delays between the gathering of price data and its appearance in published form. As an extreme example, the 1982 business census was not fully reported until 1985. Second, it is frequently difficult to determine exactly how the reported price was measured. Is it list price or average selling price? Does it reflect cash discounts or include freight? Some sources do explain what is included in the price, but others do not.

A final note on informal methods is that the two approaches (salesforce and secondary) can be combined to advantage. Indeed, this is frequently done because the cost and effort is modest and the results can be most informative. For example, salesforce reports of actual prices paid by various classes of customers can be compared with competitors' price lists to derive discount schedules. Or salesforce reports can be compared with published reports to assess the accuracy of the total monitoring system.

Formal Monitoring Approaches

As stated earlier, formal monitoring methods involve a high degree of consistency—consistency in the type of data collected, consistency in how it is measured and consistency of reporting periods. Most formal methods are also characterized by a wider range of data collected and a wider reach of locations surveyed.

The expanded range of data typically includes one or more means of classifying the customer (such as discount store versus department store), sales volume of the account, demographics of the trade area (especially for consumer goods), presence or absence of special sales or promotions and so forth. The expanded reach of locations surveyed ensures that competitors' local and regional price maneuvers, such as couponing, are detected in a timely fashion.

Greater range and reach of data naturally leads to an exponential increase in the quantity of data to be analyzed and for this reason formal monitoring systems are invariably computerized. A typical system will be capable of reporting by competitor, by customer, by location, by customer class and by product type, and many are programmed to highlight automatically price changes from previous reporting periods.

The basic choice in formal monitoring is whether to purchase the data from an outside supplier or gather the data yourself. Of course the choice is much simpler if no research suppliers sell data for your particular industry. Several firms offer data for consumer package goods as this is the most frequent and extensive use of formal systems.

Package goods data have been collected by a number of methods including consumer panels (in which a thousand or more consumers report details of their weekly purchases) and shelf audits (in which field employees of the research firm record prices in stores). More recently, the advent of Universal Product Code (UPC) scanning has made automatic scanning the method of choice by reason of its accuracy and timeliness. Nielson and SAMI/Burke are among the more widely known firms who supply scanner data, but a number of other firms also provide similar services. The *Green Book* directory identifies firms which supply panel data and scanner data or provide other forms of pricing research.

Creating an in-house formal monitoring system is not difficult from a design or computer standpoint, but does require the assurance of a steady stream of high quality input from the field. Like any other information system, one starts at the ending and works backwards. The first step is to sketch-out the desired reports, then determine what data are required to generate the reports and then determine who is to gather the data and how often. Software is usually custom-programmed for extensive systems and done on a spreadsheet package for more modest efforts.

Staffing the data-gathering process is the most common catch for the do-it-yourselfer. For obvious reasons, the salesforce comes to mind first and the salesforce is, in fact, the most common vehicle. It is worth remembering, however, that salespeople make a living by selling, not by doing extensive market research. Another stack of forms to be filled out for headquarters does not gladden the hearts of those in the sales ranks. At a minimum, system designers should estimate the time required to gather data and fill out forms (or enter on floppy disk) and then calculate the subsequent number of work-days lost by the salesforce.

Several of the more successful systems use field personnel who have extensive customer contact but who do not work on a commission basis or have important sales quotas. These may include sales trainees, technical representatives, field engineers and the like. Another, but more expensive, alternative is to contract for the services of field workers employed by market research firms at various locations.

Lastly, it is important to resist the temptation to overkill. Information has cost as well as value, even when the cost is not in "hard" dollars or budget lines. Distinguishing between "need-to-know" and "nice-to-know" will result in a system with obvious worth to all concerned, including the data collectors.

Formal versus Informal

When choosing among various monitoring methods, a number of considerations come into play. First is the cost/benefit analysis: any information system must be judged by the same criteria as other business investments. Once again, the standard of value for information is based on reduction of uncertainty—what will it cost me if I don't know? Since formal systems cost more, the greater expense must be balanced by a correspondingly high worth of current and detailed information.

One component of uncertainty is the general pricing environment. Many industries have a well-recognized and established price leader who makes the first move; others quickly follow. In these cases, an informal system is generally sufficient. In other industries, a host of competitors will be engaging in a variety of price moves on an ongoing basis, sometimes at the local level. Here a formal system is indicated.

Another factor is the number of people involved in the pricing decision. Large, complex organizations may require coordination among brand managers, market managers, account executives and financial planners in pricing decisions. With formal systems there is less chance of critical information falling through the cracks.

Also, greater numbers of products, brands, styles and models require more formal systems for adequate monitoring.

The final issue is incremental change. If two-cents-off makes a difference to your customers, then a $50,000 formal system might make real sense for your business. If a thousand bucks either way doesn't faze your buyers, just read the newspaper to see what the competition is doing.

Looking Ahead

Monitoring systems are a record of the past and a snapshot of the present, but what of the future? A good monitoring system will be capable of identifying price trends, and these trends can be extrapolated into the future for a certain length. Although this is suitable for some purposes, the approach is severely limited by its implicit assumption that business conditions in the future will mirror those of the past.

This section outlines several kinds of instances in which business conditions change markedly and exert a profound influence on price levels and price structures. Although precise forecasting of these events is a most inexact science, some degree of anticipation can be achieved. Forewarned is forearmed.

Supply and Demand

Your Economics 101 book was wrong: supply and demand don't always have that much to do with pricing in many industries. Suppose the price of table salt fell by 50% tomorrow—would you buy any extra? No; in fact, demand would probably continue to decline due to health consciousness. On the flip side, demand for BMWs is rising steadily despite (or perhaps because of) price increases.

There is, however, a supply-related factor which frequently has an enormous effect on prices and that is capacity utilization. Despite some notable exceptions (which also tend to attract the interest of antitrust lawyers) capacity underutilization is generally accompanied by price erosion of a greater or lesser degree. Several years ago, the price of artificial sweeteners dropped by over 37% when capacity utilization fell by 50%. The interesting part of the story is that demand hadn't fallen off at all: excessive additions to capacity caused the problem.

Clearly, prices would have fallen just as far had the underutilization been due to slack demand instead of additions to capacity. The key point here is that forecasting demand is not sufficient as a means of anticipating industry price level changes. Demand forecasts are only half of the equation when it comes to predicting capacity utilization rates. The other half is monitoring changes in productive capacity, including foreign capacity.

It is important to analyze your own industry's typical reaction to underutilization situations. Bus companies usually respond more moderately than airlines, and pharmaceutical companies more moderately than chemical companies. These characteristic response patterns are underlaid by a range of structural factors such as fixed overhead and labor agreements, but are also strongly influenced by the experiences and personalities of the parties involved.

Cost/Price Dynamics

In well-established industries, costs and prices tend to bear a close relationship over time. With exceptions such as price-cutting to fill excess capacity, cost/price ratios are generally stable. In the case of new products, however, cost/price relationships can be most irregular, changing suddenly and dramatically.

The early stage of the Product Life Cycle (PLC) is the most dynamic phase of an industry's history and is characterized by high levels of competitive entry, increasing product differentiation, the emergence of product line strategies and the refinement of production techniques. Due to the experience effect, unit costs decline rapidly in the early going, frequently by 25-30% with every doubling of accumulated production.

While production costs decline in a predictable fashion, the selling price commonly follows one of two distinct patterns over time, depending on the price strategy of the pioneer firms in the industry. Specifically, two pricing orientations are open to the pioneer firm: price skimming and penetration pricing. Price skimming aims to "skim the cream" off the top of the demand curve by charging high prices for the new innovation and then gradually lowering the price to reach more customers. Penetration, on the other hand, seeks to stimulate higher levels of demand right from the start by setting a low price, frequently well below the initial cost of production.

Under penetration pricing, production costs are expected to fall below selling prices as production volume increases so that the long-term price trend is fairly stable, at least in real terms. This strategy has been employed in such diverse situations as Proctor and Gamble in disposable diapers, Reynolds metals in aluminum cans and Hercules in polypropylene.

When the pioneer follows a skim strategy, two problems for the industry may develop and these may set the stage for wrenching price cuts. First, high levels of competitive entry are occasioned by the high prices and fat profit margins. Second, the price leader (usually the pioneer firm) tends to wait too long to reduce prices in tandem with falling unit costs—and this further stimulates entry. The general result is an industry shakeout, with prices falling precipitously and droves of smaller or less efficient firms forced from the market. This type of event happens frequently enough that the price path has been given a name: the price umbrella. Firms which were viable under the umbrella quickly become money losers in the price war and only those firms furthest down the experience curve survive the battle. Electronics markets typify this scenario, from pocket calculators to digital watches to personal computers, but others including soft contact lenses, smoke alarms and nonwoven fabrics exhibit the same pattern (see Figure 1).

The message here is that if you are in a young industry, watch out! Recent entrants and prospective entrants to a market pioneered with a skim strategy must understand that there may be eminent danger of a price collapse or, at the very least, considerable downside potential for prices before the market attains maturity.

Figure 1   Cost/Price Dynamics

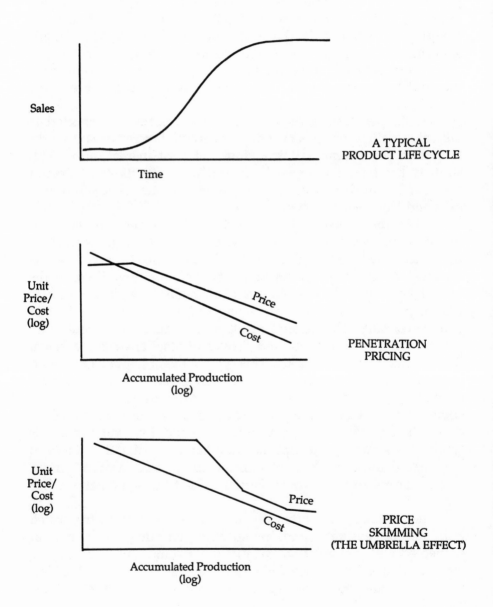

Barriers to Entry and Exit

Barriers act to prohibit, inhibit or slow the entry or exit of competitors in an industry. This has considerable implications for price levels. In effect, barriers are one of the foundations of an industry's price structure; if barrier heights change, the price structure may change as well. This is particularly true when lowered barriers result in substantial entry and much keener price competition.

Barriers come in many shapes and sizes, including legal, structural and perceptual. Legal barriers comprise patent protection, regulated monopoly and regulated competition and are among the strongest barriers to be found. On the other hand, legal barriers exist at the pleasure of the government and are therefore subject to change or removal. Recent price cutting in passenger airline and long distance telephone markets illustrates the results of removal of regulation, while severe price erosion in photocopy machines shows what can happen when patents expire.

Structural barriers include capital requirements, minimum efficient plant size and access to technology and know-how. Changes in technology, especially production technology, can render these barriers impotent. Witness, for example, the success of steel mini-mills using new, efficient steelmaking technology. Before the advent of mini-mill technology, it was thought that any new entrant would need to invest billions in order to compete with the big steelmakers.

Perceptual barriers result from extensive and longstanding brand advertising; that is, established brand awareness to the point that prospective entrants are deterred by the necessity of having to support enormous promotion expenses in order to gain recognition. For example, many experts believe that the major players in the breakfast cereal and cigarette industries are virtually immune from new competition because their brands are so well-known. Of course, the experts also used to say that about GM, IBM and Xerox.

Exit barriers become an important consideration in the decline stage of the PLC, and specialized equipment is usually the culprit. When the demand for women's stockings was replaced by demand for pantyhose, several hundred small, family-owned stocking companies were stuck with equipment which could only produce sheer tubular goods. Their only option was to convert to pantyhose production, where they were quickly dispatched by Hanes and other national producers in an episode of severe price-cutting.

For pricing purposes, the key is to look for *changes* in barriers and anticipate how these changes will impact the industry price structure (in the case of exit barriers, look for changes in demand which will bring the barriers into play). With the exception of patents, which have a set term, this may not always be an easy task. Changes in governmental regulations are usually preceded by an extended debate, but innovations in production technology may be kept under wraps right until they are put into operation. Automakers who felt secure in their brand awareness and acceptance didn't realize until too late that OPEC decisions would open the gates to low-priced imports by stimulating consumer interest in lesser known alternatives.

In summary, this section has outlined sources and causes of major changes in industry price structures or price levels. In the case of overcapacity, the changes may be transient, with a return to former price levels when capacity and demand are better balanced. In the case of price umbrellas or falling barriers, the changes are frequently permanent, at least until another restructuring occurs. The key here is to anticipate and adapt—there is little else to be done about the situation.

Conclusion

A thorough industry analysis for pricing decision making is not technically difficult and need not be expensive in most cases. But it does require effort, persistence, good planning and routine evaluation of the quality of the outputs. Like so many other undertakings, the way to proceed is from the general to the specific, from the simple to the complex, from the present to the future. Here are some pointers to keep in mind:

- *Price Structures.* In the fundamental price/quality structure, price is a positioning tool. Price defines your competitors and your customers; it creates expectations about your offering and engages certain competitors while bypassing others. Once a brand is established at a particular price/quality point, significant price changes become a very problematic undertaking unless your competitors also change.

  Within this competitive arena, the discounting substructure reveals the rules of the game for pricing tactics and the search for competitive advantage. Here the idea is to achieve the most sales at the highest average price by offering different prices to different customers. Understanding and making effective use of discounts, deals, coupons and the like leads to superior performance year after year.

- *Price Monitoring.* Both informal and formal monitoring systems have the same goal: an adequate flow of current information about competitors' prices. Here the twin concepts of effectiveness and efficiency come into play. Too little information is ineffective—it creates blind spots and undermines the quest for competitive advantage. Too much information is simply inefficient—it wastes time, money and effort. From a competitive standpoint, inefficient is better than ineffective.

- *Forecasting.* Predicting broad-scale changes in price levels and price structures is tricky business. It depends on understanding a host of business linkages and interrelationships which impact price, and then forecasting changes in those business conditions which are linked to the price.

  Anticipating changes in capacity utilization, in cost/price ratios or in barriers requires constant attention and a thorough knowledge of the industry. The same trade journals, business periodicals and industry reports discussed under informal monitoring are helpful here, but also take heed the wisdom of the veterans in your company who have probably seen it all before.

A final remark on industry analysis: stay alert. Many industries exhibit a high degree of price stability for considerable periods of time, and this can lead to laxity and inattention. None of the other controllable variables—product decisions, promotion or distribution—can change as quickly as price. A lack of vigilance can have an immediate and very costly impact on your own business performance.

Recommended for Additional Reading

Aaker, David and G. Day, "The Perils of High-Growth Markets," *Strategic Management Journal*, v. 7 (1986).

Gorton, Keith and Isabel Carr, *Low-Cost Marketing Research*, London; John Wiley (1983).

Green Book: International Directory of Market Research Companies and Services, Chicago; American Marketing Association, New York Chapter (Annual).

Herring, Jan, "Building a Business Intelligence System," *Journal of Business Strategy*, v. 9, (May 1988).

Porter, Michael, *Competitive Strategy*, New York; Free Press (1980).

Yip, George, *Barriers to Entry*, Boston; Allyn and Bacon (1982).

CHAPTER EIGHT

PRICING ANALYSIS USING SPREADSHEETS

MICHAEL V. LARIC, PH.D.

MICHAEL V. LARIC

Michael V. Laric, Ph.D., is an internationally known lecturer, writer, and consultant specializing in computer applications to marketing and sales management. He is the author of over a dozen books, three dozen articles in professional journals, numerous monographs, and consulting reports.

A frequent speaker all over the United States and Canada, he is currently Professor of Marketing at the University of Baltimore, and a principal in Ecomares International Ltd., an Economics and Marketing Research Co.

Dr. Laric has taught over 300 executive seminars, as well as Ph.D., M.B.A., and undergraduate courses at the Universities of New York, Connecticut, Rutgers and Tel Aviv. He holds a B.A. degree in economics and an M.A. degree in business from the Hebrew University of Jerusalem, Israel. His Ph.D. in marketing is from the City University of New York.

CHAPTER EIGHT

This chapter describes the benefit of using computers and spreadsheets for pricing analysis. Three pricing models which use spreadsheets are introduced. The first example begins with the cost-based breakeven model, then builds on that example to include target return. The example is further expanded to cover demand adjustments, market share calculations and return on investment. The second example is a quantity discount model which allows you to set both minimum and maximum quantity discount levels, the number of levels, and corresponding discounts. This is followed by an experience curve pricing model—the third example. The chapter concludes with descriptions of other models which can benefit from the use of spreadsheets.

The Benefit of Using Computer Spreadsheets

The first use of computers in pricing decisions can be traced to utility companies and other regulated industries in the 1950's. Sophisticated, computer-based pricing models were built by companies requiring repetitive or complicated bidding. As more and more information and accounting systems became automated, pricing became an integral domain of these systems.

In the financial industry, computers are used to identify profitable products and customers and isolate them from those less profitable. Using price adjustments or service and product modifications, less profitable products and customers are culled and reevaluated. Successful products are cloned, and profitable customers are studied so that new customers like them can be found.

167

Recently, the use of computer technology has fostered new pricing strategies which could not have been used before. The airline industry has combined computer and reservation systems to segment prices—few travellers on a flight pay the same amount for their ticket. Differences of up to 500% per ticket are possible on the same flight, and there could be as many as 50 fares on a 200 seat flight.

The above examples represent pricing models using mainframe computers. In the late 1970's, the personal computer made its debut. It opened new vistas.

Personal Computers

Desktop computers enable salespeople to provide customers with faster and more precise price quotes, especially if cost data are readily available to them. In complex selling situations, the computer can easily accommodate changes in options, and adjust the selling price instantly. Where customized delivery, installation, terms of credit, or last-minute changes once required costly delays, these corrections can now be handled almost instantaneously.

Computers also enhance the ability to conduct price analysis. Competitors' prices can be stored on some of the more sophisticated computer systems. This can facilitate the fine-tuning of negotiations over quoted prices by providing more informed conditions. With data on the number of units, package sizes, stock turnover rates and prices, sellers can better evaluate precise contribution. Retailers can more accurately gauge which lines contribute to profits and which need an overhaul.

Although there are few computer programs devoted solely to pricing, a multitude of models are available for implementation on financial modelling spreadsheets. Spreadsheets, more than any other group of applications programs, have been used as a medium through which such models were implemented.

Spreadsheets and Pricing

Spreadsheets contributed to the personal computer's development as a managerial productivity tool. While word processing, database management, and project management were in use before computers, spreadsheets were born with the personal computer. Spreadsheets electronically combine columnar and graph paper, calculator, pencil, and eraser. Spreadsheet programs such as Lotus 1-2-3 and its latest rivals, Excel, Quattro and SuperCalc5, have become commonplace in corporate offices. Managers using spreadsheets conduct more and more "What if?" analysis using their financial and marketing data.

The most vital characteristic of the spreadsheet is its ability to calculate a value in one cell based on a value in another. The added ability to retrieve, then analyze, a series of data using new values opens endless possibilities. Series of values can be calculated based on one or more numbers. For example, all sales forecasts are based on assumed prices. Changes in the price automatically affect forecast. The "What if?" analysis gives pricing managers a better understanding of the relationships between prices and sales numbers. Spreadsheets can also be used for broader evaluations of business opportunities, strategic make or buy decisions, and long-term equipment lease or buy decisions.

The second major spreadsheet feature is the ease with which spreadsheets can be constructed and then recycled for additional analysis. Once a spreadsheet is developed for an application—for example an airline ticket pricing model for a given route—it can be saved and later used for another route. This saves time, since the formulas, assumptions, and relationships have already been developed and are contained in the original spreadsheet. The ease of developing "What if?" scenarios is enhanced by the ability to easily change a spreadsheet and compare it to the previous spreadsheet.

The speed with which the above benefits are derived, plus the time savings resulting from added accuracy and the automating series of mundane calculations, affords additional time for studying relationships and thereby better understanding underlying forces. Basic relations between profits and volume, or between prices and contribution, are easier to understand (and graph) using the spreadsheet's power.

The spreadsheet is not yet up to linear programming types of solutions, but that too may be forthcoming. Already add-on and add-in programs for spreadsheets—for example, programs capable of maximizing a profit equation subject to production and raw materials constraints—are becoming available. The spreadsheet is also not yet capable of linking the pricing decision to the rest of the business decisions—strategic planning, dynamic pricing over the product life cycle, or multi-national manufacturing and selling systems.

Pricing managers who make extensive use of accounting ledgers or calculators are the prime beneficiaries of spreadsheets. Even occasional users of such tools can benefit from a spreadsheet.

Cost and Contribution Analysis

Our first example deals with cost-oriented pricing using a spreadsheet. The spreadsheet developed in this example begins with a simple break even, then builds on to add additional features. By the end, the model allows you to change variable costs per unit, total fixed costs, prices, target profits, sales estimates, market sizes, and required investments. The spreadsheet also calculates a break even in both units and dollars, and allows you to treat target profits as either fixed or variable per unit. First, a break even in units is shown, along with the formulas; next, a break even level in sales, and target profits are added. Finally, sales estimates for alternative prices and the corresponding market sizes are evaluated to derive an optimal price.

Break Even in Units

Break even analysis (BEA) is perhaps the best known form of price analysis. BEA assumes a specific time period and a cost structure which remains fixed during that period of time. A break even is achieved only if the quantity produced is sold at the asking price. If, however, that quantity is not sold, the unsold goods incur carrying charges. This translates to higher costs for the inventory sold and possibly a loss on each unit sold.

Assume that several managers of an established airline are ready to start their own airline, serving primarily executives flying between the downtown areas of Washington and Chicago. Table 1 shows a preliminary break even analysis. Three assumptions are required: unit price, variable cost per unit, and the fixed costs. Assumptions should be expressly stated in a well designed spreadsheet. In the examples that follow, all assumptions are placed above a single rule.

Table 1 A Break Even Analysis:
Examining Monthly Fare Alternatives

	Fare A	Fare B	Fare C	Total
Price Alternative	$663	$534	$312	$503
Variable Costs	$350	$312	$225	$296
Fixed Costs	$60,000	$60,000	$60,000	$180,000
Break Even in Units	192	270	690	1,152
Break Even in Sales	$127,093	$144,324	$215,172	$486,589
Unit Contribution	$313	$222	$87	$207
Contribution Ratio (%)	47	42	28	39

In Table 1 the three price alternatives are for a round trip with first class (Fare A), coach (Fare B), and supersaver ticket (Fare C). The last column gives an overall break even analysis. The variable and fixed cost are the other assumptions and are estimated.

In this spreadsheet, the relationships between the three assumptions are stated below the double line, which distinguishes between assumptions we make (subject to the "What if?" analysis) and the relationships. Thus, the break even is calculated below the double line, as are relationships between other assumptions such as price and variable cost.

The formula for break even is located in the first row below the double line:

Break even = Fixed Cost/Price Alternative – Variable Cost

The spreadsheet calculates the value and displays the number 192 for Fare A's break even. The spreadsheet further calculates the per unit's contribution as:

Unit's Contribution = Price Alternative – Variable Cost

This is placed in the cell showing $313 for Fare A. The contribution ratio is calculated on the last line as:

Contribution Ratio = Contribution/Price Alternative

An alternative formula for calculating the contribution level is:

Contribution Ratio = Sales – (Total Cost – Fixed Cost)/Sales)

Both methods yield the same results. Accounting systems frequently have readily available data for use in the latter formula.

Note that Table 1 shows three fares and a break even for the total company using these three fares. Needless to say, the fixed costs, which are currently split evenly between the three products, can easily be redistributed so as to have one fare carry more of the fixed cost, say in proportion to the revenue level or the number of seats used.

Adding Break Even Sales Calculations and Target Return

It is possible to enhance this break even by adding the level of sales revenues at which break even is added. This can be done by using the relationship:

Price per Unit * Break Even Quantity

Alternatively, one can use the contribution ratio, also known as the profit-volume ratio. Either formula can be added to the bottom of the spreadsheet. The other formula for break even sales level is:

Break Even Sales = Fixed Cost/Contribution Ratio

Dividing the break even sales level by the price per unit should produce the unit break even level.

When a profit target is sought, target return pricing can be incorporated into this analysis. The profit target is often based on a specific return on investment. This method was popularized by the chairman of General Motors, Alfred P. Sloan. While the break even analysis shows the level of output at which neither losses nor profits are derived, target return shows a break even at the desired profit level. Generally, some target profit is desired, and can be done in one of two ways.

The desired profit level can be calculated as return on assets. The amount is required regardless of the level of output and hence can be treated as an additional fixed cost. To modify the earlier break even analysis, all that is required is that an additional line be added, perhaps below the fixed costs, labeled Target Profits. As soon as that is entered and the formulas modified, the Lotus 1-2-3 break even spreadsheet will recalculate all the values, producing a "Target Return" analysis. At this new break even quantity, the mandated level of profits is earned. Table 2 shows this scenario.

Table 2 A Break Even Analysis Incorporating Target Profits: Examining Monthly Fare Alternatives

	Fare A	Fare B	Fare C	Total
Price Alternative	$663	$534	$312	$503
Target Profits (%)	0	0	0	0
Variable Costs	$350	$312	$225	$296
Fixed Costs	$60,000	$60,000	$60,000	$180,000
Target Profits	$6,000	$6,000	$6,000	$18,000
Break Even in Units	211	297	759	1,267
Break Even in Sales	$139,802	$158,757	$236,690	$535,248
Unit Contribution	$313	$222	$87	$207
Contribution Ratio (%)	47	42	28	39

Alternatively, the company may require a certain return as a percent of sales. Here it would be better to treat the desired profit level as a variable cost. Table 2 shows this scenario as an extra assumption, with 0% as the required per unit profit (above the single rule).

Incorporating Demand Considerations and Market Share

The next addition to the analysis integrates demand considerations with BEA. The break even analysis can incorporate estimates of demand for different price levels, so as to look at potential sales. A break even analysis can provide only an estimated level of break even, at a given price. At higher (skimming) prices, break even will be achieved at lower quantities. As the price is lowered, more units must be sold to break even. Which of the prices should be used? The break even analysis can be modified to help select the best price, given demand considerations. Figure 1 shows the results of such an analysis graphically.

While price decisions for existing products generally are based on previous price levels, products which are new to the market or the company require additional attention. How to price a new offering is critical, since both skimming and penetration strategies are possible.

Three different prices are examined in this model, ranging from $312 to $663 per flight ticket. It is assumed that the price differences reflect different requirements: The cheapest requires a weekend stay (Super Saver), and only a few seats per flight are made available. The highest fare has no restrictions and is associated with a limousine service on the ground, upon arrival. The coach fare requires 5 days advance booking, and has the highest demand.

The price has an effect on the marketplace, and the assumed impact is shown in an assumption. To obtain such information, knowledgeable salespeople and executives must be consulted. As can be seen, the essence of a break even analysis is retained, while sales estimates are incorporated into the analysis. Table 3 allows you to compare the relationship between three potential price levels, their break-even points, estimated sales, and corresponding profits for every price level. It shows different prices and their effects on total revenues and net profits.

With a price of $543, total profits will be higher than with either of the other price alternatives. Additionally, Table 3 shows the market share represented by the sales estimate.

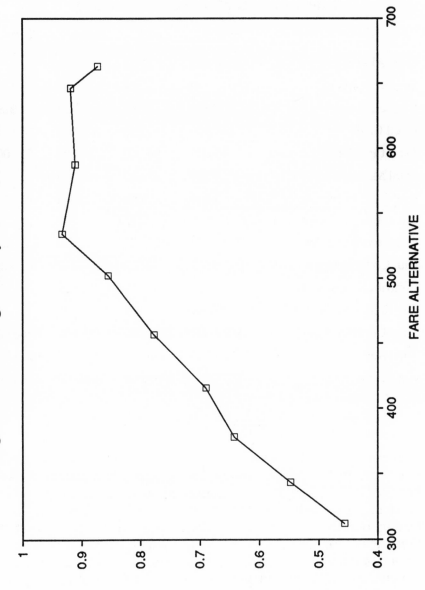

Figure 1 Examining Monthly Fare Alternatives

FARE ALTERNATIVE

Table 3 Break Even Incorporating Demand Considerations: Examining Monthly Fare Alternatives

	Fare A	Fare B	Fare C	Total
Price Alternative	$663	$534	$312	$503
Target Profits (%)	0	0	0	0
Variable Costs	$350	$312	$225	$296
Fixed Costs	$60,000	$60,000	$60,000	$180,000
Target Profits	$6,000	$6,000	$6,000	$18,000
Total Market	5,000	16,000	12,000	$33,000
Unit Sales Forecast	3,000	4,5000	6,000	$13,500
Break Even in Units	211	297	759	1,267
Break Even in Sales	$139,802	$158,757	$236,690	$535,248
Unit Contribution	$313	$222	$87	$207
Contribution Ratio (%)	47	42	28	39
Required Mkt Share (%)	60	28	50	41
Total Contribution	$939,000	$999,000	$522,000	2,460,000
Total Revenues	$1,989,000	$2,403,000	$1,872,000	$6,264,000
Net Profits	$873,000	$933,000	$456,000	2,262,000

Other Applications

This example can be easily extended to include assessments of different products in the same line or the prices of different product lines. Also, by changing the assumptions, some relationships can be changed as well. Notably, the fixed costs are considered fixed throughout the analysis. This relationship can be changed if the break even quantity is at a level exceeding current plant capacity, or one is interested in checking what would happen if fixed costs are changed by a certain percent. For example, this quantity may require additional production shifts, which raise the fixed manufacturing costs. Such added complexity can be built into the spreadsheet, allowing fixed costs to rise above certain production quantities. Alternatively, lowering of fixed costs can be checked as well. Table 4 shows the final spreadsheet, to which such additions can be made.

Table 4 Break Even Incorporating Demand Considerations and ROI: Examining Monthly Fare Alternatives

	Fare A	Fare B	Fare C	Total
Price Alternative	$663	$534	$312	$503
Target Proftis (%)	0	0	0	0
Variable Costs	$350	$312	$225	$296
Fixed Costs	$60,000	$60,000	$60,000	$180,000
Target Profits	$6,000	$6,000	$6,000	$18,000
Total Market	$5,000	$16,000	$12,000	$33,000
Unit Sales Forecast	3,000	$4,500	6,000	$13,500
Required Investment	$6,000,000	$6,000,000	$6,000,000	$18,000,000
Break Even in Units	211	297	759	1,267
Break Even in Sales	$139,802	$158,757	$236,690	$535,248
Unit Contribution	$313	$222	$87	$207
Contribution Ratio (%)	47	42	28	39
Required Mkt Share (%)	60	28	50	41
Total Contribution	$939,000	$999,000	$522,000	$2,460,000
Total Revenues	$1,989,000	$2,403,000	$1,872,000	$6,264,000
Net Profits	$873,000	$933,000	$456,000	$2,262,000
ROI (%)	15	16	8	13

This spreadsheet can also be used to determine the sales necessary to achieve a fixed profit level. To do this, assign the fixed profit as the investment and enter the target % ROI as 1.00.

These entries calculate the sales necessary to return this total amount each year.

Can competitive reactions be similarly treated? One way is to add on assumption (row) about competition. For example, a similar product introduced by a competitor is expected to capture an 11% market share, cutting into the company's sales. This can be simulated by lowering the potential market for the company's sales levels at every price alternative.

The competitive impact can be more severe at higher prices, as may be expected if a competitor's price is set at $550 compared to the $663 recommended by the aggressive strategy. A more cautious strategy may prove prudent in the long run if the aim is to keep competition out of the market. Alternatively, the competitive reaction can be likened to a price increase which results in lower sales. Clearly, the break even analysis can be easily changed to examine different assumptions about demand, competition, and other pertinent aspects of pricing.

Table 5 shows the same spreadsheet as a template, to which all these changes in relationships can be made. Obviously, assumptions too can be changed. Note that perhaps the greatest advantage of spreadsheet programs lies in the fact that they facilitate development of templates. Like boiler plate letters, as different assumptions are introduced, they quickly come to life with calculations reflecting the new assumptions.

Discounts

Discounts are frequently used as pricing tools designed to achieve specific goals. A spreadsheet calculating quantity discounts is called the discount spreadsheet. This spreadsheet is built around several assumptions. The rationale for granting quantity discounts is encouraging sales. In order to accomplish such an increase it is extremely important that the data entered in the assumptions section be carefully thought out. Such data must always be followed with sales analyses which compare total revenues and profits with and without the quantity discounts.

Table 5 Break Even Incorporating Demand Considerations and ROI Examining Monthly Fare Alternatives

	Fare A	Fare B	Fare C	Total
Price Alternative	$0	$0	$0	$0
Target Profits (%)	$0	$0	$0	$0
Variable Costs	$0	$0	$0	$0
Fixed Costs	$0	$0	$0	$0
Target Profits	$0	$0	$0	$0
Total Markets	0	0	0	0
Unit Sales Forecast	0	0	0	$0
Required Investment	$0	$0	$0	$0
Break Even in Units	ERR	ERR	ERR	ERR
Break Even in Sales	ERR	ERR	ERR	ERR
Unit Contribution	$0	$0	$0	$0
Contribution Ratio	ERR	ERR	ERR	ERR
Required Mkt Share	ERR	ERR	ERR	ERR
Total Contribution	0	0	0	0
Total Revenues	0	0	0	0
Net Profits	$0	$0	$0	$0
ROI	ERR	ERR	ERR	ERR

Table 6 shows the spreadsheet with a quantity discount structure for a ticket agent serving small business owners. The bottom quantity reflects the monthly number of tickets (4) needed for weekly flights. The next level, however, requires the purchase of 5-8 tickets, calculated so as to encourage the buyer to consider buying weekly tickets one month in advance. Buyers at this level pay only $515.85, a 5% discount. Buyers of three months' worth of tickets get a bigger discount, 10%, and pay only 464.27 per ticket.

Table 6 Quantity Discount Structure for Tire Wholesaler

4	Minimum Quantity, Below Which No Discount Applies
24	Maximum Quantity, Above Which There Is No Discount
5	Number of Breaks (1 to 5) to be Given to Large Buyers
5%	Discount per Break Level 1
10%	Discount per Break Level 2
13%	Discount per Break Level 3
15%	Discount per Break Level 4
20%	Discount per Break Level 5
$543.00	Price Per Unit With No Discount

Quantity	Unit Price	Total Sale	Total Price Reduction
4	$543.00	$2,172.00	$0.00
8	$515.85	$4,126.80	($217.20)
12	$464.27	$5,571.18	($944.82)
16	$403.91	$6,462.57	($2,225.43)
20	$343.32	$6,866.48	($3,993.52)
24	$274.66	$6,591.82	($6,440.18)
25	$274.66	$6,866.48	($6,708.52)
26	$274.66	$7,141,14	($6,976.86)
27	$274.66	$7,415.80	($7,245.20)
28	$274.66	$7,690.46	($7,513.54)
29	$274.66	$7,965.12	($7,781.88)
30	$274.66	$8,239.78	($8,050.22)
31	$274.66	$8,514.43	($8,318.57)
32	$274.66	$8,789.09	($8,586.91)
33	$274.66	$9,063.75	($8,855.25)
34	$274.66	$9,338.41	($9,123.59)
35	$274.66	$9,613.07	($9,391.93)
36	$274.66	$9,887.73	($9,660.27)

The data below the rule shows the levels, unit prices, sales volume, and the total discount given at that level. This spreadsheet can also be turned into a template by placing zeroes in every assumption. Figure 2 shows the resulting discount structure graphically.

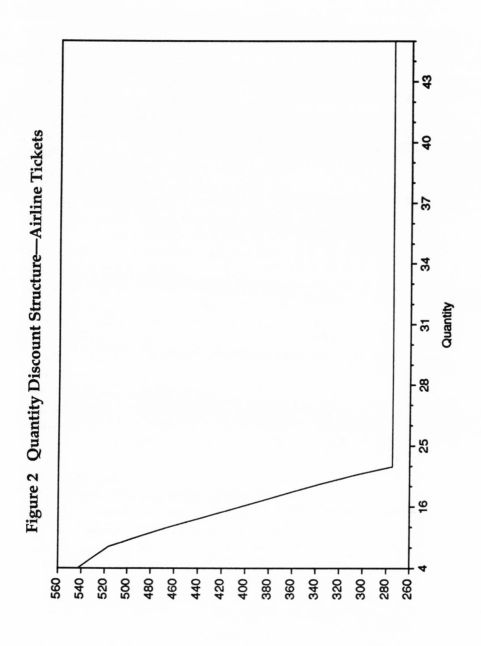

Figure 2 Quantity Discount Structure—Airline Tickets

In addition to using spreadsheets for calculating quantity discounts, there are other uses for the discount spreadsheet. For example, to develop a number for the first assumption (minimum quantity), an analysis of customers is required. A listing of all customers (or the more important ones) should be sorted by their sales level in descending order. Next the sales data should be converted to cumulative sales. This will give a list of customers, from the most important to the least important, with a corresponding cumulative sales list. Now identify three groups of customers: those corresponding to the top, middle and bottom thirds of your sales.

The minimum discount quantity can be defined as the average sales level of the bottom third of your customers. Conversely, the maximum would be defined as the average sales level of the top third of your customers. These two will give you the first two assumptions. All customers buying above the average for the top third qualify as house accounts. All those below the bottom third do not deserve a discount. The number of customers between these two levels will help you determine how many discount levels you want to have.

Several additional discounts may be customarily granted in specific lines of business: notably, cash discounts and seasonal discounts. At times, in some industries, advertising allowances are given. In other industries there are geographically based prices. Since in most of these cases calculations are rather straightforward, general purpose spreadsheets are not provided for these.

The spreadsheets shown earlier can be adopted to reflect any of these discounts. Cumulative discounts (i.e., all units bought in the course of this year are used to calculate discounts) can be incorporated into this model, as can changes which accommodate quantity discounts based on dollar volume as opposed to units. Legal considerations are of course important, since you cannot discriminate in pricing. In all cases these decisions have strong implications for both buyer and seller.

Trade discounts are given to different distributors according to their line of business. Wholesalers and retailers frequently receive discounts, but different classes of customers also earn discounts. The U.S. Government, OEM's, and different types of distributors often also get special discounts. The rationale for trade discounts lies in the savings to the seller, accrued from services performed by the buyer for the seller. Customers performing more services are rewarded with larger discounts. This rationale is important legally since, otherwise, the seller must charge the same price to all customers who are basically similar.

Though the use of trade discounts tends to follow industry practices, the amount and terms of the discount can be analyzed with spreadsheet programs.

Experience Curve Pricing

Experience curve pricing is based on the assumption that, over time, costs will decline in a predictable amount every time cumulative production doubles. Examples of successful price declines include computer memory and automobiles (the Model T Ford). It is important to remember that the cost decline is due to accumulated experience, not the doubling of production between points in time. Moreover, the decline is measured in constant dollars.

Table 7 shows an experience curve pricing calculation given the cost of the first unit, the percent growth in production, the first year in which production begins, and the assumed percent experience. Each of the assumptions can be changed to fit other parameters. Using the example of airplane manufacturing, the spreadsheet shows that while the first plane was built at a cost of 8 million dollars, that price comes down significantly, with experience.

The effects of experience curve pricing are noted by consumers and producers of electronic equipment, where dramatic price reductions coupled with demand increases are regularly expected. Calculators, portable tape players, video recorders, computers, digital watches, and compact disk players are just a few of the products for which experience leads to reduced variable costs.

Experience curve effects can also be found in "low-tech" industries. The variable costs for hamburgers, physical examinations, airline seats, and books can be reduced as a result of experience

Table 7 Experience Curve Pricing Calculation

20.00% = Learning curve constant
$8,000,000.00 = Average Variable Cost During First Period
12 = Average Production per Period

Period	Cumulative Production	Variable Cost/Unit	Percent Reduction	% Reduction as Production Doubles
1	12	$8,000,000	0.00	
2	24	$6,964,405	12.94	12.94
3	36	$6,421,932	7.79	
4	48	$6,062,866	5.59	13.38
5	60	$5,798,237	4.36	
6	72	$5,590,617	3.58	
7	84	$5,420,887	3.04	
8	96	$5,278,032	2.64	13.62
9	108	$5,155,152	2.33	
10	120	$5,047,659	2.09	
11	132	$4,952,351	1.89	
12	144	$4,866,915	1.73	
13	156	$4,789,623	1.59	
14	168	$4,719,156	1.47	
15	180	$4,654,486	1.37	
16	192	$4,594,793	1.28	13.74

gained by management. Trends which produce greater stand-ardization (McDonald's) and larger service networks (real estate agents, airline reservation systems) produce such effects.

Experience curves are product-specific. Making these forecasts is difficult, but for many products the potential variable cost savings play an important role in strategic price planning. Experience with similar products provides a starting point for establishing an experience curve; however, this approach will not identify the possibilities for more rapid learning by some competitors.

The learning curve constant permits customization of the expected effects of learning on costs. When set at .25 (instead of .20 as shown in Table 7), costs are reduced approximately 17 percent for each doubling of production. Constants above 0.50 are unrealistic for virtually all products, since with fairly brief experience costs approach zero. Therefore, the learning curve constant has a realistic range between zero and .50, with lower values more likely.

Customization of the learning curve can also be made by using a function with a different shape than shown in Figure 3. This complexity is not discussed here, but is vital in fine-tuning experience curve analyses.

Other Pricing Models

Many additional pricing models can benefit from spreadsheet use: bidding, competitive pricing and service pricing, to mention a few. These pricing models can be calculated in one of several ways, depending on the user's needs and specific environment. Some concluding comments on each follow.

Bidding

Construction companies, sellers of employee health and pension plans, and other firms selling in industrial and government markets are frequently required to submit sealed bids. It is not unusual to compete against ten to a hundred other firms when seeking government and industrial contracts. The inverse relationship between the probability of getting the contract and the quoted bid price is the dominant factor to be considered.

Other factors of importance include information about competitors, their past behavior, considerations of capacity utilization, and prospects for future or additional work on the contract. The estimates can be compiled by experienced executives or salespeople who know the competition.

The likelihood of securing a contract is generally negatively related to the bid price. The higher the bid, the lower the chances of winning. Firms that do extensive bidding can estimate the probability of securing a bid at different price levels. A spreadsheet can be constructed using as assumptions the bid price, bid costs, prob-

Figure 3 Experience Curve for Plane Buildup

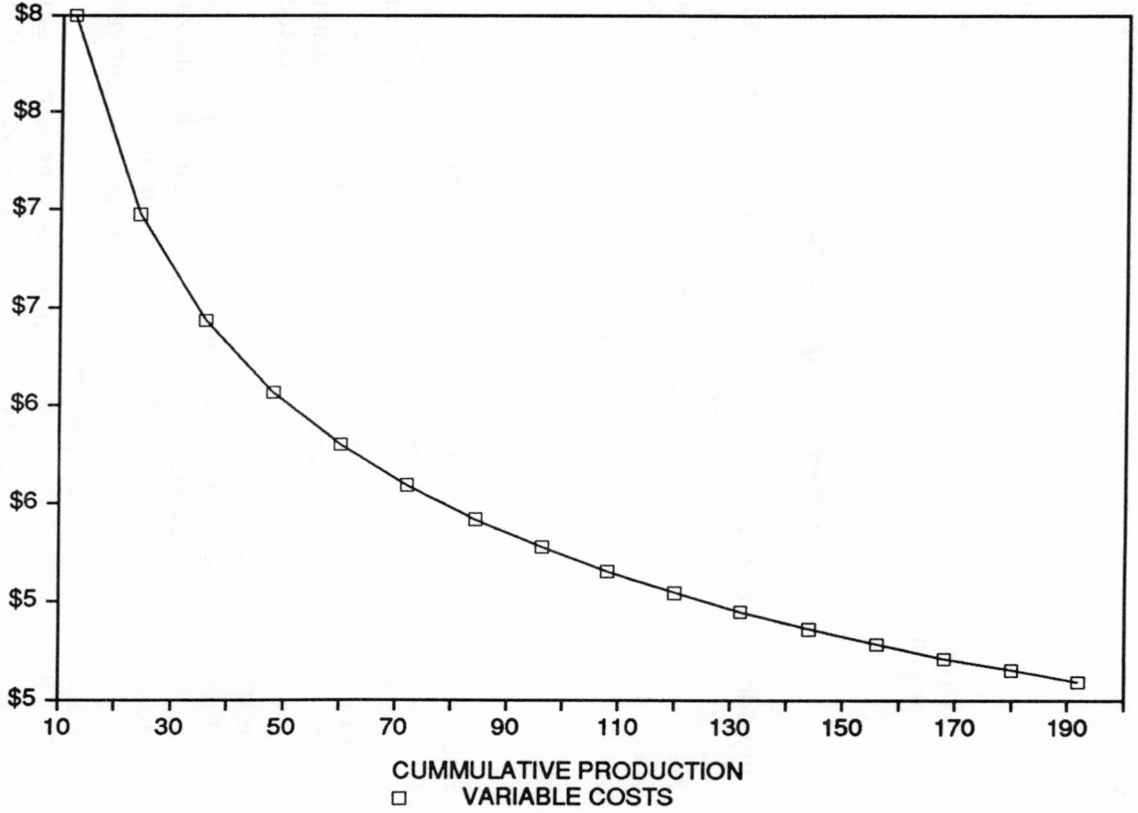

ability of award, profits, and expected value for alternative bids. Using such assumptions, the spreadsheet can calculate the profit at each price, then multiply this profit by the probability of acceptance to yield the expected value to the organization.

When additional data are available, incorporating it into the model could be useful. For example, the number of competitors who bid in the past on similar contracts, along with their prices, can be used to calculate the probabilities of success.

One consequence of the above is that many marketing managers must rely on corporate reports, profit analyses, and quarterly balance sheets which were generated for purposes other than marketing management. This forces many to perform additional analyses (often involving tedious data re-entry) just so they can use the data in a form more consistent with their needs. Data from the corporation's data processing center is not always timely, and at times simply unavailable. The above models were designed to assist in some of these tasks and provide ideas for developing spreadsheets to meet specific needs.

Service Pricing

Like airlines, theaters, hotels, sports, and other service organizations offer from 5 to 10 different prices for different service levels, such as location and degree of service provided. Limits are often set for some of the price levels, especially for deep discounted prices. This is done to minimize displacing the more expensive prices with the lower ones. A complex supply and demand problem arises in setting prices and capacity limits for various levels of service. For yet other some service offerings, such as movies and amusement parks, pricing different times at different levels is practical.

Spreadsheets provide the means for testing the relationships between costs, capacity, and capacity limits for several prices and demands. A spreadsheet showing several price levels, demands, and capacity limits for those demands can be constructed. The spreadsheet can produce a *pro forma* income statement, providing expected profits and the percent of capacity utilized.

The spreadsheet then forecasts the profits by price for each time period, specifies the maximum profits for each use, calculates the total profits for multiple uses of the same time, and estimates maximum profits. As always, the pricing policy requires strategic considerations, such as a one-price policy to reduce potential consumer confusion, remaining open at potential loss times to maintain consumer good will, or remaining open at potential loss times to provide revenue to cover at least a portion of company overhead.

Competitive Price Analysis

The pricing decision takes on special meaning when a product/service is introduced to a new market or is being repositioned by the company. At such times, the product's competitive positioning is studied so as to assure the best position. Price, in relation to target markets, other competitive offerings, and the bundle of benefits offered with the product, are evaluated.

Spreadsheets can be constructed to show how consumers rate competing products using several product attributes. Consumers are asked to allocate 100 points among the competing products for each attribute. A total score can then be calculated by multiplying the weight of each attribute by the score. Product A has the highest total score, followed by D, B, C, and finally E. The price should reflect this relative standing, if a straightforward price/value relationship is sought.

Summary

Since the great depression, price has taken on added importance as a regulatory tool, used by lawmakers to regulate the marketplace. This has resulted in many pricing decisions which were made by lawyers and accounting professionals who looked at costs as the most important driving force in pricing. Price was a highly visible attribute, closely monitored by politicians, economists, labor, and unions.

Price and the pricing decision, however, must complement other marketing mix considerations, and the entire mix needs to be evaluated before concluding which price to use. In marketing, price is but one of several tools to be used.

Computer spreadsheets provide pricing professionals with an analytical tool for better judging the effect of the confluence of all these forces on price. Demand, capacity utilization, costs, sales promotion and image must all be considered and evaluated in an accurate and speedy manner. The ability to do this using spreadsheet programs is rapidly becoming commonplace. This is perhaps the greatest contribution of spreadsheets to pricing.

Recommended for Additional Reading

"Computers deserve a tilt at those pricing decisions," by John Butcher in *Accountancy*, May, 1985.

"Micros in Accounting: Using Lotus for Pricing and Break-Even Strategies," by Joseph J. Weil in *Journal of Accountancy*, July, 1987.

SECTION II

PRICE STRATEGIES

CREATIVE PRICING OF PRODUCTS AND SERVICES:

Principles, Analysis and Applications

GERARD J. TELLIS

This paper is adapted with permission of the American Marketing Association from "Beyond the Many Faces of Price: An Integration of Pricing Strategies," *Journal of Marketing*, Volume 50 (October), 146-160, and uses concepts from, "Creative Pricing Strategies for Medical Services," *Journal of Medical Practice Management*, Volume 3 (2), 120-124. Both articles are by the author.

GERARD J. TELLIS

Gerard J. Tellis is Associate Professor of Marketing, at the College of Business Administration, The University of Iowa. As of August 1989, he will be at the University of Southern California, Los Angeles. He has a Ph.D. in business administration from the University of Michigan, Ann Arbor, Michigan. He also has a postgraduate diploma in Business Administration and worked as a Sales Development Manager for Johnson & Johnson. Dr. Tellis' research is in analyzing consumer and market response to pricing and advertising. He specializes in developing pricing strategies that incorporate complexities from multiple products, competitors and consumers.

CHAPTER NINE

Introduction

Pricing is a central variable in the marketing of products and services for several reasons. First, it is the source of revenue for sellers and the cost of the benefit for buyers. It is thus the basis for completing the transaction between buyer and seller. Because of this role, pricing is often the last strategic decision available to the seller. While the form, availability and location of products and services cannot be easily changed at short notice, the price can. So appropriate pricing can complete the transaction when all else fails.

Beyond this crucial albeit short-term role, creative pricing can be a powerful strategic tool for the manager. It is a vital means of defining new markets, differentiating products and services and gaining competitive advantage. The most important isssue in creative pricing is applying the simple principle of cross-subsidies or shared economies over consumer groups, or over products and services or over competitors. The principle of cross subsidies also has an educational advantage: together with the principle of consumer heterogeneity, it helps to classify and relate all of the pricing strategies that are described in the literature.

This chapter has three objectives. First, it discusses the principles that help us to price creatively in response to different scenarios. Second, with these principles it develops a taxonomy of pricing strategies that unifies the variety of strategies described in the literature. The taxonomy also helps to compare, contrast and apply the various pricing strategies appropriately. Third, the chapter details each pricing strategy as the unique, profit or revenue-maximizing response to a particular scenario. For ease of understanding and application, the scenarios are presented as numerical problems.

Principles Driving Creative Pricing

A pricing strategy is a reasoned choice from a set of alternative prices or price schedules that aim at profit or revenue maximization within a planning period in response to a given scenario. (In contrast, a pricing method is a heuristic or mechanical procedure that guides managers in their numerical calculations.) In most situations, the scenarios facing managers involve the interplay of many forces or principles, and a good pricing strategy harnesses these forces effectively.

The principle of cross-subsidizing or sharing costs is basic to creative pricing. In a shared economy, one customer group, or one competitive group, or one product (service) bears more of the costs than another, so the firm may more profitably serve a wider audience. A shared economy is diametrically opposite to strict accountability, where prices for each customer/product/service are assigned directly in proportion to its costs.

The second principle in creative pricing is the heterogeneity of buyers that arises from at least three sources that are of relevance to pricing. First, consumers differ in their information about products and services,—especially about prices. Because it takes some effort or time—and thus money—to gain such information, we could refer to this problem as consumers' information costs. Information costs could be high enough relative to product/service costs, so that some consumers would buy without full information. Second, consumers could also differ in the price they are willing to pay for the product (the reservation price). We could refer to this problem as a difference in consumers' price sensitivity. Third, consumers may have different transaction costs, such as travelling costs, the costs of obtaining funds, the costs of switching brands, or the cost of uncertainty (risk) in investing in the product/service.

The principles of shared economies and consumer heterogeneity help unify the variety of pricing strategies described by practitioners and researchers. The unity is evident in a simple taxonomy of pricing strategies formed by crossing the three bases of shared economies (consumers, firms and products) with the three levels of consumer hetergeneity (information costs, price sensitivity, and transaction costs). (See Table 1.) The taxonomy makes it easier to compare the strategies on various criteria and to describe their use. Table 2 further compares and contrasts these strategies on several dimensions and is discussed in the concluding section.

Table 1   Taxonomy of Pricing Strategies

Objective of Firm: Shared Economies

Characteristics of Consumers	Vary Prices Among Consumer Segments	Exploit Competitive Position	Balance Pricing Over Product Line
Some have high search costs	Random discounting	Price signaling	Image pricing
Some have low reservation price	Periodic discounting	Penetration pricing Experience curve pricing	Price bundling Premium pricing
All have special transaction costs	Second market discounting	Geographic pricing	Complementary pricing

However, the real world is more complex, and several of the conditions listed (information costs, transaction costs, and consumer heterogeneity) may occur jointly. Accordingly, in reality a firm may adopt a combination of these strategies. These tables and numerical problems demonstrate the necessary conditions for each strategy, conditions that are jointly sufficient to classify them conveniently. Similarly, the numerical problems define fairly simple scenarios where "other things are assumed constant" and only factors affecting the choice of a strategy are allowed to vary.

The list of available strategies also is affected by the legal environment. Because of the potential for pricing abuses, especially against weak competitors or weak or uninformed buyers, Congress and the states have passed laws that regulate the pricing strategies that firms can adopt. These laws ban collusion among competitors, deception of consumers, explicit discrimination among industrial buyers, or attempts to manipulate the competitive structure. Some of these laws rule out certain pricing options whereas others include new possibilities, and these effects are dis-

Table 2 Comparison of Pricing Strategies

Criteria	Differential Pricing			Competitive Pricing			Product Line Pricing		
	Second Market Discounting	Periodic Discounts	Random Discounts	Penetration and Experience Curve Pricing	Price Signaling	Geographic Pricing	Price Bundling	Premium Pricing	Complementary Pricing
Characteristic of price strategy varies systematically over:									
Consumer segments	Yes	Yes	Yes	No	No	No	No	No	No
Competitors in market	No	No	No	Yes	Yes	Yes	No	No	No
Product mix	No	No	No	No	No	No	Yes	Yes	Yes
Characteristics of consumers	High transaction costs: physically separated segments	Only some with low reservation price; price sensitive segment	High search costs: some uninformed about price	Some with low reservation price: price sensitive segment	High search costs: some uninformed on quality; uninformed prefer high quality	High transportation costs: geographically distinct markets	Some prefer one product, others, another: asymmetric demand	Only some prefer basic products at low prices	High transaction costs: risk aversiveness or store or brand loyalty
Product and cost characteristics	Unused capacity	Economies of scale or unused capacity	Economies of scale or unused capacity	Economies of scale or experience, or unused capacity	Signaling firm has higher costs or suboptimizes or cheats on quality	Higher production costs in adjacent market; economies of scale or unused capacity	Perishable product or purchase occasion	Joint economies of scale across products; features with low cost increase relative to price increase	Patents, superior technology
Variants	Generic pricing, dumping	Price skimming, peak-load pricing, price discrimination, priority pricing	Variable price merchandising, cents-off, coupons	Limit pricing	Reference pricing	FOB, base point, uniform, zone, and freight pricing	Mixed bundling, pure components, pure bundling	—	Captive pricing, two-part pricing, loss leadership
Relevant legal constraints	Explicit price discrimination illegal	Explicit price discrimination illegal	Explicit price discrimination illegal	Predatory pricing illegal	—	Price collusion, explicit price discrimination, predatory pricing illegal	Explicit price discrimination, pure bundling illegal	—	(Minimum) retail price maintenance illegal, tie-ins illegal

cussed in the appropriate place. The laws are not always fully explicit, but the general motivation of the laws and the spirit in which they have been interpreted by the courts indicate that no strategy should reduce the impact of competitive forces unless it is to the benefit of consumers.

Differential Pricing Strategies

The pricing strategies discussed here all arise primarily because of consumer heterogeneity, so the same product can be sold to consumers under a variety of prices. The three strategies discussed refer to consumer heterogeneity along three dimensions: transaction costs that motivate second market discounting, demand that motivates periodic discounting, and search costs that motivate random discounting.[1] These conditions enable a firm to discriminate implicitly in the prices it charges its consumers. In industrial and wholesale markets, explicit price discrimination whereby a firm charges different prices to two competing buyers under identical circumstances is illegal under the Robinson-Patman Act's (1936) amendment of the Clayton Act (1914), unless the price-cutting firm can meet specific defenses. In the consumer market, explicit price discrimination would lead to the ill-will of consumers. Aside from the special motivations for each type of discounting to be discussed hereafter, discounting in general has a sales-enhancing effect, probably because consumers overwieght the saving on a deal in relation to the cost still incurred in buying the product at the discounted price. If the product were regularly at the discounted price, many of these consumers may not buy it at all!

Second Market Discounting

Consider a competitive firm that sells 100,000 units of a product $10 each, when variable costs are $1 and fixed costs are $500,000 for a capacity of 200,000 units. The firm gets a request to sell in a new market for a negligible loss of sales in the first market and a negligible increase in fixed or variable costs. What is the minimum selling price the firm should accept?

This is a classic problem in incremental costing and the solution is well known. The minimum acceptable price would be anything over $1, because any price over variable costs would make a contribution to this ongoing business. Generics, secondary demographic segments, and some foreign markets provide opportunities for profitable use of this strategy. Often pioneering drugs are faced with competition from identical but much lower priced generics after the expiry of the patent. The pioneering firm has the options of either maintaining its price and losing share or dropping price and losing margin. The relevant strategy would be to enter the generic market segment with an unbranded product and arrest loss of sales to that segment without either foregoing margin or position in the branded segment. The same principle also holds for a firm changing to a mixed brand strategy after selling under a manufacturer label only or a private label only. A second illustration of this strategy is the discounts to secondary demographic markets such as students, children, or new members.

Similarly, for some countries the foreign market represents an opportunity rather than a threat if the same theory is applied. Often a firm's selling price or even current average cost in the home market may be higher than the selling price in the foreign market. However, if its variable costs are sufficiently below the selling price in the foreign market, the firm can export profitably at a price somewhere between the selling price in the foreign market and its variable costs. The term "dumping" is sometimes used to describe the latter strategy in the firm's selling price in the foreign market is below its average costs.

The essential requirements for this strategy are that the firm have unused capacity and consumers have transaction costs so there is no perfect arbitrage between the two markets. In terms of profitability, additional revenues from the second market should exceed all increases in variable and fixed costs and loss of profits from the first market. Note, here, that the first market provides an external economy to the second, because the latter market gets goods at a lower price than it would otherwise. (For this reason some economists are not critical of dumping. Others, however, stress that there may be long-term damage to the foreign economy from lost wages and production facilities.) The second market provides neither an economy nor a diseconomy to the first in the short run.

Periodic Discounting

Consider a firm faced with the following pricing problem. Average economic costs[2] are $55 at 20 units and $40 at 40 units. Forty consumers per period are interested in its product only at the beginning of each period even if they have to pay $50 per unit. The other half are price sensitive and would take the product at any time but will pay no more than $30 per unit. At what price should the firm sell its product?

Initially it may seem that the firm cannot bring the product to market profitably because costs exceed acceptable prices for each segment. However, in effect, the firm can produce and sell profitably if it exploits the consumers' heterogeneity of demand by a strategy of periodic discounting. It should produce at the level of 40 units per period at a cost of $40 per unit, price at $50 at the beginning of each period, and systematically discount the product at the end of the period to $30. In this way it would sell to the fussy consumers at the beginning and to the rest at the end of each period. Note that its average selling price is $40, which equals its average economic cost.

This is the principle often involved in the temporal markdowns and periodic discounting of off-season fashion goods, off-season travel fares, matinee tickets, and happy hour drinks, as well as peak-load pricing for utilities. Similarly, this is the principle involved in the discounting of older models, the priority pricing of scarce products, and the strategy of price skimming for new products. Because of the circumstances in which this discounting strategy has been used, it often is referred to by different names. However, a more general label would be "periodic discounting," because of the essential principle underlying this strategy: the manner of discounting is predictable over time and not necessarily unknown to consumers (unlike random discounting discussed next) and the discount can be used by all consumers (unlike second market discounting).

An interesting issue in periodic discounting is that both segments of the market provide an external economy to each other.[3] The first segment provides a "venture" price at the beginning while the second segment provides a "salvage" price to the firm for unsold items at the period's end. This intuition suggests that, even if the demand for the product is not exactly known, a strategy of pricing high and systematically discounting with time is likely to ensure that the firm covers its costs and makes a reasonable profit. However, the first segment provides a greater external economy than the second, because it bears more of the production costs.

Random Discounting

Consider a firm that has a minimum average economic cost of production of $30. Assume a distribution of prices for the same product between $30 and $50 because there are several other firms with other cost structures and $50 is the maximum consumers will pay for it. It takes one hour to search for the lowest price, $30. If a consumer does not search but buys from the first seller, he/she may if lucky get a $30 seller but if unlucky may get a $50 seller. Further, assume consumers' opportunity cost of time ranges from $0 to well over $20 per hour. What is the best shopping strategy for consumers and the best pricing strategy for firms? For consumers, the problem is fairly simple. Let us assume that the distribution of prices is such that on average a consumer who does not search and is uniformed about prices pays $40 for the product. Then on average a consumer who searches and is informed saves $10. Hence consumers earning more than $10 should not shop and the rest should. Let us assume that at least some consumers search and others buy randomly. What strategy should the firm with an average economic cost of $30 adopt?

The answer is a strategy of random discounts, which involves maintaining a high price of $50 regularly and discounting to $30. However, the manner of discounting is crucial. It should be undiscernible or "random" to the uninformed consumers and infrequent, so that these consumers do not get lucky too often. The uninformed consumers will not be able to second guess the price; they will buy randomly, usually at the high price. In contrast, the informed will look around or wait until they can buy at the low price. In this way the firm tries to maximize the number of informed at its low price instead of at a competitor's low price, while maximizing the number of uniformed at its high rather than its low price. Research on the intransitivity of preferences indicates some interesting twists to the appeal of discounts and coupons. First, searches are likely to oversearch. They spend more time shopping than is justified by their gains, the result of what researchers call the "endowment effect." The real saving from the discounts is overweighted in relation to the opportunity cost of time. In contrast, nonsearchers are likely to undersearch for high cost products. This behavior can be explained by the psychophysics of pricing. Consumers relate the benefits of search to the cost of the good rather than to the cost of the time it takes to search.

Most discounting today by specialty stores, department stores, services, and especially supermarkets is of this type. Out-of-store coupons or features are of this type unless motivated by periodic discounting, inventory buildup, or damaged goods.

The vast volume of business in this category has increased the importance of understanding the issues involved. The basic condition for this strategy is heterogeneity of perceived search costs, which enables firms to attract informed consumers by discounting. All consumers know there is a distribution of prices and have the same reservation price. However, for high-income individuals, hunting for the lowest price may not be worth their time. For others the opposite holds.

The individual firm should adopt a strategy of random discounts if the increased profit from new informed consumers at the discounted price exceeds the cost of administering the discount.

It is interesting to examine the implications of this strategy. First, note that the uninformed consumers provide a diseconomy to other uninformed consumers and to informed consumers. Inefficient firms that produce above $30 or efficient firms that price above $30 can exist because some consumers do not search. As a result, prices vary, so that the informed must search for the lowest price. Similarly, the average price paid by the uninformed is higher as the proportion of uninformed increases. In contrast, the informed provide an external economy to the uninformed by encouraging the existence of low price firms, thus lowering the average price the uninformed pay. From a public policy perspective all consumers as well as the efficient firms would benefit from a mechanism that could disseminate price information in the market at relatively low cost.

Competitive Pricing

This category covers a group of pricing strategies based primarily on a firm's competitive position. Penetration pricing and experience curve pricing attempt to exploit scale[4] or experience[5] economies, respectively, by currently pricing below competitors in the same market to drive them out. Predatory pricing means pricing low to hold out competition with the sole objective of establishing monopolistic conditions and subsequently raising price; this practice is illegal under Section 2 of the Sherman Act and the Robinson- Patman Act of 1936. Many states also have laws that forbid a firm from pricing below cost for extended periods of time. A third strategy is price signaling,[6] whereby a firm exploits consumer trust in the price mechanism developed by other firms. A fourth strategy, geographic pricing, involves competitive pricing for adjacent market segments.

Penetration Pricing

Consider the periodic discounting example with the following two modifications: the economic cost price at 40 units is $30 and other competitors can freely enter the market with the same cost structure. How should the firm price now?

The firm could still adopt a strategy of periodic discounting, producing 40 units a period at $30 each and selling to the first set of consumers at $50 and to the second at $30. Now, however, because its average cost price is $30, it would make an excess profit of $10 per unit. Given this scenario, any other firm would be willing to come in and sell the same product for an average price that is less than $40 but more than $30. To preempt competition and stay in business, the firm would have to sell at $30 to all consumers.

The same logic underlies penetration pricing, a strategy proposed for new products as an alternative to periodic discounting (or price skimming). Periodic discounting is obviously preferable for a firm, even if its costs are lower than demand prices (as in the modified example here), as long as there is no immediate threat of competitive entry. Besides being used for new products, penetration pricing can be observed in the growth of discount stores and in the consolidation of manufacturers during the "shake out" phase of the life cycle. A variation of penetration pricing is limit pricing, whereby a firm prices above costs but just low enough to keep out new entrants.

Penetration pricing is relevant only when the average selling price can or does exceed the minimum average cost. Other essentials for penetration pricing strategy are price sensitivity on the part of some consumers and the threat of competitive entry. In penetration pricing, unlike periodic discounting, the presence of the price sensitive consumers and of competition provides a benefit to the price insensitive segment, who can now buy the product at a price lower than they were willing to pay.

Experience Curve Pricing

Assume a competitive market with experience effects as shown in Figure 1. There are four firms (A, B, C, and D), each with per period volume of 2000 units but the first having the most experience and average costs of $3.75 per unit. Current prices are $5 per unit. Consumers are price sensitive and react immediately to price changes. What would be a good pricing strategy for firm A?

Note that currently firm A makes more profit than the others and that, given the projections, cost declines will be less prominent after year 6. A good strategy for firm A would be to price aggres-

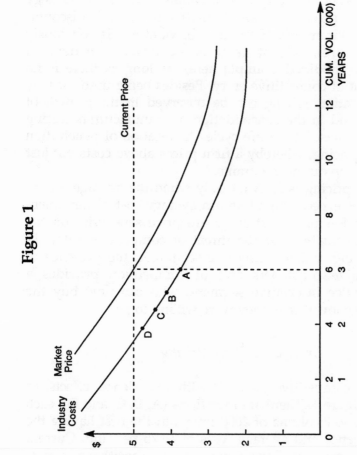

Figure 1

sively, even below current costs, at $3.75. This strategy has two advantages. First, it will be uneconomical for firms B, C, and D, which may have to leave the market. Firm A is then faced with less rivalry. Second, firm A can benefit from the share of the others and gain experience more rapidly. Indeed, it would sell a cumulative volume of 12,000 units as early as year 4 and its costs would have dropped by then to $2 per unit. In addition, the low price is likely to encourage more consumers to enter the market, giving firm A an opportunity to exploit economies of scale. As a result the firm will soon be profitable again and total revenue and profits could be much higher in the future. The strategy for the other firms is less clear. In general, unless there are other competitive advantages, it is inadvisable for the others to start a price war as they have a cost disadvantage to firm A.

Experience curve pricing, like penetration pricing, is an alternative strategy to periodic discounting. In this strategy the consumers who buy the product early in the life cycle gain an external economy from late buyers, as they buy the product at a lower price than they were willing to pay. They get this discount, however, because of economies of experience and active or potential competition that forces prices down.

The essential requirements for adopting an experience curve pricing strategy are that experience effects are strong; that the firm has more experience than competitors; and that consumers are price sensitive. Typically, these conditions occur for durable goods in the early or growth stage, when a relatively large number of competitors are striving for a strong long-run position. The different sources of economies for penetration pricing and experience curve pricing must be clearly understood, because the circumstances in which they are applicable are often very similar but the mechanisms for tracking costs and pricing products are very different.

Price Signaling

Consider a market in which firms can produce products at two different quality levels, under the constraint that the minimum average economic cost is $30 for the low-quality product and $50 for the high-quality product. Assume that, to avoid image conflicts, each firm chooses to produce only one quality but may sell at either price, $30 or $50. Let us assume for convenience that there are at least a few firms selling the high quality product for $50 and the low quality product for $30. Consumers can easily find the lowest price (in negligible time), say by a phone call or by consulting a price list. They generally prefer high quality, but it takes them 1 hour of study and consulting manuals to tell quality differences. Let these consumers have a distribution of opportunity costs of time as in the random discounting example. What are consumers' shopping strategies and firms' pricing strategies?

Firms can choose among three pricing strategies (no firm would sell the high-quality product at less than $50). First, they could produce the low-quality product and sell it at $30. Second, they could produce the high-quality product and sell it at $50. Third, they could sell the low-quality product at $50, with the intention that some consumers who cannot tell high-quality but want it will be fooled. The last strategy is called "price signaling." Consumers also have three strategies. Those with low costs of time could study quality and buy the high-quality product at $50. Those with high costs of time could adopt a risk aversive strategy and always buy the low-priced product, or could buy the high-priced product with the hope of getting a high-quality product.

Extensive research in marketing has indicated that consumers may use price to infer quality. Three underlying conditions are necessary for price signaling to be an equilibrium strategy. First, consumers must be able to get information about price more easily than information about quality. Second, they must want the high quality enough to risk buying the high-priced product even without a certainty of high quality. This motive is especially necessary because consumers tend to underweigh the values of uncertain events (the so-called "certainty effect"). Third, there must be a sufficiently large number of informed consumers who can understand quality and will pay the high price only for the high-quality product. This third condition ensures a sufficiently positive correlation between price and quality so those uninformed consumers who infer quality from price find it worthwhile to do so on average.

The issue of pricing in the presence of quality variation and asymmetric consumer information is typical of durable goods, though not uncommon for services and nondurable goods where it may involve less risk. For durables, quality is an important attribute yet consumer information on quality is low because of the difficulty of determining quality by inspection, the large number of brands, and the high innovation rate relative to repurchase time. One result is the possibility of consumers using price to infer quality. However, another result is that the correlation between price and quality is low and consumers may often be mistaken. Price signaling is probably most common for new or amateur consumers in a market, who do not know the quality of competitive brands but find quality important. The purchase of a high-priced wine by the casual buyer is a good example. The success of several high-priced, inferior quality brands, as reported by *Consumer Reports*, is another illustration of consumers either buying randomly or using price to infer quality.

There are some other variations of price signaling that firms can adopt to exploit consumer behavior in other circumstances. Image pricing, discussed subsequently, and reference pricing are two common examples. In reference pricing, a firm places a high-priced model next to a much higher priced version of the same product, so that the former may seem more attractive to risk aversive uninformed consumers. The latter model serves primarily as a reference point, though consumers who infer quality may buy it. Researchers call this aspect of consumer behavior the "isolation effect": a choice looks more attractive next to a costly alternative than it does in isolation. The strategy is sometimes adopted by retailers of durable goods. A more common variation is for firms to state that a product is on sale, with the "regular" sticker price adjacent, when actually the regular price is on for less than half the time. To minimize deception on the part of firms, several states now define minimum time periods for the regular price.

In this context it is worthwhile to consider the welfare aspects of such strategy. The most important point is that all consumers would be better off with a mechanism that provides information on quality at low cost. Second, those firms that sell the low-quality product for the low price and those that sell the high-quality product for the high price would also be better off if information on quality were disseminated, because they would not lose customers to firms that sell the low-quality product at the high price. The last category of firms would vanish. Therefore, heterogeneous search costs on quality create benefits for some firms at the expense of others. Third, firms could sell the low-quality product at the high price for many reasons. Some could adopt such a strategy accidentally, others because they are inefficient producers, and still others because they intentionally cheat. Fourth, consumers who use price to infer quality may not necessarily be worse off. To the extent that obtaining information on quality is difficult for them, the correlation between price and quality is positive, and they prefer the high-quality product, they may profitably use the high price to infer quality. In such a situation there is an external economy from the informed to the uninformed who gather information via the price mechanism.

Note that price signaling is independent of the strategy of random discounting. Both are used in situations in which consumers have heterogeneous search costs, but differ on other dimensions. For price signaling, products must differ on quality, information on quality must be more scarce than that on price, and quality must be important to consumers; further, each firm need adopt only one price level always and at least some efficient firms are necessary to establish consumer trust in the price mechanism.

Geographic Pricing

Consider two adjacent markets X and Y, of 20 consumers each, where all consumers have a reservation price of $50 for the product and incur a cost of more than $10 for purchasing the product in the adjacent market. A firm operating in market X is faced with free competitive entry and the following cost structure: the economic cost price for the product is $40 at 20 units and $30 at 40 units, with an added cost of $10 per unit to ship the product to the adjacent market. The cost of production is higher in market Y. What pricing strategy should the firm adopt?

The firm should produce 40 units and sell to both markets at an average economic cost price of $35 ($30 + $10 x 20 ÷ 40). To avoid competitive entry, the firm must set the average selling price over both markets at $35. However, the firm has several options for pricing the product to the two markets, called "geographic pricing strategies," depending on the competitive condition in market Y.

If the competitive price in market Y is above $40, the firm can sell the product at $30 in market X and $40 in market Y to reflect the transportation costs of $10 per unit to the latter market. Because price equals average costs, the price would be profitable yet ward off entry. This strategy is called "FOB." If the competitive price in market Y is a little over $35, the firm could sell at $35 in both markets and still achieve the same competitive effect. This strategy is called "uniform delivered price." Zone pricing is a strategy between the two when more markets are involved. When using zone pricing, the firm would charge different prices for different zones depending on the transportation costs to each, but within each zone it would charge one price, the average of all costs to all points in that zone. Basing point is still another variation of uniform delivered price: the firm chooses a base point for transportation costs to points other than the point of production.

If the competitive price is a little over $30 in market Y, the firm could sell profitably to both markets by pricing at $30 in market Y and $40 in market X. This strategy is called "freight absorption cost," because market Y bears none of the transportation cost it incurs for the product. In a monopolistic situation, the firm may absorb the transportation cost or pass it on to consumers in market X. However, in a competitive market such as this one, all the transportation costs are borne by market X.

Geographic pricing strategies can be thought of as being between price penetration and second market discounting (see Table 1). As in price penetration, in geographic pricing the firm seeks to exploit economies of scale by pricing below competitors in a second market segment. As a result, the second market generally provides a benefit to the first. However, in geographic pricing the two segments are separated by transportation costs rather than by reservation prices. In this respect, geographic pricing is similar to the strategy of second market discounting, where two markets are also separated by transaction costs. In second market discounting, however, the firm explicitly attempts to exploit the differences between the two segments, providing considerable savings to the second market. By contrast, in geographic pricing the firm attempts to minimize differences between the two markets by sharing or "absorbing" the transportation costs between them. In spite of the transportation costs and because of economies of scale, the second market does not provide a diseconomy and generally provides an economy to the first.

Some of the geographic pricing strategies discussed may be illegal in certain circumstances. Three general principles can be used to guide policy in this respect. First, a firm should not discriminate between competing buyers in the same region (especially in zone pricing for buyers on either side of a zonal boundary) because such action may violate the Robinson-Patman Act of 1936. Second, the firm's strategy should not appear to be predatory, especially in freight absorption pricing, because such a strategy would violate Section 2 of the Sherman Act of 1890. Third, in choosing the basing point or zone pricing the firm should not attempt to fix prices among competitors because such action would violate Section 1 of the Sherman Act.

Product Line Pricing Strategies

Product line pricing strategies are relevant when a firm has a set of related products. In all of the cases considered, the firm seeks to maximize profit by pricing its products to match consumer demand. However, in each of these strategies, the nature of either the demand or the cross-subsidies varies among the firm's products. A firm uses price bundling when it faces heterogeneity of demand for nonsubstitute, perishable products. A firm uses premium pricing when it faces heterogeneity of demand for substitute products with joint economies of scale. Image pricing is used when consumers infer quality from prices of substitute models. Complementary pricing (including captive pricing, two-part pricing, and loss leadership) is used when a firm faces consumers with higher transaction costs for one or more of its products.

Price Bundling

Assume a distributor of two films, "Romancing the Stone" and "Places in the Heart," is faced by the following demand for these films from two movie houses, Astro and Classic Theatres, that serve the same market.

	Maximum Prices ($'000) Paid By:	
For:	Classic Theatres	Astro
"Romancing the Stone"	12	18
"Places in the Heart"	25	10

What is the best pricing strategy for the distributor to adopt if we assume it cannot explicitly discriminate in price or use tying contracts (force a theatre to buy both movies)?

An explicit price discriminating strategy, charging each distributor the most it will pay for each movie, would yield a total revenue of $65K, but this practice is illegal. Assume the buyers are sufficiently informed and the products perishable so that differential pricing by periodic or random discounting is not possible. A penetration strategy is to price the first movie at $12K and the second at $10K, but in that case total revenue is only $44K from both theatres (2 × (12 + 10)). A "pure components" strategy is to price the first at $18K and the second at $25K, for a total revenue of $43K.

The best solution is to price the first movie at $18K, the second at $25K, and offer both at $28K for a total revenue of $56K. Note that Classic Theatres will take both movies at no more than $37K and Astro at no more than $28K. Thus both theatres will accept the package for $28K, which is the profit-maximizing strategy. This strategy is called "mixed bundling" to contrast it with a pure bundling alternative in which case only the package is available for $28K. Pure bundling may be illegal as a tying contract. The mixed bundling strategy has the added advantage of creating the reference price effect: the package is offered at a much lower price than the sum of the parts.

Examples of such a strategy are the lower prices for season tickets, buffet dinners, packages of stereo equipment, and packages of options on automobiles. The basic requirement for mixed bundling is nonsubstitute (i.e., complimentary or independent), perishable products with an asymmetric demand structure. Because the products are not perfect substitutes, it is possible to get consumers to buy both (or all). Because the products are perishable, the differential pricing strategies of periodic or random discounting are not feasible. The perishability of food items or seats for shows is apparent. The perishability in the purchase of durable goods is the purchase occasion, at which time it is in the interest of sellers to maximize revenues within consumers' demand schedule by price bundling. For example, consumers may buy automobiles once in 3 or 5 years. Each of those times is an opportunity for a firm to sell a maximum number of options by appropriate pricing.

The strategy of price bundling must not be confused with that of "trading up," in which consumers are persuaded to buy more or higher priced models than they originally intended. As the numerical example shows, a passive strategy of correctly bundling the prices of related items is all that is needed to maximize profit. It is also in the interest of consumers to buy at the price bundle. Thus, all consumers and sellers are better off with the mixed bundling strategy than with the pure components strategy.[7]

Premium Pricing

Consider a firm faced with the following pricing problem. There is free entry and average economic costs (for production and marketing) are $50 at 20 units and $35 at 40 units. At any volume, it costs the firm an additional $10 per unit to produce and market a superior version of the product. Assume that any fixed costs of marketing two products instead of one are negligible. Forty consumers per period are interested in its product. Half of them are price insensitive and want the superior version of the product even if they have to pay $50 per unit. The other half are price sensitive and want the basic version of the product but will pay no more than $30 per unit. In what version and at what price should the firm sell the product?

As in the periodic discounting example, costs seem to exceed prices if the firm chooses to sell to only one segment or at only one price. However, it can solve its problem by a premium pricing strategy that exploits consumer heterogeneity in demand. It should produce at 40 units, half of which will be of the superior version, for an average economic cost of $40. It should sell the basic product for $30 and the premium for $50, which price is profitable and wards off entry. Relative to its costs, the firm takes a premium on its higher priced version and a loss on its lower priced version. However, by exploiting joint economies of scale and the heterogeneity of demand, it can profitably produce and sell the product.

Premium pricing applies in a large number of circumstances in markets today. It is used in the pricing of durable goods, typically appliances, for which multiple versions differing in price and features cater to different consumer segments. It also could apply for the pricing of some nondurable goods such as basic and specialty breads or common and exclusive perfumes. A similar strategy is used for the pricing of alternate service plans such as term and preferred insurance policies, front and rear auditorium seating, and deluxe and basic hotel rooms. As is well-known in the case of autos, firms do not find their lower priced models "very profitable," but typically make their profits on the premium versions. Often these premium versions differ from the basic only by features and options, whose production costs generally are not high enough to justify the higher markup. Why does the firm produce the lower priced version and why do other firms not enter the market with only the higher priced version? The preceding explanation is based on heterogeneity in demand and joint economies of scale. Notice that the firm, by using a premium strategy, sells at exactly its economic cost price, which is compatible with a competitive market with free entry.[8] No firm could enter and profitably produce only for the price insensitive segment.

Premium pricing also is used in retailing, where it enables retailers to carry some otherwise unprofitable products desired only by select segments. The pricing of by-products, though generally considered different from premium pricing, involves the same principle. A by-product may carry a cost of disposal to the firm, which may add to the price of the main product. In some cases a by-product may be worth much more than it costs the firm to produce, which advantage can subsidize the price of the main product.

The essential difference between premium pricing and price bundling is that the former applies to substitutes and the latter to complementary products. Both require heterogeneity in demand, but premium pricing emphasizes segment differences by pricing substitutes differently, whereas price bundling bridges segment differences by selling at the lowest common package price. The difference between premium pricing and price signaling is that in the latter each firm produces only one type of product, which is sold at different prices to differently informed consumers. In the former, a firm produces two types of products to exploit joint economies of scale and markets them to heterogeneous but fully informed consumers.

The welfare aspects of premium pricing parallel those of periodic discounting. The main difference is that periodic discounting involves price variation over time for any one brand; premium pricing holds for any one time with price variation over related models. As in the periodic discounting example, each segment provides an external economy to the other; however, the advantage to the price sensitive segment is greater because they buy a product below its average cost.

Image Pricing

By image pricing, a firm brings out an identical version of its current product with a different name (or model number) and a higher price. The intention is to signal quality. This strategy is between price signaling and premium pricing in that the demand characteristics are similar to those of price signaling and the cost aspects are similar to those of premium pricing (see Table 1). Thus the firm uses the higher priced version to signal quality to uninformed consumers and uses the profit it makes on the higher priced version to subsidize the price on the lower priced version. Image pricing differs from price signaling in that the prices are varied over different brands of the same firm's product line. It differs from premium pricing in that differences between brands are not real but only in the images or positions adopted. This strategy may account for some of the variation in prices of alternative brands of cosmetics, soaps, wines, and dresses that differ only in brand names.

Complementary Pricing

Complementary pricing includes three related strategies—captive pricing, two-part pricing, and loss leadership.

Captive pricing: Consider a firm that produces a durable good whose economic cost price is $100 and life span is 3 years. During that time the product needs supplies that have an economic cost price of $.50 a month. All consumers are willing to pay at most $50 for the product and $2 per month for supplies. Assuming all buyers will keep on purchasing supplies regularly and the discount rate for future earnings is zero, what pricing strategy should the firm adopt?

Under these given assumptions, the firm would do well to price the basic product at $50 and the supplies at $2. The accumulated premium over the life of the product would equal $54 (3 × 12 × $1.5) and would more than compensate for the loss at the time of selling the basic product. In actually computing the minimum price of the product, the firm would have to include as costs a discount for future earnings and the risk that consumers would not purchase supplies. The firm also needs to consider the potential gains from this strategy. For example, consumers may not view the basic product they purchased as a sunk cost, and may try to "recover" their investment by buying the accessories and using it (the "sunk cost effect"). Alternatively, they may get involved in the product and use it more than expected. This possibility has led some authors to label this strategy "captive pricing".

An interesting question is whether consumers would buy the package with the product at $100 and the accessories at $.50 if they were informed they were incurring the same cost the other way around. Probably they would not. A consumer may be reluctant to incur a big immediate investment (a certain loss) for an uncertain future satisfaction: ("the certainty effect"), or may not have the funds for the purchase. In either case, the consumer has a transaction cost," which the firm apparently absorbs.

The chief restraint on the use of captive pricing for durable goods and accessories is that there are often no major shared economies in the manufacture of the basic product and its accessories. Thus, if the premium on the accessories is too high, marginal producers of the accessories may enter the market and drive down prices. In some circumstances, as in the automobile industry, the accessories are themselves produced by smaller firms. Consequently this strategy has limited importance unless consumers are source loyal and would like to buy supplies from the original source even at a higher price. In other circumstances, manufacturers hold patents or are the only source of the technology for the production of the supplies. In this case captive pricing is crucial for the success of the product. In no circumstances may the firm bind the buyer to purchase the supplies from it. Such a strategy of tying contracts may be illegal under the Sherman Act of 1890 or the Clayton Act of 1914.

The well-known examples of captive pricing are razors and blades, cameras and films, autos and spare parts, and videos or computers and software packages. In the case of services, this strategy is referred to as "two-part pricing" because the service price is broken into a fixed fee plus variable usage fees (e.g., the pricing by telephone companies, libraries, health or entertainment clubs, amusement parks, and various rental agencies).

In retailing, the corresponding strategy is called "loss leadership," and involves dropping the price on a well-known brand to generate store traffic. The drop in price should be large enough to compensate consumers for the transaction cost involved in making the extra trip, switching from their normal place of purchase, or foregoing the cheaper basket of prices they pay at the alternative store. However, in many cases the drop in price may not be exactly that high, primarily because consumers may see the price drop as a real gain while underestimating the transaction costs. Nevertheless, to ensure the success of this strategy, retailers normally feature several "super buys," on nationally branded products.

Manufacturers of nationally branded products have always disapproved of loss leadership for two reasons. First, a product that is often available on discount may give consumers the impression that the quality is inferior. Second, specialty stores that depend on the branded products for their source of income may lose sales to discount stores and therefore cease to distribute the product. Manufacturers have sought to restrain loss leadership by a strategy of retail price maintenance. However, (minimum) retail price maintenance is now illegal under a federal statute, the Consumer Goods Pricing Act of 1975.

The reverse case, maintaining maximum retail prices, is not illegal. This situation occurs when a retailer charges too high a price for a branded product over which it has exclusive or selective distributorship. In such a case the retailer may suboptimize the manufacturer's profits. The manufacturer can control this practice by listing or advertising the "suggested (maximum) retail price." High-priced durable goods such as appliances and automobiles are examples of products for which this strategy is used.

Complementary pricing is similar to premium pricing in that the loss in the sale of a product is covered by the profit from the sale of a related product. However, there are two important distinctions. First, premium pricing applies to substitutes and complementary pricing to complements. Second, complementary pricing requires variation in transaction costs over the products, whereas premium pricing requires variation in preferences over consumer groups. So there is no sharing of economies among customer groups in complementary pricing.

An Integration and Comparison of Strategies

The preceding discussion demonstrates the variety of pricing strategies available to a firm. The theory underlying some of them has only recently been analyzed in the economics literature, though they all have been discussed in some form in the marketing discipline. A major contribution of this chapter is that all these strategies are discussed on the same basis and are compared in a manner that is theoretically rich yet typologically simple. The most important contribution is that the strategies are shown to have a common denominator—shared economies. This proposition makes possible an enlightening classification of the strategies and a summarization of their underlying principles. The classification is based on two dimensions: the objective of the firm in exploiting these shared economies and the consumer characteristics necessary for each strategy (see Table 1).

The relevance of the central idea of shared economies is summarized here with respect Table 1. A more detailed explanation is given in the description of the welfare aspects of each strategy. In the class of differential pricing strategies, one product is sold to two segments at different prices. By this means the firm exploits economies of scale and each segment provides an economy to the other. In addition, in second market discounting and periodic discounting, one segment buys the product at a higher price and incurs more of the costs so the product can be made available to the other segment at its lower acceptable price. In random discounting, the searchers ensure that the product is available at a lower price at random periods, thus providing a lower average price to the nonsearchers.

In the class of competitive pricing strategies, firms sell one product to one or more market segments at the same price, but the pattern of shared economies is more complex. In price signaling, the searchers provide an economy to nonsearchers, who can get the quality they desire at an acceptable risk of an error by observing prices. In penetration, experience curve, and geographic pricing, the two segments provide a simple cost economy to each other, enabling the firm to exploit economies of scale or experience. In addition, in penetration and experience curve pricing the common price is that of the more price sensitive segment, which therefore confers a greater economy to the price insensitive segment. In geographic pricing, the lower the competitive price in the adjacent market, the higher the price and hence the greater the diseconomy borne by the home market.

In product line pricing strategies, the shared economies are primarily over the production or marketing of the products in the line. In image pricing, premium pricing, and complementary pricing, one product is sold at a "loss" which is then recovered from the higher price of a complimentary product sold to the same segment or of a substitute product sold to a less price sensitive segment. In price bundling, there is an asymmetric demand by two consumer segments over two nonsubstitute products. The optimum price is the lower of the joint reservation prices of both products. In this way the firm sells one product below the acceptable price of one segment, but compensates by selling both products to both segments. In all of these cases the creative dimension of pricing is to identify the source and pattern of shared economies that can be exploited for the benefit of the individual firm and its consumers.

Besides delineating the classification scheme, this chapter compares and contrasts the various strategies with closely related alternatives. In addition, a summary comparison based on five criteria is in Table 2. The five criteria are: the characteristics of the strategy; the necessary consumer, product, and cost characteristics; the relevant legal constraints; and the variants of this strategy. The table demonstrates that the multiplicity of names distracts from the essential similarity among the strategies and the common principles that unify them. A small, theoretically based set of labels, like the one suggested here, enhances understanding and communication on the issues.

Endnotes

[1] There are also other motivations for discounting, the most common being damaged goods, overstocking, or quantity purchases. These discounts are not considered pricing strategies because they are merely adjustments for costs, often of an *ad hoc* nature. The term "price discrimination" has been used in the literature very broadly to mean charging different customer groups different prices for the same or related products.

[2] The term "average economic cost" means all costs, production and marketing, fixed and variable, plus acceptable profit divided by number of units.

[3] The discussion of welfare applies only to the competitive case as in the example described. Some of the applications of this strategy have been to the monopolistic case, where the price sensitive buyers are the primary beneficiaries. However, monopoly is not a necessary condition for periodic discounting, though some authors mistakenly say so.

[4] "Economies of scale" refers to the decline in average total costs with scale, due to superior technology or more efficient organization or cheaper purchases (Mansfield 1983; Palda 1969). Average total costs may increase beyond a certain point because of the difficulty of managing very large operations.

[5] "Experience curve" or "experience economies" refers to the decline in average total costs in constant dollars with cumulative volume (see Figure 1). Define C_1 as average costs at volume V_1, let V_1 hold for n_1 periods; define C_2 as average costs at volume V_2, let V_2 hold for n_2 periods. Then economies of scale are captured by the elasticity, ε_s, defined by

$$\frac{C_2}{C_1} = \left(\frac{V_2}{V_1}\right)^{\varepsilon_s}, V_2 \neq V_1 \qquad (1)$$

and economies of experience by the elasticity defined by

$$\frac{C_2}{C_1} = \left[\frac{\sum\limits_{i=1}^{n_2} V_{2j} + \sum\limits_{i=1}^{n_1} V_{1i}}{\sum\limits_{i=1}^{n_1} V_{1i}} \right]^{\varepsilon_e} \tag{2}$$

$$= \left(\frac{n_2\, V_2 + n_1\, V_1}{n_1\, V_1} \right)^{\varepsilon_e} = \left(1 + \frac{n_2\, V_2}{n_1\, V_1} \right)^{\varepsilon_e}$$

Note that change in the scale of operation, measured by V_2 / V_1, affects the value of ε_s and ε_e, which are therefore related. However, ε_s does not *cause* ε_e or vice versa. Moreover, unlike ε_s, ε_e, is defined even if $V_2 = V_1$, and when $V_2 \neq V_1$ may still be dependent primarily on n_2 / n_1, the time parameters. The strategic implications of the experience curve were best documented and popularized by the Boston Consulting Group (1972). The decline in costs due to experience could be caused by a number of factors, most importantly labor efficiency and newer process technology. Two important issues when pricing are that economies of experience can occur independently of scale (as shown above) and that their decline generally takes place fairly constantly with cumulative volume. Because cumulative volume increases at a faster rate in the first few years of a product's production history, experience effects are most noticeable at that time period. Because of competitive pressures, prices also decline with costs.

[6] Here the term means firms signaling quality to consumers by price. It must be distinguished from various interfirm signaling strategies that firms may use to "implicitly collude."

[7] In this example all cost issues are ignored, which could lead to at least three scenarios. First, a monopolistic situation in which the costs are sufficiently low that any of the pricing options would be profitable. Second, a cost situation in which only the mixed bundling option would be profitable. This could hold for monopoly or pure competition. Third, a situation in which costs are sufficiently low that any option would be profitable, but due

to free entry, firms would use only penetration pricing ($10 for the first and $12 for the second movie), always the best option for consumers.

[8] In some oligopolistic or monopolistic situations a firm could market profitably only to the premium segment. However, there are several reasons for marketing to both segments. First, dealers, especially of high-priced durables, are more likely to accept an exclusive dealing strategy if the manufacturer has a complete line of products. Second, with a complete line it is easier to develop brand loyalty, especially as consumers tend to buy better versions of durables with each subsequent purchase. Third, a low-priced basic version may be used to attract consumers into stores, and then motivate them to buy the higher priced versions.

Recommended for Additional Reading

Nagle, Thomas (1984), "Economic Foundations for Pricing," *Journal of Business*, 57, 1, 2, 53-526.

Scherer, F.M. (1980), *Industrial Market Structure and Economic Performance*, Chicago: Rand McNally College Publishing Company.

Tellis, Gerard J. (1986), "Beyond the Many Faces of Price: An Integration of Pricing Strategies," *Journal of Marketing*, 50, 4 (October), 146-160.

Thaler, Richard (1985), "Mental Accounting and Consumer Choice," *Marketing Science*, 4,3 (Summer), 199-214.

CHAPTER TEN

IMPLEMENTING PROACTIVE PRICING:

Navistar International Corporation

STEVEN HYDE

The opinions expressed in this chapter are those of the writer and do not represent Navistar International Transportation Corporation's official policy.

STEVEN HYDE

Steven R. Hyde is Manager, Truck Pricing at the Navistar International Transportation Corporation. His responsibilities include the establishment of pricing strategies for a $3 billion truck wholesale business as well as being an active participant in the product planning process at Navistar. He has held several other positions at Navistar including Manager, Business Planning in which he established a comprehensive product line information system. Mr. Hyde holds an M.B.A. in Finance and Economics from the University of Chicago and has studied at the London Business School.

CHAPTER TEN

Navistar International Corporation, the successor company to International Harvester company, emerged in early 1985 from five years of economic turmoil in which its principal businesses had all suffered huge losses. During the early 1980s, International Harvester restructured, divested businesses, reduced manpower, closed factories, and shrank its international operations. Business strategies for continuing operations out of necessity became secondary to developing a financial and operating structure that could survive a sustained economic downturn. The Company's management tried—and ultimately succeeded—in accomplishing a remarkable turnaround from an economic situation which appeared intractable in 1982 and 1983. By early 1985, International Harvester had sold its construction business to Dresser Industries, its gas turbine business to Caterpillar, and finally, its 150-year old agricultural equipment business—and its name—to Tenneco. The cost of this transformation was very high:

| | Year End | |
	1979	1985
Employment	100,000+	17,000
Stock price (per share)	$40	$7
Sales (continuing operations)	$8.5 billion	$3.5 billion
	Businesses then:	*Businesses now:*
	• Agricultural Equipment	• Trucks/Engines (N. America)
	• Trucks/Engines Worldwide	
	• Construction Equipment	
	• Gas Turbines	

225

The restructured company began 1985 with many strengths: its profitable core business of trucks and engines; solid and up-dated product lines in its principal markets; the leading market share among all North American truck producers; an excellent distribution network of franchised dealers. The Company also had identified many shortcomings: a lack of corporate identity and strategy; intensifying competition, including offshore threats; and a very costly fixed cost structure for pension and health/welfare costs related to the restructuring.

Navistar developed a new transaction-based pricing approach to this core business as part of a number of fundamental changes designed to transform its corporate strategy. This chapter describes the steps involved in implementing this new approach to pricing.

Business Environment

Navistar is a holding company whose assets consist of Navistar International Transportation Corp. and other (future) holdings. The Transportation company is organized into four major related business segments: trucks, service parts, diesel engines, and financial services. Fiscal 1988 sales totaled $4.1 billion, and income from continuing operations was $259 million. Figure 1 displays the current organization structure.

Truck Industry

Navistar is the leading manufacturer of medium and heavy duty trucks in North America, and ranks second worldwide behind Mercedes-Benz. Principal competitors include Ford and GMC in medium duty, and Freightliner Corp. (owned by Mercedes Benz), Volvo, Mack (owned by Renault), and Kenworth and Peterbilt (both owned by Paccar Corporation).

The truck industry uses gross vehicle weight (GVW) to classify vehicles. Classes 1-4 (under 14,500 lbs. GVW) are small pickup truck-type vehicles, which share componentry and are derivative of automobile styles. Because of economies of scale, only the

Figure 1 Corporate Structure Business Segments

Navistar International Corporation

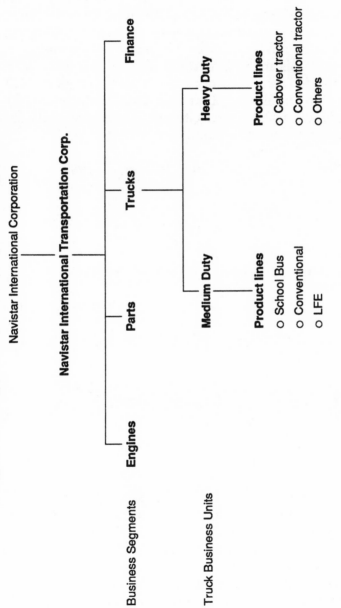

Navistar International Transportation Corp.

Business Segments

Engines   Parts   Trucks   Finance

Truck Business Units

Medium Duty   Heavy Duty

Product lines
○ School Bus
○ Conventional
○ LFE

Product lines
○ Cabover tractor
○ Conventional tractor
○ Others

○ Corporate mission unites all businesses.

○ Sales/Profit objectives established for each business segment.

○ Profit and market share objectives are established for each product.

largest automotive companies, both North American and Japanese, participate. Class 5-7 trucks (14,500-32,500 lb. GVW) are classified as medium duty; 90% of these vehicles are sold by GMC, Ford, and Navistar although imports are becoming an increasingly important factor in this market. Medium duty trucks are used typically in in-city delivery operations (such as beverage trucks), in construction and similar applications. Class 8 (over 33,000 lb. GVW) are typically used in inter-city line haul applications, severe service trucks, and many specialized applications.

North American Truck Industry—1988

	Medium Duty	Heavy Duty	Total Rank	
	GVW (5–7)	GVW (8)		
Industry size (units)	164,800	148,400	313,200	
Market Share (%)				
Navistar	30.8%	22.8%	27.0%	1
Ford	28.1	10.0	19.5	2
GMC	30.3	0.9	16.4	3
Paccar	0.6	22.1	10.8	4
Mack	3.0	14.7	8.5	5
Freightliner	—	16.3	7.7	6
Volvo/GMC	0.9	11.5	5.9	7

Source: MVMA (Motor Vehicle Manufacturers Association) Data.

The customer base is very diverse, ranging from small businesses which may purchase only one unit every several years to giant transportation and leasing companies, such as UPS and Ryder Systems, which purchase thousands of units per year. The degree of customer sophistication and purchase criteria vary greatly by the size and type of customer. However, regardless of customer type, initial purchase price is a very important factor in the buying decision in the truck business, as in most capital goods industries.

The truck business is intensely price sensitive, for two fundamental reasons:

- *Deregulation.* The deregulation of the trucking industry, beginning in 1980, had a dramatic effect on regulated common carriers, which form a large portion of the heavy duty industry. Freight rates fell, high-cost trucking companies failed, and the entire industry became sensitive to the basic economics of their business: equipment cost, fuel cost, and wages. The result for truck manufacturers was demand for lower total cost of ownership...and falling prices.
- *Product development.* Product improvements are evolutionary in nature, and a few large suppliers (Eaton, Dana, Rockwell, Bendix, Cummins, and Caterpillar) provide major components common to all manufacturers. Engines, transmissions, axles and other components in general, do not serve to differentiate one manufacturer from another, particularly in heavy trucks. The result is the increasing perception of trucks as commodities. In this situation, and in the absence of non-product advantages (service, financing, etc.), price becomes the major purchasing criterion.

The truck manufacturing industry has experienced falling real prices since the early 1980s. Navistar's—and the industry's— traditional strategies have been to develop state-of-the-art products, and reduce manufacturing and overhead costs, while shifting focus to distribution services and an emphasis on durability and reliability as the means to influence purchases.

Pricing Process

The structure of truck prices is similar to that for automobiles. Manufacturers establish suggested "list prices" for the base (standard) vehicle and for optional equipment. Manufacturers establish a wholesale (dealer) price, usually as a percentage discount from the list price for the base chassis and optional equipment. As with automobiles, the manufacturer participates from time-to-time in retail sales, with factory incentives and other sales programs. Most sales are through franchised, independent dealers (who may carry more than one brand), although large nationally based customers, such as Ryder, may be served directly by the manufacturer.

Unlike the automobile business, however, truck pricing is increasingly managed by the manufacturer (not just the dealer) on a deal-by-deal basis, sometimes even on single unit transactions. Intense discounting, in most cases, has eroded the value of the published price list as a guide to transaction price.

Given this price-sensitive environment, the key to profitability—and long-term survival—lies in correctly managing transaction prices to achieve both profit and volume goals. Changing management style at Navistar to permit profit-based transaction management required extensive changes in organization, management attitude, and in decision support systems. For many years the Company had controlled costs and had developed complex systems to manage and report expenditures in finite detail. Revenues were left to manage themselves. The fundamental change that Navistar had to make was to recognize that managing revenues was at least as important as managing costs, and to create a new process to manage the transaction-based pricing environment.

Corporate Strategy and Identity

With the birth of the new company in 1985, executive management was finally freed from the problems of International Harvester, and could devote the large amount of time necessary to develop a corporate strategy and accompanying marketing strategies for its core truck business. The development of this strategy required the active participation of senior management, and was guided to a successful conclusion of the planning phase with the assistance of a large general management consulting firm.

The corporate strategy and identity which emerged from this lengthy process had two features which were essential for success: a deep commitment by executive management and a belief that fundamental changes could and would be accomplished.

In very broad summary, a new corporate identity—Navistar—was adopted, with a theme of the continuity of an existing successful business in the framework of a new company. "Navistar" would start out as simply a word, but over time the name would become invested with the significance that its shareholders, customers, suppliers, employees, and competitors created.

In keeping with the corporate identity, we created mission and strategy statements—which management continually reinforces—for the holding company and for the transportation company. Each mission statement and the related strategies, for both the holding company and the transportation company, are appropriate to the served customers of that entity:

Navistar International Corporation (Holding Company)
- Increase shareowner value through serving the customer base better than competition.
- Selective growth in new businesses which add value.
- Redeploy resources where returns fall short of objectives.

Navistar International Transportation Co.
- Service to customer as primary means of improved profitability.
- Growth in highly profitable parts and diesel engines.
- Increase truck profit margin and market share by improving customer service, quality, and productivity faster than competitors.

These general statements in turn permitted the detailed development of marketing, sales, and pricing strategies.

Pricing Strategy

We began an investigation of all aspects of the pricing and transaction management process, including information systems, decision processes, approval authorities, organization structure, and finance and accounting systems. We evolved a pricing strategy and a structure for implementing this strategy using both internal resources and the assistance of a general management consulting firm. In the course of our research, we noted a remarkable convergence of opinion among the many experts we consulted: success depends on changing attitude and behavior, in breaking down internal barriers to achieving superior performance, and in having the top-level commitment of executive management to continually reinforce the need for change.

In summary, we evolved a proactive approach to pricing, with the goals of managing the transaction-based pricing process according to the fundamental economics of each transaction and focusing resources and prioritizing sales efforts on high-margin, high- potential business. We developed a marketing strategy and a customer segmentation to lead this process. This strategy represented a major departure from past practice, which was volume-based and which in most cases ignored the economics of specific transactions.

Implementing this strategy required major changes in information flow and organization structure:

Information
- Profit data to guide transaction pricing.
- Product line profit objectives to guide executive decisions.
- Customer targeting and business priorities.
- Communication of strategies to all management responsible for profit performance.
- Measurement of performance consistent with objectives.

Organization
- Unified pricing structure: only one organization with pricing authority.
- Incentives based on performance to profit and market share objectives, instead of purely volume-based incentive.
- Finance and accounting change to profit measurement from cost tracing.
- Redirection and retraining of the sales force.
- Improvement and strengthening of the dealer network.

We began to implement these ideas at the end of 1986—about 20 months after the process of identifying strategies and action plans began. This seems like a long time to get to the starting point of an implementation plan. Large organizations, however, do not change rapidly; planning objectives typically can be articulated far in advance of a supporting organization structure and information flow. In the case of Navistar, a great many changes to accepted means of doing business had to be understood, and accepted by the managers who would have to put them in effect.

Implementing a Pricing Strategy: Defining the Problem

In the case of Navistar, the first and most formidable problem in beginning a profit-based pricing strategy was the lack of basic profitability information. Financial information systems simply were not equipped to report on profit by business unit (truck, engine, parts, finance) or product line (medium duty truck, heavy duty truck, etc.), let alone on individual transactions. Financial reporting supported departmental cost budgets, standard costs and inventory valuation, but not profit information. In short, the information structure supported very well the old way of doing business, but when the business changed, management information began to fail. We recognized this problem early on, and out of necessity created management information outside of normal reporting and MIS channels. The information we developed was not in complete conformity with accounting accuracy, but it was certainly good enough to guide our pricing strategy and provide decision support for transaction management.

We began a review of pricing effectiveness, and developed data on the profitability of specific transactions. We then focused on the profitability of our optional equipment. One example of our investigation was the relationship between stated selling price (dealer net price) and profit margin. We expected to see a strong positive relationship between price and profitability: as the price of the product increased because of added optional equipment, we should observe an increase in margin. Figure 2 expresses the expected relationship.

Figure 2 Expected Relation Between Price and Margin.

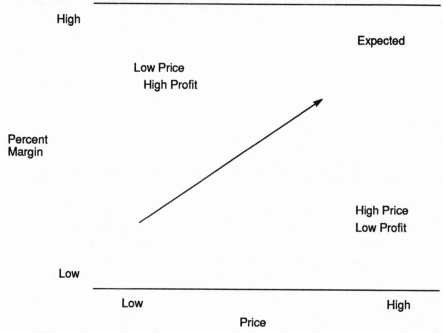

What we found, however, was just the opposite: no relationship, or a negative relationship. Figure 3 shows one product line—a high-volume truck model. There is a clear correlation: high profit and low price, an low profit and high price.

The review of price-profit relationships underscored two important points:

- Transaction-based pricing management must be supported with transaction-based profit analysis. Decisions based on average margins will lead to the perverse results of underpricing low-margin transactions, while discouraging high margin transactions.

- Causes of the observed price-profit relationships were not understood, indicating several shortcomings in costing, accounting, and reporting systems. For example, there was no systematic reporting of the profitability or the costs of optional equipment, or even a means of tracking which customers purchased specific product features.

Figure 3 Actual Relation Between Price and Margin.

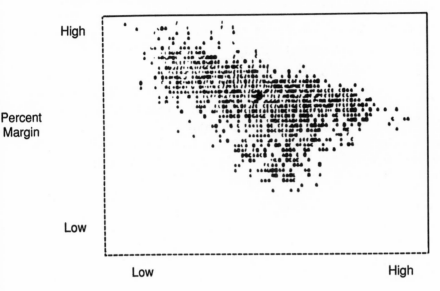

The result was a concentration on new cost-price-profit information systems, which has proved to be one of the most difficult parts of completely implementing our strategy. Cost information is na integral part of the financial system, and any changes to past practice have far-reaching effects. In addition, financial reporting systems are at the heart of incentive compensation and performance measurement, and there is immense organizational pressure to resist changes. Navistar is still in the development stages of the numerous systems changes which will be required to make profit-based management fully operational.

Despite these practical difficulties, we succeeded in gathering the improved information needed for driving the pricing decision process. We accomplished this long before formal systems improvements could be made. We used both PC and mainframe ad-hoc systems to integrate information from numerous sources to provide transaction-level profit and cost data. The types of information which we now review routinely include:

- Customer history (profitability of past transactions).
- Prototype or "what if" profit review.
- Optional equipment cost and profit.
- Profit performance tracking.

The other major problem we encountered was in the organization of the pricing process. At least three different organizations were involved in the old structure. First, published prices were established within the marketing organization. Since prevailing wisdom held that published prices mattered little when every transaction was subject to discounting, the marketing organization had little influence on the actual pricing process. Formal control of transaction pricing was in the finance and accounting organization, while the sales organization was responsible for achieving volume objectives. The pricing process was inherently unstable, since there was no formal authority responsible for resolving conflicting objectives.

Once the two major problems of information and organization had been identified, the general solution was obvious: create profit-based information systems, and consolidate and increase the visibility and authority of the pricing function, while reorienting the sales, marketing, and finance organizations to profit-based incentives and reporting systems.

These simple-sounding formulas proved both difficult and time-consuming to implement. Navistar has nearly completed the process of establishing the right internal structures and information systems for successful proactive pricing, but behavior changes (motivated by better communications and rationalized financial incentives) are likely to take much longer to become complete.

Implementing Proactive Pricing: Organization

The study, review, recommendation, and approval process for Navistar's new approach to pricing, marketing, and sales consumed almost one year. Because of structural changes required in many organizations, and the complexity of the issues uncovered in the review process, implementation was phased in over a period of several months.

Key points of Navistar's pricing and marketing restructuring toward profit-based management include the following changes:

- Product managers were named with broad responsibility for product development, marketing plans, and product line profitability.
- A new pricing organization was created, led by a senior executive with broad general management experience.
- All aspects of the pricing process were consolidated in the new pricing organization. The visibility, level of authority, and status of the pricing function was greatly elevated.

We have accomplished the establishment of a profit-based, customer-oriented marketing and pricing structure. Our intention is to manage revenue—and therefore, profitability—by means of improved knowledge of the customer base, directing product, marketing, and sales resources toward those priority customer segments that have the largest potential for profitable business. We intend also to de-emphasize efforts on marginal business, on those customers who require large resources to serve or who offer a low probability of success. The objective is to manage the deals that are lost just as carefully as the ones that are won, and avoid the futile pursuit of a 100% market share.

This structure has been in place for over two years, and we are achieving our objectives. There remain many difficulties: incentives have not been established to fully complement profit- based management; the volume orientation of the sales force is very difficult to change, and the knowledge and skills of management is not fully developed. However, we are convinced that this structured approach is the only long-term solution to the basic economic problem of competing in a mature industry with the likelihood of continued declining real prices.

Implementing Proactive Pricing: Information

As we have noted, information drives the transaction-based pricing process. Developing new information structures that can complement the new organization structure remains the most challenging part of the efforts to establish profit-based management and to support the overall corporate mission.

Our development of information systems has taken several paths. We first established a framework to report the Company's actual and planned financial performance on a basis consistent with the company's organization. This process, which we called profit generation analysis, reports results for the Transportation Company by its business segments (truck, parts, engine, finance) and by product line within the truck business.

This has proven to be a difficult and complex task, which we only recently concluded successfully. It is essential, however, to have this view of financial performance in order to define and communicate achievable profit objectives and create the basis for incentive compensation tied to measurable financial goals, starting with executive management, but including all levels of the organization.

The second action taken was to develop transaction-based profit reporting to support the pricing process. Implementation of this phase began early, as noted before, and two years in advance of formal systems development, which is now nearing completion. It is always the case that decision support systems can be developed quickly, cheaply, and far in advance of formalized accounting and sales systems. There are two immediate benefits to improved decision support information. First, of course, better decisions are made. Equally important is the ability to identify problem areas in systems and organizations that were ignored previously. In the cost-price-profit example cited earlier, a number of costing system deficiencies were noted and corrected when we investigated why certain transactions had exceptionally low or high reported margins. We discovered that changing to profit- based management requires fundamental changes to many financial and accounting systems. Improvements to these systems are in the planning phase and are likely to take several more years to complete. The principal reasons for the length of time required to accomplish these changes are the complexity and age of existing systems and the need to maintain current financial reporting with current systems.

The results of implementing the new pricing and marketing strategy have been a much elevated awareness among senior management of the need for information that complements the operating structure of the business. With awareness has come the commitment to change, which is essential to success. And most important, from a practical point of view, has been the development of a continuing process to re-evaluate and restructure the way the business is managed.

Implementing Proactive Pricing: Conclusion

The new pricing, marketing, and product management has been in place at Navistar for over two years. We have achieved significant success in developing a structured approach to marketing and pricing, and have achieved measurable, significant, financial benefits during these two years. We found the essential elements of success to be the following:

- Commitment to change from the highest level in the Company.
- Investment in organization and information.
- Incentives tied to financial performance.

Many implementation issues remain, including the need for better systems and more timely means to change systems, policies, and procedures. The process has taken a long time to accomplish; large organizations do not change quickly, and there are many technical and organizational barriers which must be overcome. Changing pricing strategies amounts to changing management behavior; the difficulty and length of time it takes to be successful is easy to underestimate.

Having completed a significant portion of the process, we have concluded that the real challenge of transaction-based pricing management is to manage details: establish accountability performance objectives and information systems to report on performance, and create a means to resolve conflict at each level of the organization so that the pricing process—and therefore profit management—is forced to work correctly. In a mature industry, managing revenues requires at least as much effort as managing costs.

Recommended for Additional Reading

Braham, James, 1986. "The Price is Wrong," *Industry Week*, December 8, p. 28.

Eliashberg, Jehoshua and Abel Seuland, 1986. "The Impact of Competitive Entry in a Developing Market upon Dynamic Pricing Strategies." *Marketing Science*, Winter; p. 20.

Ross, Elliot B., 1984. "Making Money with Proactive Pricing," *Harvard Business Review*, November-December, p.145.

MANAGING DEMAND AND ADJUSTING INVENTORY:

Pricing Strategies in the Hotel Industry

MARGARET SHAW
WILLIAM H. HECK

MARGARET SHAW

Margaret Shaw is Professor of Marketing in the Department of Hotel, Restaurant and Travel Administration at the University of Massachusetts/Amherst. In addition to her M.B.A. and Ph.D. from Cornell Univeristy, she has had extensive sales and marketing experience with the Sheraton and Hyatt hotel corporations. Dr. Shaw is the author of several hotel-related articles in hospitality publications and an active participant through speaking engagements and seminars with the American Hotel & Motel Association and the Hotel Sales & Marketing Association International.

WILLIAM H. HECK

William Heck is a hotel developer and operator as well as a consultant to the hotel industry. From 1975 through 1988 he was a principal and Executive Vice President of Hotels of Distinction and General Manager of the Copley Plaza hotel in Massachusetts. Mr. Heck is an honors graduate of the Hotel, Restaurant and Institutional Management School at Michigan State University. He sits on the Board of the Greater Boston Hotel Association, has chaired and currently serves on the Advisory Board of Boston University's Hotel and Food Administration Program and is the former President of the Boston Executives Association.

CHAPTER ELEVEN

In simple terms of barter, pricing is the sellers' determination of the maximum amount that can be charged for goods and services while maintaining the buyer's perception of a worthwhile purchase. Price is the *quid* of the *quid pro quo*.

The price of hotel rooms is viewed in different ways by different people. To the owner, pricing is based upon the need to satisfy issues of liquidity. To the operator (which we refer to as the hotelier), price is determined by the reality of the marketplace, reflecting the very real ramifications of supply and demand, both on the micro and macro levels. To the consumer, who feels the impact of supply and demand, pricing is the accepted, shopped for, or negotiated cost to get rooms.

A noted professor of hotel management recently said that when he was a practitioner in the hotel business, there was one rate: "rack." (Rack-rate is an industry term for full-rate. The name refers to a mechanical rack that once held small slips of paper known as duckets, which stated the retail room rate. This system dominated prior to the development of computers.) Those days are over.

Today, hoteliers practice targeted marketing to well-defined markets. Targeted marketing prompts the hotelier to tailor both product offering and price in order to gain incremental occupancy points from primary and secondary markets.

The rack-rate serves as an important tool in determining market position for hotels because it defines their respective product "classes." All other rates are simply efforts to make a property more attractive to different market segments. As a result, rack-rate sales constitute one of the smallest market categories for most hotels in today's marketplace. Why? Because there is a great deal of price competition, there are new and complex business conduits, and there is much more and better data that permit more sophisticated target marketing. Additionally, these forces have contributed to greater demand for travel and have successfully increased the size of demand overall. The world has changed a bit since the professor was a practitioner, but the relevance of supply and demand has remained the same.

Hotel room pricing assumes a market scenario in which elasticity (or inelasticity) of demand and the relative availability of supply guides prevailing rates. When pricing hotel rooms, it is fundamental that a hotelier anticipate the relative availability of room supply in the marketplace. If he knows the details of room supply in the market, the hotelier can manipulate his segmented inventory of rooms, in view of demand, and maximize revenue potential. A change in the available supply of rooms has the same effect on the remaining rooms inventory as the shiller who drives up the price at an auction.

This scenario is common and complex, but the apparent vagueries are not vague at all to the hotelier. The hotelier seeks to manipulate the number of available rooms in order to reduce the remaining inventory, which becomes more precious. As a result, there is immediate reason to revalue remaining inventory and adjust pricing strategies accordingly.

Hotel room pricing is generally framed within an oligopolistic market structure with supply that is fixed in size, at least for the short term, and which is perishable with each passing day. Hotel room rate pricing is truly dynamic. It is of great issue in this business of fixed short-term room supply, that whenever demand removes some of this supply from the marketplace it causes the remaining supply to become more scarce. If demand continues, prices rise. If demand is very weak, the market structure becomes far more competitive and the sale of the perishable commodity becomes imperative.

The full-service hotel business is characterized by 24-hour-per-day operations that never close to the public. It is a business with high fixed costs and high breakeven points. A hotel's primary markets produce strong seasonal revenue flows that must offset shoulder season and off-season losses. Pricing is one of the key marketing tools available to the hotelier, and as we will see in this chapter, it must be used strategically and in concert with other strategies to produce consistent maximization of revenues and, consequently, profits.

Managing Demand

Demand determines the highest rate that can be charged, i.e., "what the market will bear." Demand, however, fluctuates for hotels by demand periods and those demand periods are a result of the markets targeted by the hotel.

Hotels are designed, built, marketed and operated to cater to pre-determined primary markets and secondary markets. Hoteliers analyze the marketing opportunities in terms of their product and their potential markets. They also analyze their competitors' opportunities. Based on the conclusions of the analysis, the hotelier allocates both current and future daily room-inventories to various market segments and prices the allotted rooms accordingly.

Primary markets for hotel rooms tend to be price-inelastic during the prime demand periods. For example, the Copley Plaza, located in the heart of Boston's fashionable Back Bay area, targets the upscale business traveler for both group and transient business. This primary market is typical of first-class metropolitan hotels both in the United States and worldwide. Because business travellers consider the timing of a trip important, they are willing for the most part to pay a reasonable price for the use of a hotel guestroom during the peak travel days of the week. In other words, they tend to be less price-sensitive during these prime demand times than other market segments. They are not necessarily price insensitive, however, because timing of the trip is weighed heavily in the price-value relationship of the hotel guestroom purchase for this market.

Top rate usage for any hotel occurs during its peak periods. Yet during shoulder and off-peak periods, the top rates usually are lowered considerably. The hotel then targets its secondary target markets, because there is an absence of its primary markets and it still has all its rooms available.

In Boston, business travel, related business meetings and conferences are heaviest in autumn and spring. The shoulder and off-
peak periods are in winter and summer. During these shoulder
and off-peak times, more price-sensitive secondary markets are
targeted to offset the "temporary" loss of the primary business
market. Typically, these price-sensitive markets include the
regional association markets, educational and fraternal markets,
weekend-pleasure travel markets, and so on. Direct selling and
promotion techniques commonly are used to pursue these markets
with price incentives as bait to attract them. Table 1 gives examples of peak and off-peak rates by market segment for the
Copley Plaza.

Table 1   Peak and Off-Peak Room Rate Examples—
Copley Plaza Hotel, Boston

Demand Period	Market Segment	Rate Range
Peak	"Pure" Transient	$150 – $190
	Corporate Rate Program Transient	$135 – $155
	National, Association and Corporate Groups	$135 – $155
Off-Peak	Weekend Pleasure Traveler	$95
	Educators	$75 – $105
	Religious/Fraternal	$75 – $105
	Regional Association	$110 – $130

Note: Rates are for single occupancy excepting the weekend pleasure traveler
package. "Pure" transient is noncorporate rate program individual business.

Corporate rates, company rates and other such "flat" rates are
common in hotel room-rate pricing strategies. They are offered to
companies and other users who present hotels with high and consistent volume opportunities throughout the year. These "flat"

rates are usually positioned somewhere between top rates during peak periods and deeply discounted rates during vally periods, depending on the volume of business and the period in which it occurs. In other words, when business travel from a particular company is fairly consistent throughout the year, cutting across the normal peak and off-peak periods, astute management tries to capture this business by offering an attractive annual flat rate. High volume users, such as corporations, usually prefer flat rates.

In a business where demand is highly seasonal and is coupled with a non-storable or perishable product as with sleeping rooms in the hotel business—efforts to smooth out or manage demand and then to properly allocate daily inventories of rooms, both current and future, enhances customer service, customer use, revenue and profitability. Though revenue and profit margins may be diminished in peak periods by this practice, it is the increased revenue gained during off-peak periods that contributes to long-term maximum profit. Not coincidently, customer use, customer service and customer satisfaction result.

"Discounting-based-on-availability" is another technique used by hotels to help manage demand and supply. This price-elastic technique has been mastered by the airlines on a grand scale. The hotel industry has learned much from the airline industry regarding the whole process of marketing availability through discounted prices to its customers. Airlines and hotels are very similar to each other in many ways. Perhaps the only major difference between the two industries is that airplanes can be moved to another route if business is not good, whereas hotels must remain wherever they are built.

The airlines do a superb job of managing and marketing the excess availability of supply by means of manipulating demand with various discounted fare structures. Furthermore, the airlines have caused the public to accept the ever-changing availability, or lack of availability, of these discounted fares. This customer acceptance permits the airline to open and close the discounted fare's availability, thereby enabling the airline to capture as much of the price-elastic market as is available, while not interfering with the potential price-inelastic demand. This manipulation of demand enables the airline to fill its planes optimally by serving the maximum number of customers, by serving the greatest number of routes and, thus, maximizing its revenues.

Adjusting Inventory

While demand provides important input to pricing decisions, understanding its relationship to supply is imperative. Though a hotel's room supply and the marketplace's room supply are essentially "fixed," this is only relative to demand in any given period. The supply of guestrooms made available to identified market segments fluctuates depending on the demand situation.

The classic questions when dealing with price determination are: is demand greater than supply, or, is supply greater than demand? In the hotel industry, these questions, specifically, are asked for each period and each market segment. Hotels have the ability to determine what portions of their inventory will be made available to which market segments on any given day. In other words, total supply does not change but the relative available supply does change.

Many hotels adjust their room inventory depending on the demand period in question. For the Copley Plaza, as can be seen in Table 2, the lucrative corporate-transient market merits a fairly large rooms-inventory allocation. It is largest in the peak period, giving way to secondary group-market business in the off-peak period. Group business booked during peak times is largely made up of high-rated corporate or national association business. During shoulder and valley periods, group room allocations increase, which directly relates to the weaker demand from the prime corporate and national association markets. Group business in these softer periods expands to include the fraternal, religious and educational groups that cannot afford the higher rates charged during peak periods.

Pricing decisions are not based solely on the price sensitivities and other needs of these various market segments. Hoteliers assess how competitors adjust their room inventories as well. In other words, hoteliers try to determine just how much supply is really available to the buyers. For example, the 1,200 room Marriott

Table 2 Guest Room Inventory Example—
Copley Plaza Hotel, Boston
(1989 Estimates)

Demand Period	Market Segment	Inventory Allocation
Peak	"Pure" Transient	100 rooms
	Corporate Rate Program Transient	100 rooms
	National, Association and Corporate Groups	200 rooms
Off-Peak	"Pure" Transient	50 rooms
	Corporate Rate Program Transient	50 rooms
	Group Business— General	250 rooms
	Special Promotions	50 rooms

Copley Place Hotel, also in the Back Bay area of Boston, similarly targets the corporate transient market. Given its larger size, however, a larger portion of its inventory is allocated for large convention business during peak periods. Yet during the slower winter and summer months, this hotel also aggressively pursues the more price sensitive markets and adjusts inventories accordingly. Having a good understanding of how competitors manage their inventories is important for effectively managing one's own inventory, and thus making the best price decision possible.

Monitoring the Competition

Hotel market structure essentially refers to the availability of substitutable hotel room products for similar buyers. As discussed above, hotel markets or market structures change across demand periods, and as a result, a hotel's pricing strategies are reviewed frequently. In the hotel business this involves determining how many rooms are available for the transient buyer and/or the group buyer for a given demand period. Analyzing the anticipated market structure for the demand period in question helps a hotelier make optimal pricing decisions.

An oligopoly is a market structure which tends to favor a "seller's" market scenario. It assumes very high costs to get supply into the market, few supply competitors, like or similar products, and pricing that is generally controlled to some extent. This market structure typifies many hotel marketplaces, especially in peak periods. It gives hoteliers a greater degree of control in the pricing decision than they could exercise in other, more competitive, market structures. Also, in oligopolistic hotel markets, management needs to be particularly sensitive to the anticipated pricing strategies of its direct competitors. Because the number of sellers are few, this is not an impossible task.

Hotels continuously monitor their competitors' rate schedules. Published rates are readily available in countless directories. Current rates, corporate rate programs, special promotional rates and other rates can be defined by simply calling the hotel and asking for them. Hyatt Hotels now actively publish their corporate rates for selected hotels in a national advertising campaign showing rate comparisons with major competitors (see Figure 1). Discerning privately negotiated group-rates is far more difficult. Nonetheless, these rates can and must be estimated in order to determine how the competition is pricing its inventory allotments.

One example of a hotel pricing strategy is the opening of the Hyatt Regency Cambridge in the mid-1970s. During the opening period of this 400-room hotel, the general pricing strategy involved being priced above convention hotels in the city. At that time, the convention hotels were the 1,200-room Sheraton-Boston Hotel and the 1,000-room Park Plaza Hotel. It further involved being slightly above direct competitors (the 400-room Copley Plaza and 400-room Marriott-Newton) and slightly below a premiere competitor (the 225-room Ritz Carlton) for full-rated transient business. On a weekly basis, rates of these primary competitors were monitored, along with those of other secondary competitor hotels in the city. When a change in rates was observed, the situation was analyzed immediately and price decisions were made accordingly.

There has been a burst of new hotels opening in the Boston market in the 1980s, but the market structure during peak periods continues to be essentially oligopolistic for both the transient and group markets. This is especially true for the group and convention market. In peak demand periods, the convention hotels heavily target their convention markets, offer some rooms to the transient market (but a limited supply), and focus their attention on monitoring the relative supply of rooms and the rates of other convention hotels.

The current convention-room supply in Boston consists primarily of four hotels—the Sheraton-Boston, the Marriott Copley Place, the Westin and the Boston Park Plaza. In a highly concentrated market structure such as this, there is a greater degree of control in price determination. At the same time, there is a high degree of vulnerability to sudden changes in strategy by competitors. When one of these hotels significantly lowers (or raises) its rates, there is a direct impact on the pricing tactics of its competitors. They may be forced to follow suit, or, at minimum, to review their own pricing strategy given the competitor's change in tactics.

The transient and smaller capacity group hotels (the Copley Plaza, Marriott Longwharf, Hyatt Cambridge, Parker House, etc.), as well as the transient and non-group hotels (the Ritz-Carlton, Bostonian, Meridien, etc.) are less highly concentrated but nonetheless represent oligopolistic markets to some extent during peak periods. As with the convention market hotels, demand exceeds supply for the general market during peak demand periods. This combination of demand greater than supply and concentrated markets gives hotel management a higher degree of control for setting rates.

Moving from peak demand periods to shoulder and off-peak demand periods, prime market demand falls and supply becomes greater than demand. This marks the move from an oligopolistic market structure to that of a more straightforward competitive market environment. Hotel inventories are shuffled and repriced to attract as much of the potential business available as possible. Simply stated, the supply dynamics switch from a market controlled by a few players to one with many players. Convention hotels lose their prime convention market, transient and small-capacity-group hotels lose their prime corporate buyers. Each competitor then looks to secondary markets to help fill this void, and competitors vie directly for the same business, unlike the situation during peak demand periods.

Not surprisingly, price becomes a major marketing tool to attract more price-sensitive markets. Price-elastic buyers are in an excellent position to dictate the prices they are willing to pay. Astute buyers go one step further and persuade hotels to drop prices even lower through open competitive bidding, especially in group-business negotiations. At this point hoteliers must pay much more attention to price quotations, particularly those given to savvy buyers. In other words, hoteliers often lower rates or risk losing business to a competitor who is more willing to do so. The questions now become: How low to go on a quote? What costs are relevant to the pricing decision?

The Costs of Business

To borrow accounting terms, we all recognize that in the long-run both fixed and variable costs need to be covered to achieve profit objectives. Bertram Rashkow, in his article, "How to Set the Right Price," succinctly distinguishes between variable and fixed costs by referring to them as costs of doing business versus costs of being in business:[1]

> Fixed costs are those that generally do not change with reasonable increases or decreases in business volume. They are the costs of *being* in business: rent, depreciation, executive and administrative salaries, and insurance for example.
>
> Variable costs are those that do change with changes in volume: materials, direct labor, a portion of overhead, and sales commissions for instance. They can loosely be described as the costs of *doing* business.

Variable costs for hotel guestrooms are essentially housekeeping labor, bathroom amenities, laundry, and the like. Being service commodities, these costs are not incurred until the room is occupied. Variable costs are relatively low, ranging from $10 to $50 depending on the service level of the hotel, location (rural, metropolitan, suburban) and occupancy of the hotel. During high occupancy periods hotels often incur overtime costs for labor. The Copley Plaza's variable costs range from $25 to $40. These costs are similar to those incurred by other hotels in the Boston area in this hotel class.

In the short run, it is the variable costs that are relevant to the pricing decision. These costs of simply doing business need to be covered and, thus, are the minimum threshold for pricing decisions. Any revenue exceeding these costs contributes something to overhead, which is better than no contribution at all.

Hoteliers recognize that profit margins can and will be lower in off-peak periods. Their focus is on contribution margins that shrink during off-peak periods, but nonetheless contribute to the fixed costs of being in business.

Many potential group clients look at the big picture when buying. They add all of the component costs to compute a total cost for their conference, meeting or trip. These clients look at more than just the room-rate when making the purchase decision. Other factors include the cost of meals, meeting rooms, receptions, travel, entertainment, and so on. Also, there are preferences to style, location, and other factors that enter into the price/value buying decision.

Hoteliers will reduce prices for varied services and facilities such as sleeping rooms, meeting rooms, health and fitness facilities, and parking in order to generate greater overall revenues. It is common to under-price some hotel offerings, from time to time, in order to generate or create demand for other full-priced hotel services. Such strategies are appropriate when it is determined that the operation's aggregate contribution margin will be greater because of the incremental revenue generated by this type of pricing strategy.

A senior executive from a major hotel chain commented that general managers who are overly concerned with profit margins lose sight of the importance of revenue. "The short-sightedness of it is they are limiting revenue...costs overall will only be paid for when the revenue is large enough...Until you have reached a certain projected volume of revenue, pricing for revenue takes precedence over pricing for profit."[2]

All too often a profit orientation rather than a revenue orientation dominates in hotel pricing decisions. Profit is not a variable or input for the pricing decision—it is a result. And as such, pricing objectives need to focus on the revenue side of the profit equation, not the cost side.

Pricing Objectives

Pricing objectives need to be clearly stated when making hotel pricing decisions. The ultimate objective for any operation is long-term profit maximization. Some marketers will disagree, citing long-term customer satisfaction as the ultimate goal. It is our contention they are essentially saying the same thing—through customer satisfaction, long-term profit maximization is realized.

Short-run pricing objectives for hotels are also similar to most other industries. Typically, they include maximizing revenue, achieving market penetration, generating market development and market growth, inducing trial, maintaining market share, and so on. In the hotel business, lowering rates to fill rooms in valley periods is a common strategy to maximize revenues. During peak periods it is also common practice for revenue maximization to offer few, if any, discounted rooms to price-sensitive markets.

In contrast, market penetration strategies are designed to reach more of a current target market—for instance, corporate business from the Northeast corridor. Frequent-traveler programs, similar to those of the airlines, recently have been adopted by many hotel chains (see Table 3). The goal is market penetration through increased usage by the frequent business traveler. These programs are not special promotions; rather, they are a form of discount awarded to repeat customers in addition to their corporate-rate program privileges. (There is current debate in the industry over whether or not these programs indeed pay for themselves in terms of increased revenues resulting from the program.)

Table 3 Selected Hotel Frequent Traveler Program

Hotel Company	Basic Program	Maximum Award	Fee to Join
Hilton	10 points per dollar spent as registered hotel guest	Two arount-the-world airline tickets and 14 hotel nights. (500,000 points)	None
Holiday Inn	1 point per dollar spent as registered hotel guest	Two round-trip tickets to selected destinations in the Far East or most Pan Am destinations (25,000 points)	$10
Hyatt	5 points per dollar spent as registered hotel guest	10-night vacation at any Hyatt Resort including all transportation expenses (300,000 points)	$25/annual
Mariott	10 points per dollar spent as registered hotel guest plus 100 points for each night registered	Three four-night hotel stays, four round-trip coach tickets with airline partner, 15 days free rental car (350,000 points)	None
Radisson	10 points per dollar spent as registered hotel guest	48 hotel nights, 11 airline awards (250,000 points)	None
Sheraton	4 points per dollar spent as registered on nonregistered hotel guest	Porsche 911 Carrera (2,500,000 points) or each dollar of Sheraton lodging free for each 100 points earned	$25/annual
Stouffer	1 point per dollar spent as registered hotel guest	Resort vacation or $1,750 merchandise certificate or $3,500 U.S. Savings Bond (35,000 points)	None

Source: Hotels and Wall Street Journal, 3/18/88

Market Development

"The Copley Plaza Celebrates 75 Years"

Market development is reaching for new markets in tandem with enlarging current target markets. A recent set of marketing objectives for the Copley Plaza included introducing the hotel to broad new potential market segments, increasing business volume in off-peak periods, and implementing these steps in a fashion compatible with the hotel's established image as Boston's Grande Dame.

The hotel's 75th anniversary offered an excellent opportunity to carry out these objectives and a special promotion was developed. The Copley Plaza invited the public to join in the celebration by enjoying a $75.00 room-rate during the entire year of the anniversary. The promotion was targeted to primary feeder markets in the Northeast, with advertisements in the *New York Times*, the *Wall Street Journal*, and the *Boston Globe* (see Figures 2 and 3). This price promotion is an excellent example of tying together the managing of demand and adjusting inventories without compromising the premiere position of the hotel.

Managing Demand. The special rate package gave very price-elastic consumers the opportunity to afford the luxury of staying at the "Grande Dame of Boston." Even regular customers of the Copley Plaza returned on weekends with their spouses to take advantage of the special offer. The price of $75.00 was below market value for this product class and it was perceived as an excellent price/value opportunity by both new and existing customers.

Adjusting Inventory. The offer was available on any night, subject to availability, which in hotel vernacular means subject to anticipated levels of demand from various target markets. The Copley Plaza analyzed and forecasted demand of its primary and secondary markets and then made appropriate inventory allocations for the 75th Anniversary rate package. Simply stated, a larger number of rooms were allocated during projected "softer" periods.

Figure 2 Winter Promotion

Figure 3   Summer Promotion

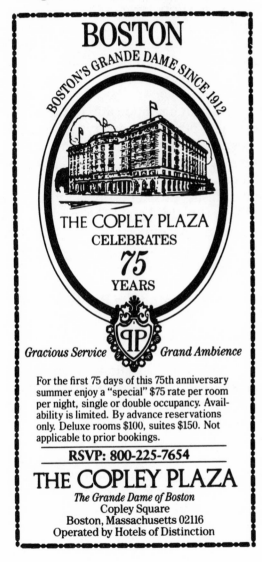

Positioning. One of the best features of the promotion was that it was consistent and very supportive of the Copley Plaza's positioning in the marketplace. Though indeed it was a discount, it did not convey a negative "discount house" image. Rather, it was an invitation to enjoy a happy celebration of the Grande Dame's successful 75 years of gracious service.

The Results. The price/value relationship of the offer, coupled with the storyline of the 75th Anniversary, combined to create a tremendous success. Year-end results reflected an 11% increase in the overall occupancy from the previous year, an increase in the tangent sales of food and beverage by virtue of the increased number of overnight guests, excellent publicity for the hotel, and numerous new clients to the hotel. The package also gave very price-elastic consumers the opportunity to afford the luxury of staying at the "Grande Dame of Boston."

Positioning the Product

Hotels are created to meet anticipated demand from predetermined selected target markets. The point at which a hotel is conceived and designed—when location is chosen, when square footage is allocated, when facilities and services are specified, and when decor is determined—is also the point at which a hotel has the differential uniqueness and the necessary elements to effectively position itself in the marketplace. This is why some hotels have 700 rooms instead of 400 rooms, or two pools instead of one or none, or 10,000 square feet of space designated to meeting space instead of 3,000 square feet, or a tea court instead of a coffee shop. Hoteliers further position their hotels with pricing strategies.

All pricing decisions need to support the "positioning statement" of a hotel. Pricing is a marketing tool used to satisfy target market customers and to communicate the image of a hotel to the general public. A consumer's judgment regarding his or her perception of a hotel is directly influenced by the price of that hotel. A simple analogy is the $30,000 sticker price for a Jaguar versus the $10,000 Chevrolet. These products are not in the same product class, and that is how the consumer perceives them. The same is true for hotels.

While pricing for positioning has little to do with the cost of operations, such pricing serves to introduce and/or position a hotel in a competitive environment by instituting forces of demand elasticity. This is significant because the stated rack-rate or full price actually serves to exclude certain markets. Any further pricing modifications within the retail price range is within the targeted market's acceptance zone.

A rate range of $135-170 for a hotel in Boston suggests a first class, full-service hotel. The customer expects 24-hour room service, fine dining, valet service, and similar services. Frequent business travelers, for the most part, who are seeking these kinds of amenities expect this price range for this type of hotel during peak demand times. But they do not and probably will not pay a rate of $200 or more. As noted earlier in this chapter, the *customer* really sets the rate—or at least, the rate range—which he or she is willing to pay.

Conclusion

Pricing hotel rooms, though difficult to explain to the normal customer, really does pivot around supply and demand, sometimes seemingly merciless to the customer and at other times seemingly merciless to the hotelier.

The General Manager of the Copley Plaza, with 16 years at that position, has a favorite story about price elasticities of demand: "A guest rents the Presidential Suite for $750 a night for three nights. She dines, with parties of 4 to 6, each night in the 4-star Cafe Plaza, with 20 to 30 year-old Bordeaux wines, Champagne, excellent cognac, nothing spared...everything the best. Yet, in the morning, she walks across the street to Dunkin' Donuts and carries back to her suite a couple of donuts and a cup of coffee in a paper bag for breakfast!"

What price to charge? In the end, the customer dictates. And for some customers, perhaps the hotelier can do nothing to surpass the temptations of the ubiquitous Dunkin' Donuts.

Endnotes

[1] Rashcow, Bertram, "How to Set the Right Price," *Inc.*, (February 1981), p. 54.

[2] Shaw, Margaret, "An Analysis of the Hotel Room Rate Pricing Decision," Ph.D. Dissertation, Cornell University, 1984, p. 119.

Recommended for Additional Reading

"Pricing Augmented Commercial Services," by Roberto Friedmann and Warren A. French in *Journal of Product Innovation Management*, no. 4, 1987, p. 33-42.

"Business at Any Price," by James C. Makens in *The Cornell H.R.A. Quarterly*, August, 1987, p. 13-15.

PRICING, PRODUCT DIFFERENTIATION AND THE DOMINANT FIRM:

Borden's ReaLemon Foods

DAVID I. ROSENBAUM
PHIL HALL

DAVID I. ROSENBAUM

David Rosenbaum is Assistant Professor of Economics at the University of Nebraska-Lincoln and a consultant in antitrust-related matters. His research interests include dominant firm strategies and interactions in markets containing few firms. He received his Ph.D. in Economics from the University of Wisconsin-Madison.

PHIL HALL

Phil Hall is Assistant Professor of Management at the University of Nebraska-Lincoln. Dr. Hall publishes and consults in the area of strategic management for profit and non-profit organizations. He attended graduate school at California State University, Sacramento and completed his doctorate at the University of Nebraska.

CHAPTER TWELVE

Industry dominance is the dream of most product managers. Achieving this goal requires establishing a total competitive advantage. Maintaining dominance, however, may take additional strategies. This chapter examines one dominant firm's maintenance strategy, emphasizing the role of pricing. ReaLemon has been the dominant brand of reconstituted lemon juice in the United States for several years. Yet ReaLemon has faced periodic competition from a handful of unadvertised regional competitors. The chapter examines the promotional pricing strategy implemented by ReaLemon to maintain and to reinforce its dominant position.

Borden, Inc.—ReaLemon

In 1962, Borden, Inc., purchased the ReaLemon-Puritan Company and formed that company into ReaLemon Foods, a separate unit of its Borden Foods Division. The principal product of ReaLemon Foods has been ReaLemon brand reconstituted lemon juice. ReaLemon has been the only national brand and the only significant advertiser of reconstituted lemon juice in the United States. The main reason for Borden's advertising strategy was to differentiate ReaLemon from any and all other reconstituted lemon juices. ReaLemon officials speculated that "heavy emphasis on the ReaLemon brand name through its media effort should create such memorability for that brand, that an almost imaginary superiority would exist (for ReaLemon) in the mind of the consumer." So even though ReaLemon and other reconstituted lemon juices may have been chemically similar or identical, in most consumers' minds they were distinctly different products. Borden's efforts at image advertising established this dominant competitive advantage based on product differentiation.

ReaLemon faced some competition from a handful of local and regional competitors. None of these competitors distributed its own brand of reconstituted lemon juice nationally and none advertised. Some, however, were significant in regional markets. For example, while ReaLemon's national market share was 88.2 percent in August 1970, its market share in Pittsburgh was only 62.5 percent at that time.

ReaLemon and Its Rivals

Reconstituted lemon juice is manufactured by adding water, a preservative or preservatives, and lemon oil to pure lemon juice concentrate which is purchased in bulk, often in tank cars, by large producers. The ingredients are mixed according to a simple, well-known formula, using uncomplicated, relatively inexpensive equipment of the sort employed by any juice bottling operation. The production process for making reconstituted lemon juice exhibits few sunk costs, low fixed costs, and no appreciable economies of scale. Production among firms is so similar that ReaLemon Foods officials stated "reconstituted lemon juice is virtually indistinguishable one brand from another."

If a supermarket had room for only one brand of reconstituted lemon juice, that brand would be ReaLemon. When a supermarket had additional room, it would take on only one alternative brand of reconstituted lemon juice and that brand would be the cheapest of the "second" brands available. This meant there was competition among the regional producers to become the second brand in a market. As a consequence, while ReaLemon faced competition from several producers across all its markets, within any one market or region it typically faced competition from only one brand.

ReaLemon's pricing strategy had two components. The country was divided into three zones. Each zone had its own list price. ReaLemon also offered three or four trade promotions per year. These promotions usually covered the periods around Memorial Day, mid-summer, and Thanksgiving-Christmas, and were sometimes offered during Lent. The trade promotions were intended to induce a retailer to promote ReaLemon and to offer it for sale at a reduced price. Some promotions required certain actions or "performance" on the part of retailers. Other promotions did not. For the promotions that did require performance, one of the performance options was generally a reduced retail price. In 1972 ReaLemon sold approximately 71 percent of its largest selling size during promotional periods, in 1973 about 84 percent, and in 1974 an estimated 77 percent.

Regional reconstituted lemon juice producers competed with ReaLemon on retailer margin and retail price. These competitors recognized that "only the presence of a price differential [between their brand of reconstituted lemon juice and ReaLemon] sufficient to induce the supermarket to stock their brand, and motivating the consumer to buy it, enabled them to survive." In the early 1970s, regional competitors' reconstituted lemon juices were priced as much as 25 to 30 percent below the average 65 cent retail price for 32 ounce bottles of ReaLemon. When ReaLemon lowered its price, the regional competitors had to lower their prices as well.

ReaLemon's Pricing Strategy

The dominant firm follows a differentiation strategy to make its product uniquely perceived by consumers. The undifferentiated regional rivals of the industry-wide dominant firm use price as their basic competitive tool. These are lower price alternatives for buyers who don't perceive the leader as either unique or of substantially greater quality to justify a higher purchase price. The dominant firm has to continue to do everything to pursue effective differentiation. For instance, it may continue advertising and promotional campaigns. The dominant firm also has to remain price-conscious, and has to make pricing decisions to compete directly against lower priced niche competitors.

The dominant firm already has established a major competitive edge with its differentiated position. ReaLemon was the reconstituted lemon juice market; therefore, Borden could establish an aggressive pricing strategy to thwart the growth of regional competitors. A decision to decrease the price of ReaLemon juice would either force competing brands to lower their prices too or give consumers the opportunity to buy the perceived highest-quality product at a price relatively close to the low-price, regional competitor. These regional competitors would already have smaller margins than the dominant firm and would resist prices decreases if possible. ReaLemon also had the advantage of selective use of the pricing strategy. It could decrease the price in any geographic region where competitive rivals were the most effective and maintain the higher margin prices where the differentiation strategy was sufficient for competitive advantage.

In 1970 ReaLemon Foods decided its market share in certain regions was falling too low and that one regional competitor in particular was gaining too much market share in too many regions. To counter the advances of these producers, ReaLemon management stated that:[1]

> In those markets where competition has been making inroads, tentative plans are to increase the size of the [promotional] allowances to as much as $1.20 per case, or 10 cents a bottle. Based on past history, it is hoped that the trade will reflect reduced retails of as much as 15 cents per unit. We will again be specifically attacking the problem of the retail price spread between ReaLemon and competition. In general terms, competitive activity exists in the Eastern half of the United States. In the Western half, promotional allowances will be limited to a range of 60 to 75 cents per case.

In essence, ReaLemon management felt it could regain market share by manipulating the spread between retail prices for ReaLemon and its competitors' brands. Also, management decided that the best way to manipulate the retail price spread was through selective changes in promotional allowances where these promotions typically required reduced retail prices. In those regions where ReaLemon faced competition, promotions were increased. In those regions where ReaLemon did not face competition, promotions were not increased.

Reconstituted Lemon Juice Industry Pricing

Through its product differentiation Borden was able to put other equally efficient producers at a marketing disadvantage. The disadvantage forced other firms to maintain a price differential between their brands of reconstituted lemon juice and ReaLemon. Given this differential, Borden's pricing strategy allowed it to sell ReaLemon at a profitable price and also forced its competitors to sell their products at considerably less profitable prices.

The following section develops the model of this strategy of adding a price decrease to a differentiation advantage. This model calculates the highest wholesale price that a regional competitor can charge a food retailer for its brand of reconstituted lemon juice while still remaining competitive based on its price position relative to ReaLemon. In essence, ReaLemon can lower its price and force the regional competitor to respond. The regional competitor has to consider its maximum wholesale price, average variable cost, profit margins, and competitive position when formulating its response. In the extreme, the regional competitor may decide to leave the market.

An Economic Model

There are two brands of reconstituted lemon juice: Borden's ReaLemon and a regional competitor's reconstituted lemon juice. ReaLemon is an established brand. It is advertised nationally and has a strong consumer franchise. In contrast, the regional competitor's brand is relatively new to the market. Its position is more tenuous. The regional competitor is concerned with gaining retailer and consumer acceptance of its product. To accomplish this the regional competitor has to maintain a sufficient spread between its price and Borden's—both wholesale and retail.

To a degree, Borden's promotional activities benefited consumers. The ReaLemon trade name conveyed important information. Consumers could be assured that their purchases were of a high and consistent quality. This is not to say, however, that competing brands were actually inferior in quality. The fundamental problem facing regional competitors was convincing consumers that their products were equal in value to ReaLemon. In essence, Borden's tenure in the market, along with its promotional activities, created an information asymmetry problem. To overcome this problem, in the short run at least, competitors had to price their brands at a discount.

For the regional competitor to sell its product, it had to satisfy two agents in the food distribution system. It had to (1) convince a retailer to carry its product and (2) convince consumers to purchase its product. Consider first the problem of getting a retailer to carry the product. Retailers will accept a new item if that item will increase the retailer's gross profit dollars. A new product has to bring in more money than the product it replaces. Switching products has to provide a positive marginal gain in gross profits.

The marginal gain, or the change in gross profit dollars from stocking one brand as opposed to another, is measured per unit of shelf space over a specific period of time. For a retailer, the marginal profit from carrying a regional competitor's reconstituted lemon juice instead of ReaLemon is the gross profit derived from selling the regional competitor's product minus the gross profit foregone by not stocking that shelf space with ReaLemon.

The gross profit a retailer can derive by selling either brand of reconstituted lemon juice is influenced by three factors. The first factor is retail price. Let $P_B^R(t)$ represent Borden's retail price in period t, and let $P_C^R(t)$ represent the regional competitor's retail price in period t. Within this model, the superscript R denotes a retail observation. The superscript W denotes a wholesale operation. The subscript B denotes Borden and the subscript C denotes the regional competitor.

The second factor determining the gross profit available from either brand is its gross margin. Gross margin is the difference between the retail price and the wholesale price of a product, calculated as a percentage of retail price. Denote the gross margin a retailer can earn on any product it sells as M. If $P_B^W(t)$ denotes Borden's wholesale price in period t and $P_C^W(t)$ denotes the regional competitor's wholesale price in period t, then the gross margin a retailer can earn on Borden's ReaLemon can be described as:

$$M_B(t) = \frac{P_B^R(t) - P_B^W(t)}{P_B^R(t)} \qquad\qquad 1$$

Similarly, the gross margin a retailer can earn on the regional competitor's brand of reconstituted lemon juice can be described as:

$$M_C(t) = \frac{P_C^R(t) - P_C^W(t)}{P_B^R(t)} \qquad\qquad 2$$

Borden's trade promotions frequently affected the retailer's gross margin on ReaLemon. Certain actions were often required of retailers in order to qualify for Borden's promotional discount. One of the performance options available to retailers was a reduced retail price. This would establish the retailer's gross margin on ReaLemon as a function of Borden's own pricing strategy.

The final factor determining a product's gross profit is the number of units sold. Define $N_B(t)$ as the marginal sales of ReaLemon a retailer loses by stocking one less unit of shelf space with ReaLemon. For example, if the shelf space devoted to ReaLemon is reduced from 10 to 9 facings, and 10 fewer cases are sold, $N_B(t)$ is equal to 10. Define $N_C(t)$ as the marginal number of units of the regional competitor's reconstituted lemon juice a retailer can sell if the retailer stocks one more unit of shelf space with that brand.

For a retailer to have an incentive to carry a regional competitor's brand—and consequently not fill that shelf space with ReaLemon—the marginal gross profit from switching to that brand must be positive. It must be that for at least one unit of shelf space:

$$P_C^R(t) \bullet M_C(t) \bullet N_C(t) - P_B^R(t) \bullet M_B(t) \bullet N_B(t) > \emptyset \qquad 3$$

That is, the gross profit from stocking one unit of shelf space with the regional competitor's brand must be greater than the gross profit foregone from not stocking that shelf space with ReaLemon.

To convince a retailer to carry its product, the regional competitor must make its reconstituted lemon juice attractive to consumers as well. The regional competitor can do this by making its brand of reconstituted lemon juice relatively less expensive than ReaLemon. Define d(t) as the difference between the retail price of Borden's ReaLemon and the retail price of the regional competitor's reconstituted lemon juice, or as:

$$d(t) = P_B^R(t) - P_C^R(t) \qquad 4$$

This model assumes that as d(t) rises, given any absolute price level, the regional competitor's reconstituted lemon juice becomes more attractive to consumers. So as d(t) rises, the regional competitor can expect to gain market share. Similarly, as d(t) rises, Borden can expect to lose market share.

To counteract these losses, Borden can attempt to reduce d(t). Theoretically, when d(t) reaches zero, the competitor cannot offer consumers a better deal on its brand of reconstituted lemon juice than Borden, and more than likely will be forced from the market. Given consumer preference for ReaLemon, it can be assumed that retailers require some minimum price difference between the two products in order to carry the regional competitor's reconstituted lemon juice. Call this difference:

$$\text{mind}(t) = \begin{array}{l} \text{minimum required difference between retail prices for} \\ \text{ReaLemon and a regional competitor's reconstituted} \\ \text{lemon juice} \end{array} \qquad 5$$

Combining equations (1) through (4), and rearranging, provides the equation:

$$P_C^W(t) < \frac{P_B^W(t)}{(1 - M_B(t))} \left(1 - \frac{N_B(t)}{N_C(t)} M_B(t)\right) - {}^{min}d(t) \qquad 6$$

This equation describes the *highest* wholesale price the regional competitor can charge for its brand of reconstituted lemon juice in any period. This price is a function of Borden's wholesale price, the gross margin on ReaLemon, and the minimum retail price margin. Given Borden's pricing strategy, this price will allow a competitor to (1) offer retailers sufficient marginal revenues to carry the competitor's brand, and (2) maintain at least a minimum retail price spread between its brand of reconstituted lemon juice and ReaLemon. If Borden sets its wholesale price or retailers earn a gross margin such that the wholesale price in equation (6) is above the regional competitor's average variable cost, a regional competitor can remain in the market. If Borden sets its wholesale price or retailers earn a gross margin so that the wholesale price shown in equation (6) falls below the regional competitor's average variable cost, then the competitor is forced from the market.

Model Solution

In April and May of 1973, retailers earned a gross margin of 9.3 percent on ReaLemon, on average. This was a nonpromotional period. During promotional periods, Borden typically changed its wholesale price and allowed reduced retail prices as performance options. So it is not unreasonable to expect the gross margin in promotional periods to be different from the average gross margin in certain nonpromotional periods.

During December 1973, Borden charged Acme Markets an effective wholesale price of $4.05 per case of ReaLemon to induce Acme to sell ReaLemon for $.39 per quart. At a price of $4.05, and a suggested retail price of $.39 per quart or $4.68 per case of 12 quarts, Acme's gross margin on ReaLemon in December 1973

274 • DAVID I. ROSENBAUM & PHIL HALL

would have been 13.5 percent. This figure will be used for the retailer's gross margin on ReaLemon in equation (6). Borden's wholesale price of $4.05 will be used in the model as well.

A retailer only would have restocked a unit of shelf space with the regional competitor's brand if it expected more gross profit from that brand than from ReaLemon. The sales ratio, $N_B(t)/N_C(t)$, compares the volume of ReaLemon sales lost by removing it from one unit of shelf space to the volume gained by the regional competitor's brand when it was substituted for ReaLemon on the unit of shelf space.

The way a product is displayed influences how well it sells; when the amount of shelf space allocated to a product increases, sales of that product increases as well. The absolute increase in sales volume will be a function of the initial amount of shelf space allocated to the product as well as the amount of space gained. It can be inferred that sales volume increases at a decreasing rate with increases in shelf space.

Curve R_O in Figure 1 shows a hypothetical example of the functional relationship between ReaLemon shelf facings and ReaLemon sales volume. When ReaLemon has N facings, its sales volume is K units. When ReaLemon has N-1 facings, its sales volume falls to K' units. If a competitor were to enter the market, the functional relationship between ReaLemon shelf facings and sales volume may shift from R_O to R_1. At every number of shelf facings ReaLemon sales volume would fall. This shift would be because of substitution between brands. Some consumers would be willing to switch from ReaLemon to a lower-priced alternative brand. The magnitude of this shift will depend on the relative price difference between the two brands and the number of shelf facings given to the competing brand.

The effect of entry on ReaLemon shelf facings is important in determining ReaLemon's total losses in sales volume. Suppose entry occurs and ReaLemon does not lose facings. (This implies that when entry occurs, shelf space is taken from a product unrelated to reconstituted lemon juice and given to the regional competitor.) Substitution between brands would imply that ReaLemon would lose and the regional competitor would gain sales volume equal to A in Figure 1.

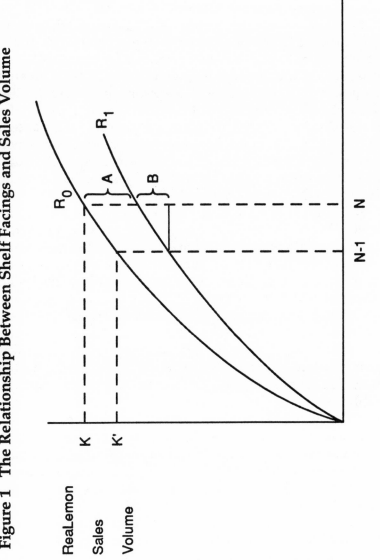

Figure 1 The Relationship Between Shelf Facings and Sales Volume

A more reasonable assumption, however, may be that retailers keep the total amount of shelf space allocated to the reconstituted lemon juice category as fixed. Then, every facing given to the regional competitor's product would be one facing taken from ReaLemon. Suppose entry occurs under these conditions. If the regional competitor were given one facing, ReaLemon would then have N-1 facings. Not only would ReaLemon lose A sales because of substitution between brands, but according to Figure 1, Rea-Lemon would lose B sales because of the bowed nature of the sales function. A reduction in shelf facings would reduce sales absent any substitution. In this example, when entry occurs, ReaLemon sales losses (referred to as N_B in this model) would equal A+B and the regional competitor's sales gains (N_C) would equal A. Then the sales ratio, N_B/N_C, would equal (A+B) /A.

But there is another component to consider when calculating the sales ratio. When the regional competitor enters the market, it does so with a retail price that is lower than ReaLemon's retail price; therefore, the regional competitor's brand may draw new customers into the market. These customers would buy this brand because its price was low enough, in absolute terms, to get these consumers to try reconstituted lemon juice. These customers would not be substituting between brands. They would be entering because the retail price for the regional competitor's brand was below their reservation price for reconstituted lemon juice in general. Call this increase in sales C. Then the sales ratio would be equal (A+B)/(A+C).

Unfortunately, we do not have all the information necessary to calculate $N_B(t)/N_C(t)$, so the maximum wholesale price a regional competitor could charge for its reconstituted lemon juice will be calculated using several estimates. This should provide some insight into how the minimum price would change if different ratios are assumed.

Sales ratios either greater than or less than 1.0 are reasonable. When the sales ratio exceeds 1.0, ReaLemon sales losses as a result of reduced shelf space outweigh the gains in sales from new customers. When the sales ratio is less than 1.0, the opposite is true. The extreme value the sales ratio may take is 0.00. This would occur if Borden lost no sales when one unit of its space was given to the regional brand; however, this seems unreasonable. It is clear that Borden was losing market share. For Borden to lose market share without losing sales, the regional competitor would have had to obtain its sales exclusively from new customers to the reconstituted lemon juice market. It seems much more plausible that the regional competitor was taking at least some customers from Borden. For this reason it seems most reasonable to expect the sales ratio to be above zero but probably below 2.0.

Only a difference in retail prices allowed the regional competitor to sell its reconstituted lemon juice. A retailer would have required some minimum retail price difference to carry the regional competitor's brand because the price difference would have allowed that brand to gain at least a minimum market share. In all probability, the price difference would not be independent of other demand influences such as the number of facings given to the regional brand. A retail price difference of 5 cents is probably far less than the differential needed to cause purchasers to abandon the premium ReaLemon brand for a relatively unknown new entrant. While this does not indicate the exact price difference needed to gain the minimum market share, it does suggest a probable lower bound. Results will be calculated using several values for ^{min}d.

Model Results

This section presents results of the maximum wholesale price model in equation (6). Again, given certain market parameters and Borden's pricing strategy, it is possible to calculate the maximum wholesale price a regional competitor could have charged while still remaining competitive. Remaining competitive means (1) that the competitor offered retailers greater gross profits by carrying its brand than by filling equivalent shelf space with ReaLemon and (2) that the competitor's brand was sold to consumers at an absolute cost saving in comparison to ReaLemon. If this maximum wholesale price was above the regional competitor's average cost, the regional competitor could have remained in the market. If this maximum wholesale price was below the regional competitor's average cost, the regional competitor would have been excluded from the market.

Results of the maximum wholesale price model are shown in Table 1. These results were calculated using several values for $N_B(t)/N_C(t)$ and ^{min}d, and using Borden's wholesale price charged to Acme Markets of $4.05 per case and a gross margin of 13.5 percent.

Table 1 The Regional Competitor's Maximum Wholesale Price as a Function of the Sales Ratio and of the Minimum Retail Price Spread

$N_B(t)/N_C(t)$

^{min}d (in dollars per case of 12 bottles)	1.9	1.6	1.3	1.0	0.6	0.3	0.0
0.00:	$3.48	$3.67	$3.86	$4.05	$4.30	$4.49	$4.68
0.36:	3.12	3.31	3.50	3.69	3.94	4.13	4.32
0.60:	2.88	3.07	3.26	3.45	3.70	3.89	4.08
0.84:	2.64	2.83	3.02	3.21	3.46	3.65	3.84
1.08:	2.40	2.59	2.78	2.97	3.22	3.41	3.60
1.80	1.68	1.87	2.06	2.25	2.50	2.69	2.88
2.40	1.08	1.27	1.46	1.65	1.90	2.09	2.28

$M_B(t) = 0.135$ or 13.5%

$P_B^W(t) = \$4.05$

The maximum wholesale price varies as the sales ratio (N_B/N_C) varies and as the minimum retail price spread (^{min}d) varies. For example, if the sales ratio equaled 1.0 and the minimum retail price spread equaled 5 cents a quart or 60 cents a case, the regional competitor's maximum wholesale price would have been $3.45. When Borden sold ReaLemon to food retailers at a promotional wholesale price of $4.05 and retailers took a 13.5 percent gross margin, the most a regional competitor could have charged retailers for its brand of reconstituted lemon juice would have been $3.45. At that price, the regional competitor would have given retailers an incentive to switch from ReaLemon. Whether $3.45 was above or below the regional competitor's average variable cost would have determined whether the competitor remained in the market.

Holding the minimum retail price spread to 60 cents, if the sales ratio was .60 instead of 1.0, the regional competitor's maximum wholesale price would rise to $3.70. A sales ratio of 0.30 raises the maximum wholesale price to $3.89. The sales ratio represents the ratio of sales lost by ReaLemon to sales gained by the regional competitor. As the sales ratio falls the regional competitor adds increasingly more to the sales of reconstituted lemon juice relative to the loss in ReaLemon sales. The more sales are increased by the regional brand, the lower the necessary per-unit profit margin to food retailers. With a low sales ratio the regional competitor could have maintained the requisite retail price spread, charged a higher wholesale price, and still allowed retailers higher gross profit dollars by carrying its brand.

For any fixed value of the sales ratio, as the minimum retail price spread (^{min}d) increases, the regional competitor's maximum wholesale price falls. Suppose for example the sales ratio equaled 1.0. If the minimum retail price spread equaled 84 cents per case, the maximum wholesale price a regional competitor could have charged to remain competitive would have been $3.21. A minimum spread of $1.08 per case would have forced the maximum wholesale price to $2.97.

Whether ReaLemon's pricing strategy would have forced a regional competitor from the market depends on the regional competitor's wholesale price relative to its costs. To determine whether a price of $4.05 would have excluded a rival, the calculated maximum wholesale price a regional competitor could have charged must be compared to the regional competitor's average variable cost.

In a planning document a Borden official estimated the manufacturing costs for its regional competitor.[2] Estimated cost parameters for the regional competitor are reproduced in Table 2.

Variable costs would have included the cost of goods, distribution costs, and part of the selling costs. Selling expenses that go toward salaries of salesman, sales office space, and the like, would have been considered fixed costs. Approximately 14 percent of Borden's average selling expenses were fixed costs. Applying this same percentage to the regional competitor's selling expenses, average variable costs are estimated as $3.51 per quart of reconstituted lemon juice.

Table 2 Estimated Manufacturing Costs for a Regional Competitor

	Regional Competitor's Estimated Cost
Glass	$1.048
Caps	.061
Labels	.079
Product	1.574
Direct Labor/Fringe	.067
Cost of Goods	2.83
Distribution	.50
Selling	.21
Advertising/Promotion	.10
Overhead	.20
Average Total Cost	3.84
Average Variable Cost	$3.51

Comparing this figure of $3.51 to results in Table 1, it is clear that under certain conditions Borden's pricing strategy could have placed great pressure on the regional competitor. Given the assertion that Borden set its own wholesale price at $4.05 and retailers earned 13.5 percent gross margin on ReaLemon, there are several combinations of minimum retail price spreads and sales ratios that would have forced a regional competitor to sell its output for less than its variable production costs. For example, if the sales ratio equaled 0.6 and the minimum retail price spread was 84 cents per case (or 7 cents per quart), the maximum wholesale price a regional competitor could charge would have been below its own variable cost of $3.51 per case. Under those conditions, the regional competitor would have been placed at an extreme competitive disadvantage.

One could argue that the sales ratio and the minimum retail price spread in fact take on values not shown in Table 1. Clearly, both will be bounded below by zero. Their maximum values, however, may be above those shown in Table 1. While this is true, it is not necessarily germane to the problem. Equation (6) shows that both ^{min}d and $N_B(t)/N_C(t)$ have a negative influence on the regional competitor's maximum wholesale price. Therefore, as one increases, the other would have to decrease to keep the maximum wholesale price at some fixed level.

When the sales ratio is zero, the regional competitor's maximum wholesale price falls below its average variable cost when the retail price spread surpasses $1.08 per case, or 9 cents per quart. If one were to argue, therefore, that the minimum retail price spread indeed was above 9 cents per quart, the value of the sales ratio would be irrelevant. Since the sales ratio can never be negative, a price spread greater than 9 cents would always exclude the regional competitor. Similarly, if one were to argue that the sales ratio was indeed greater than 1.9, the value of ^{min}d would become irrelevant. If the sales ratio was greater than 1.9, there would be no positive values that the retail price spread could take, so that the regional competitor's maximum wholesale price would be above its variable production cost of $3.51. Once again, the regional competitor would always be excluded.

This effectively places a boundary on values that must be considered. Given that Borden charged a wholesale price of $4.05 and retailers took a gross margin of 13.5 percent, the relevant values of the sales ratio would fall between 0 and 1.9. The relevant values of the retail price spread would fall between 0 and $1.08 per case. Within these bounds the model may give an ambiguous result. If either parameter took a value outside these bounds the result would be clear—the regional competitor would be excluded.

The dashed line in Table 1 indicates the probable boundary marking reasonable from unreasonable values for the minimum price difference and the sales ratio. It seems unlikely that the sales ratio would have been below 0.3 or that the minimum price difference would have been less than 60 cents per case or 5 cents per quart. Once again, given that Borden charged a wholesale price of $4.05 and retailers took a gross margin of 13.5 percent, there are very few combinations of the sales ratio and minimum price difference within the area below and to the left of the dashed line that would not have excluded an equally efficient, though lesser known rival. One can conclude from this that it is likely Borden's promotional wholesale price of $4.05 and gross margin of 13.5 percent greatly increases its ability to compete effectively against a regional rival.

Conclusion

A dominant, differentiated firm can add promotional pricing to its competitive arsenal to maintain and strengthen its market position. The competitive advantages can become strong enough to force regional rivals to reconsider remaining in the market. This was shown to be the case for ReaLemon reconstituted lemon juice. Product differentiation forced competitors to sell at a discount relative to ReaLemon. Promotional pricing on Bordon's part almost certainly forced competitors from the market.

The only major drawback of this two-fold strategy of product differentiation and promotional pricing is the threat of complaints of predatory pricing. Corporations and government entities frequently scrutinize exclusionary pricing behavior for evidence of predation. The lower bound of prices that are considered predatory is fairly well established. Several antitrust authorities, however, have argued that prices above this boundary can be predatory as well. Hence some caution must be exhibited when using promotional pricing to force undifferentiated rivals from a market.

Endnotes

[1] ReaLemon Foods, *1971 Marketing Plan*, p. 7.

[2] 92 *Federal Trade Commission Decisions* 669, p. 744.

Recommended for Additional Reading

Richard A. Posner, *Antitrust Law: An Economic Perspective* (Chicago: The University of Chicago Press, 1976), p. 188.

F.M. Scherer, "Predatory Pricing and the Sherman Act: A Comment," *Harvard Law Review* 89 (March 1976): 869-90.

Oliver E. Williamson, "Predatory Pricing: A Strategic and Welfare Analysis," *Yale Law Journal* 87 (December 1977): 284-341.

CHAPTER THIRTEEN

SMALL BUSINESS, BIG OPPORTUNITY:

Developing a Successful Pricing Strategy

MATTHEW W. PIERSON

MATTHEW W. PIERSON

Matthew W. Pierson is Vice President of Marketing and Sales for CYPLEX. CYPLEX designs and manufactures a wide variety of data communications products used in factory and warehouse automation and utility communication applications. Prior to joining CYPLEX, Mr. Pierson was Vice President of Marketing at Power Electronics Corporation and held several other senior marketing positions in the hi-tech industry. Mr. Pierson is an active promoter of international trade and in June, 1988, organized and attended a trade mission to the People's Republic of China, representing the State of New Hampshire and ten high tech manufacturing firms.

CHAPTER THIRTEEN

W hy is pricing in smaller companies so difficult? There are a number of answers common to most smaller manufacturers. In order to understand them, one must look at how a small business develops. Typically, a business is started by an entrepreneur or group of individuals with a product idea. Most have experience in a larger company with a similar product or in a similar market. Early sales are made by the founder going out and knocking on doors. Overhead is minimal and a high percentage of the sales dollars in excess of direct labor and material costs is regarded as profit. Virtually all of it goes back into the business to fuel growth.

At this point in time, pricing is based on the founder's feelings for costs and competitors' pricing. In a small company this is quite workable. The founder can control costs and see how "profitable" the company is by looking at the checkbook balance. As the company grows, more overhead is added and the founder cannot directly control all areas. Sales, engineering, purchasing, and other administrative personnel are added.

The change in the cost structure often requires a different pricing policy than the one used in the past. For example, a penetration pricing strategy might be an effective option in the early stages of a company's growth cycle; however, the continued use of the strategy may not provide sufficient margins to cover the costs of sustaining growth.

Amherst Control Products was started in 1980. The founder was an engineer with a substantial background in motor controllers. Starting with two part-time employees and working out of a small storage shed, sales of motor controllers grew from $80K in 1981 to $380K in 1982. At this time, the need for more capacity led the company to move into 8,000 feet of leased manufacturing space. In addition, the founder hired a sales manager. The company's plan was to continue to grow by offering motor controllers at a slightly lower price than their two largest competitors in the area, both divisions of much larger companies.

The company continued to grow. Six months later, shipments were running at a rate of $700K/year, the company had 18 employees, and was running out of money. Based on past performance, a local bank was glad to loan the company $250K. This money was used to finance inventory and additional production equipment. A year and a half later, losing money and $400K in debt, Amherst Control Products sold out to a competitor at a loss.

What went wrong? In examining Amherst's income statement and cost structure, it's easy to see While sales grew rapidly, expenses increased even faster. (See Table 1.)

The company made a mistake common in smaller business. It focused on sales and growth and lost sight of expenses and profitability. It failed to recognize that the drastically changed cost structure in 1983 required a change in the pricing strategy. For example, while sales increased 335 percent between 1981 and 1984, rent increased 661 percent, indirect labor increased 488 percent, and interest payments, which were zero, now accounted for 4.8 percent of sales. Overall, expenses rose from 34.8 percent of sales to 44.7 percent between 1981 and 1984. In that same time period, the gross profit margin increased by only 2 percent, due to lower parts costs associated with higher quantity purchasing. Had the company increased prices by only 5 percent and differentiated itself by offering higher quality, better or faster service, or such, the company would have continued to be profitable.

This chapter focuses on the many problems and opportunities faced by smaller manufacturing companies in developing and implementing an effective pricing strategy. It examines internal cost, external competition, market factors, and the means of selecting a macro pricing strategy that fits with the overall business plan.

Table 1 Amherst Control Products: Income Statement

	1980	1981	1982	1983	1984
Sales:	80,000	168,000	380,000	650,000	730,000
C.O.S.:					
Director Labor	24,000	48,600	106,200	189,800	203,200
Material	26,000	52,000	118,600	198,300	219,100
Total C.O.S.	50,000	100,600	224,800	388,100	422,300
Gross Profit:	30,000	67,400	155,200	261,900	307,700
Expenses:					
Rent	6,000	6,600	7,200	48,000	50,200
Utilities	2,000	2,800	3,400	19,400	21,500
Selling Expenses	1,500	3,500	8,000	17,000	22,000
Indirect Labor	0	24,000	81,000	127,000	141,000
Owner's Salary	0	20,000	30,000	45,000	45,000
Prof. Serv.	500	1,000	1,400	3,400	3,900
Legal	200	200	500	2,500	4,000
Misc.	150	350	1,100	3,900	3,700
Interest	0	0	0	0	34,900
Total Expenses	10,350	58,450	132,600	266,200	326,200
Profit Before Taxes	19,650	8,950	22,600	(4,300)	(18,500)

Know Where You Want to Go

An element which must be considered in every pricing strategy is management's (i.e., owners/investors in a small company) objectives. How is the effectiveness of the pricing strategy going to be measured? While net profit is the most obvious answer, this is not necessarily the main objective in many cases, especially in early business formation years.

Among the possible objectives are:

1. R.O.I. (Return on Investment):
   A. On actual cash invested
   B. On total value or cash invested plus debt

2. Market Share
3. Gross Sales Volume
4. Cash Flow
5. Profit Margins
6. Net Profit:
   A. Before taxes
   B. After taxes

Return on Investment

For most small investors, R.O.I. is an all-important factor. Typically, an investor will expect a level of return on an investment over a given period of time. In cases where money is invested in early R&D the expected R.O.I. is zero for one, two, or even five to ten years. Pricing in the early stages is not as critical as developing a marketable product that will be profitable in future years. For owner/investors putting money into an existing company with established products, a return on investment is often expected immediately. Depending on the owner/investor, they will measure R.O.I. based on the actual cash invested or on cash invested plus money borrowed. Generally, investors are swinging towards the latter method. For either R.O.I. method, a time frame must be specified. In a smaller company this may be measured in years, versus the large corporate mentality of "Quarterly Profit Reports."

Market Share

In marketing new products, many companies set a pricing strategy which will allow them to grab the largest market share fastest. This is particularly true where companies market complimentary products, have follow-on sales, and/or hope to gain customer brand loyalty. For existing products, market share can be equally important. Consider the ongoing battle for market share in the auto, beverage, and cigarette industries among the corporate giants. In these cases, market share is closely related to profitability as cost structures are similar. Trends up or down are also good indicators of future profitability. For smaller companies the relationship between market share and profits must be quantifiable with specific, set objectives. It's no good to gain 90 percent of the market and never turn a dime of profit. In addition, the impact on cash flow must be analyzed. Cash resources must be available if reaching the objective requires going into a period of negative cash flow.

Gross Sales Volume

Management, in some companies, chooses to measure the effectiveness of its pricing strategy by the gross sales volume. This is especially true where fixed costs are exceptionally high and additional volume requires little or no investment of capital. In this case, additional sales made at a level above the cost of materials and direct labor increase profit. Smaller companies whose management desires to "grow" the company and then sell out or go public often will consider gross sales volume as a very important factor in the pricing decision. To be successful, most companies that issue public stock need a gross sales volume of $5 – 10 million annually as a bare minimum. In smaller companies where management is planning to remain private or closely held, profits are generally more important.

Cash Flow

Every smaller company without a "sugar daddy" or group of venture capitalists behind it knows the importance of cash flow. While large corporations can often rely on retained earnings, eliminated dividends, stretched accounts payables, or a new stock issue, smaller companies often don't have these options available. Cash flow requirements and availability often dictate the selection of pricing strategies in smaller companies. While you may be able to garner a 40 percent market share by using a six-month penetration strategy, and thus a higher level of profit a year from now, if your cash flow isn't sufficient you may not be around in a year to enjoy them.

When faced with this possibility, smaller companies must recognize they have a number of choices. Among them are:

- Seek additional capital.
- Use penetration strategy for a shorter time period.
- Raise prices above what was originally intended.
- Evaluate cost structure and see if reductions are possible.

The primary management objective is to stay in business; profitability is a close second. Therefore, it is necessary to recognize the implications of any pricing decisions on cash flow.

Profit Margins

Profit margins are used by many companies as a benchmark to gauge the effectiveness of the pricing strategy, the ability to control costs, and to quantify competitive pressures. Steady profit margins allow companies to reinvest profits into market development and expansion. Declining profit margins indicate the need for cost control or pricing adjustments, as well as continual evaluation of participation in a market. Generally, profit margins are a secondary level of evaluating the pricing strategy. However, in smaller companies that specialize in low volumes in a number of areas, profit margins are more critical. Consider a company that makes specialized laboratory test equipment. If the market for the product is very small, the profit margin must be very high to warrant the investment.

Net Profit

Net profit can mean a lot of things and be measured in a number of ways. In a smaller business it's probably more important to measure the impact of net profit after taxes on management. Are there tax consequences that make it more advantageous to invest in capital equipment this year than next? Is there a loss carry forward that is needed to offset taxes in another area? These are just two of many questions that may come into play and impact pricing.

In general, management is more concerned with profitability and how it fits into their long-term objectives, than with a specific net profit figure. Is management looking to milk the business or grow the business? Is management interested in acquiring new businesses or disposing of "assets"? Is a public stock offering planned? By defining management's objectives for the company over the next six months to ten years, it is possible to develop a corresponding pricing strategy. It's important not to get caught penetrating a new market when management is looking at profits so the company can be sold next month.

Understanding the Cost Structure

Understanding, monitoring, controlling, and allocating costs in a smaller business can be the single largest determinant in making a profit. The reason is simple: it's the one area where guesswork can be virtually eliminated. While market factors such as demand and competition are beyond direct control and must be estimated, costs are not. This is not to say you can control costs for every component you buy. What you can do is establish a system to identify cost changes, or potential changes, and be prepared to make pricing adjustments accordingly. In this way you can "control" costs and pricing.[1]

Understanding the cost structure initially involves classifying cost components. Table 2 breaks down the types of costs found in a manufacturing operation and their relationship to activity levels.

On a day-to-day operating basis, raw materials and direct labor are generally the largest cost components as well as the most difficult to monitor and control. Other direct components are easier to identify and/or change slowly over time. Indirect and general costs pose another problem. They are often overlooked or ignored when costing a product.

Monitoring and Controlling Direct Costs

On the surface, one would think it easy to take a bill of materials, cost each component, extend the totals, and *presto*—have a mater-

Table 2 Cost Classifications

Classified Acording to Variation w/Activity Rate	Cost Components	Attributable
Costs vary linearly with activity rate	Raw Materials Utilities shipping Royalties Sales Commissions	Direct
Costs vary with activity, but not zero at zero activity	Operating Labor Direct Supv. Maintenance Plant Supplies	Direct
Costs do not vary with activity level	Rent Insurance Taxes Depreciation	Direct, but independent of activity level
	Payroll General Plant Overhead Storage Facilities Medical and Safety	Indirectly traceable or attributable to a product or segment
	G&A Sales Administration Market Research R&D	Common or general

Source: Adapted from Donald R. Woods, *Financial Decision Making in the Process Industry* (Englewood Cliffs, NJ: Prentice-Hall, 1975), pg. 212.

ial cost for the product. Those who have gone through this process know it's not this simple. Many variables in addition to unit costs affect material costs beyond the process described above:

- Minimum lot sizes
- Minimum delivery sizes
- Set-up fees
- Tooling fees
- Engineering fees
- Transportation expenses

These costs should be realistically allocated to the unit cost of the product before it is priced.

> You have a new product you plan to build 1,000 units of over one year. The lot size you expect to manufacture is 100 units. The sheet metal chassis the product is assembled in costs $23.00 unit/1,000 pieces. However, in 100-unit releases, the cost is $28.00/unit. There is a one-time tooling fee of $2,000. The company decides to conserve cash and purchase in 100-unit lots. The cost should be recorded as $30.00/unit when priced. This is true even if 1,000 units are purchased because this is the actual expense.

Unit price	$28.00/unit
Tooling fee amortized over 1,000 units	$ 2.00/unit
	$30.00/unit

Conversely, if the same component is purchased for multiple products, the costing should reflect the actual quantity pricing you receive.

> You have a new product which will use 10,000 pieces per year of a Texas Instruments chip. Several other existing products use this same chip and you have a blanket order in place at the 50,000 piece price of $1.08/unit, versus $1.42/unit for 10,000 pieces. Your cost should be $1.08/unit.

The concept is straightforward but implementation can be somewhat more difficult. To simplify costing and ordering, many companies group components into categories such as A,B,C, and so on. An "A" item would be a low-cost, short lead time, blanket order item used in multiple products and purchased on a minimum/maximum buy basis. A "D" item would be a high cost, long lead time item used on unique products and purchased based on orders received.

There are several benefits to classifying components using this or a similar system. When costing a bill of materials, "A" items are immediately purchased on volume blanket orders. "D" items should be costed based on the actual quantity required. In addition, the cost of "D" items may be monitored on every order received or lot produced and reflected in the pricing.

> Power Electronics manufactures power supplies for a major video game manufacturer. Typically, orders are for 1000 units delivered in weekly shipments of 100 units. Lead time is 8-10 weeks. The selling price is $70.00/unit. The bill of materials contains two "D" items, the transformer and the printed circuit board. A major cost of the transformer is copper wire, the price of which fluctuates weekly. In July, the price of copper wire is $72.00/100 lbs. and accounts for $3.80 per transformer in copper wire cost. Based on present costs, Power Electronics accepts an order for 1000 units with deliveries scheduled to start in mid-September. By early September the cost of copper wire is up to $168.00/lb., or $8.87 per transformer. This cost increase of $5.07 per unit effectively eliminates the company's profit on a $70,000 sale.

What could Power Electronics have done? One option would have been to add in a certain amount of "slush" to cover unexpected cost increases. In a competitive marketplace this "slush" might have increased the cost of the product to the point the company might have lost the sale. Another alternative might have been to add in a provision in the quote for such a material increase. This is not uncommon when quoting items with raw material or component costs that are subject to rapid change. In addition, companies with exceptionally long lead time products or with multiple year contracts peg automatic price increases to changes in the Consumer Price Index (CPI). A third option is available, although more difficult for customers to accept. Power Electronics could have gone to the customer, explained the circumstances, and asked for a fair price increase. This option should not be ignored, especially if the cost increase was unexpected and well documented in the industry. A final option is to simply notify the customer that the product cannot be delivered at the quoted price. If the order is large enough to jeopardize the health of your entire organization, this may be a last resort alternative.

Monitoring Purchasing

Beyond establishing costs for individual products, smaller companies should continually monitor their overall purchases. Most companies can recite a basic material cost for their products, say 32 percent. A way to verify this is to compare purchases over time with shipments. To simplify things, a purchase order log should be kept listing each purchase order, date, vendor, part, quantity, and value. Periodically (every quarter seems to work well without too much disruption), total the dollar value of purchase orders issued and compare this with actual shipments over the same period. The ratio should be similar to the expected parts cost. If it's substantially higher and you haven't placed a higher than average number of blanket orders in this period, check the inventory level. Has it grown by the difference? If not, you may be paying more (or less) than you think for materials.

Determining and Allocating Real Expense

Calculating the direct labor content of a product involves: (1) knowing the cost of your direct labor, (2) inclusion of each operation in the cost estimate, and (3) an accurate estimate of time required per unit/operation. Virtually every company begins the process of determining direct labor cost by taking the base hourly rate and adding in taxes, insurance, benefits, and so on. Once this is done, there are many alternatives to choose from. Should QC be included as direct labor? How about group leaders and line supervisors? What about the shipping clerk? There is but one firm answer to these questions: make sure they are included somewhere on a consistent basis!

The best possible advice is to use common sense. If you manufacture products where it is easy to attribute quality control personnel to a particular job or product, it may make sense to consider them direct labor. On the other hand, if they're involved with multiple products and it's difficult to identify the time spent on each one, they should probably be considered indirect and reflected in overhead expense.

The inclusion of each operation in your cost estimate appears on the surface to be a simple concept. In fact it is, but it is also one that eludes virtually everyone. First, it's natural for people to group multiple operations into one and forget some of the tasks involved. Second, whoever does the costing estimate (engineering versus purchasing versus sales/marketing), may not know all the operations.

Power Electronics decided to break down direct labor costing by department. Their list was as shown:

Labor Estimate
Model _____ Kit Quantity _____ Date _____

Department	Amount Time per Unit	Labor Cost/Hr	Cost/Assy
1. Kit Prep	___	___	___
2. Board Loading	___	___	___
3. Touch-up	___	___	___
4. Sheet Metal	___	___	___
5. Magnetics	___	___	___
6. Final Assembly	___	___	___
7. Test	___	___	___
8. Burn-In	___	___	___
Total	___	___	___

When the estimates were compared to actual results, they were off by 50 percent. And yet, everyone swore they spent only so much time per operation. Further analysis indicated certain operations were left off the list. A new, more inclusive list was generated, as follows:

Labor Estimate
Model _____ Kit Quantity _____ Date _____

Department	Amount Time per Unit	Labor Cost/Hr	Cost/Assy
1. Kit Prep			
A. Component Forming	_____	_____	_____
B. PCB Masking	_____	_____	_____
C. Lead Termination	_____	_____	_____
2. Board Load			
A. Line Set-up	_____	_____	_____
B. Loading	_____	_____	_____
C. Wave Solder	_____	_____	_____
D. Wash	_____	_____	_____
3. Touch-up			
A. Transformer Insertion	_____	_____	_____
B. Solder Touch-up	_____	_____	_____
4. Sheet Metal	_____	_____	_____
A. Shear	_____	_____	_____
B. Mill	_____	_____	_____
C. Tap	_____	_____	_____
D. Chromate	_____	_____	_____
5. Magnetics			
A. Main Power Transformer	_____	_____	_____
B. AC Power Transformer	_____	_____	_____
C. Torroids	_____	_____	_____
D. Chokes	_____	_____	_____
E. Inductors	_____	_____	_____
6. Final Assembly			
A. Heat Sink Assembly	_____	_____	_____
B. Final Board Assembly	_____	_____	_____
C. Enclosure Assembly	_____	_____	_____
7. Test	_____	_____	_____
8. Burn-In	_____	_____	_____

Six months later, direct labor estimates were within 10 percent.

Accurately estimating time required is certainly helped by detailing each operation. In most smaller companies there is no time/production engineer to evaluate the validity of the time allocated to each operation. This task typically falls to the design engineer, manufacturing manager, or an over-eager marketing person. A trap that often ensnares us is reasoning thus: "We can sell it for this, we should be able to build it in ...." When one thinks about this objectively, one can appreciate its non-sensical humor. To overcome this, several steps may be taken. First, where possible, take each operation and compare the labor content to a similar operation. Second, explain the operation to a line manager or supervisor who has hands-on experience. Ask them for their estimate and what could be done to improve it. Third, conduct a pilot run. It may point out some over-or under-estimates in certain operations.

For the best results, monitoring direct labor hours per unit/job should occur on a regular basis within each department. To make this easy for the busy line supervisor, a simple form should be included with the traveller for each job or distributed each week on the production line. It should list the operation, date, and estimated hours required, and should have room for actual hours spent. As in the case with verifying overall material cost, direct labor assumptions can also be checked over a period of time. By comparing quarterly direct labor payroll to shipments, management can gauge the actual versus estimated performance.[2]

Cost Allocation Methods

In smaller companies the efficient use of both human and material resources is of the utmost importance. Both are in limited supply and need to be applied wisely in ways that maximize their value. One way to judge how effective a company is using its resources is to use a realistic cost allocation process. Cost allocation allows you to compare expense with results and gauge your effectiveness in resource utilization.

Out of the vast number of costing methods available, we will look at two: direct costing and full absorption method. Knowing the difference is important because it may point out that your profitability on an item or product line is different than you think. Direct costing involves taking actual costs incurred in manufacturing and allocating them to a product or product line. This is fairly easy with materials and direct labor, but less accurate with overhead and indirect cost allocation. Full absorption method is a common, and often desirable, approach to allocating overhead costs. Typically it takes the percentage of sales of a product or product line from the overall company sales and applies that percentage to the total overhead and indirect costs.[3]

In companies where the product maturity, engineering, sales effort, and manufacturing processes are similar across product lines, this is an accurate method of reflecting costs. However, in some companies that have considerable differences between product lines in these terms, the full absorption method may not be indicative of reality.

Gilbert Cellular Corp. manufactures two similar product lines, one consisting of standard "off-the-shelf" products and the other custom products. Each product line accounts for roughly 50 percent of sales. The custom product line has an average unit selling price of about 15 percent higher than the standard line. Material costs and direct labor are very similar to the standard line, making the custom line look very profitable. The company uses full absorption costing, and the profitability statement for the past year looks like this:

	Custom Product Line	Standard Product Line
Sales	$2,000,000	$2,000,000
Cost of Goods Sold:		
Materials	510,000	600,000
Direct Labor	170,000	200,000
Total CGS	680,000	800,000
Gross Profit	1,320,000	1,200,000
Expenses:		
Engineering Payroll	160,000	160,000
Sales/Marketing Payroll	180,000	180,000
Purchasing Payroll	75,000	75,000
Rent	190,000	190,000

(continued)

Utilities	55,000	55,000
Sales/Marketing Expenses	200,000	200,000
G&A	248,000	248,000
Interest	100,000	100,000
Total Expenses	1,208,000	1,208,000
Net Profit	$112,000	$(8,000)

Using the full absorption method, the custom product line appears to be quite profitable while the standard line looks like it's operating at a small loss. However, at the urging of the standard product sales manager, a closer study of costs revealed that 61 percent of all purchase orders placed were for custom products; that 62 percent of all engineering hours were spent on custom products; and that the marketing department estimated 65 percent of its time was spent on the custom product line.

The standard product sales manager took these data and prepared a new profitability statement for each product line based on "direct costing" as accurately as possible. The results were as follows:

	Custom Product Line	Standard Product Line
Sales	$2,000,000	$2,000,000
Cost of Goods Sold:		
Materials	510,000	600,000
Direct Labor	170,000	200,000
Total CGS	680,000	800,000
Gross Profit	1,320,000	1,200,000
Expenses:		
Engineering Payroll	198,000 (62%)	122,000 (38%)
Marketing/Sales Payroll	234,000 (65%)	126,000 (35%)
Purchasing Payroll	91,000 (61%)	59,000 (39%)
Rent	190,000	190,000
Utilities	55,000	55,000
Sales/Marketing Expense	200,000	200,000
G&A	248,000	248,000
Interest	100,000	100,000
Total Expenses	1,316,000	$100,000
Net Profit	$4,000	$100,000

A much different and more accurate picture of profitability appears. This new analysis points out that the resources applied on the custom product line are not generating the expected results. Either pricing needs to be adjusted higher or resources need to be reallocated.

This example points out the need to understand fully your costs. Quite often the costs considered "hidden" aren't really that difficult to gauge. Whether the yardstick for measurement is engineering hours spent or purchase orders issued, it's important for management in smaller companies to have a consistent and realistic method to determine indirect cost allocation and its impact on profitability.

Competition and Market Factors

In general, knowledge of the costs of manufacturing a product dictates a pricing "floor." The pricing strategy of your competition and overall demand for your product help establish a price "ceiling." In a smaller business it's often more profitable to look at niche markets. While business opportunities may be smaller, there is typically less competition and greater chance for above-average pricing, or a higher "ceiling." This section will briefly look at the role competition plays in developing pricing strategy.

Identify Your Competition

A key element in evaluating the pricing structure and strategy of the competition is knowing who they are. Narrow-mindedness commonly leads to mistakes about who or what the competition is. Sometimes it's not the company that makes a similar product, but a new technology that is the real competition. (Ask the slide rule manufacturers, if you can find any!) While most companies have some idea of the nature of the competition, more thorough research into competition can be particularly valuable to smaller companies.

Evaluate Your Competition

Once you've identified your competition, try to evaluate their cost structure. You can do this in several ways:

1. Look up their annual report, if available, and see what their overall material, direct labor, and overhead costs are. Are they similar to yours? If not, try to understand why.

2. Do your competitors perform any manufacturing operations off-shore? What is the cost impact?

3. How does the competition distribute its products? Do they sell direct, through distribution, or reps? What is their commission structure?

4. What is the size of their promotion budget? How do they spend their promotion budget?

5. What is their warranty period? What are their normal terms and conditions of sale?

By understanding your competition you can do a better job of out maneuvering them when it comes to pricing.

The Role of Market Research

The following section was contributed by Richard Nagele, President, Advantage Research Corporation, North Kingstown, Rhode Island.

Research can help determine what industrial or retail buyers are willing to pay for goods and services. It is a tool the smaller manufacturer can easily and successfully use in developing a successful pricing strategy. But many people are confused about research—it often seems more like "gazing at the crystal ball" than a sound business procedure. Not true.

In its simplest form, research is nothing more than an organized way of asking questions. While it can be extremely sophisticated (psychographics or life style research, computer simulation or forecasting), smaller budget research, asking basic questions, can still be done to reduce risk and increase the precision of pricing decisions.

A good starting point in the research process is the identification of all products that meet the same basic needs as the concept being tested. Gather price history and unit sales information on these products. If the product is new, look to the next best method or combination of products and services that come closest to solving the customer's problems. At the same time, estimate the cost to potential users for not solving the problem. This process will provide an initial range of values and prices for management consideration. Once the alternative products are identified, analyze the manufacturers of these products as well as other companies that are likely to "knock off" your product or innovate an alternative. Estimate their cost structure (as it relates to producing the product category being examined) and their pricing policies. Now management has insight into both the price range buyers may be willing to pay and an overview of likely competitive reaction, including pricing options used.

Conducting this research is basic. As the information is collected, organize it by product and by competitor. Maintain records over time to see how strategies/tactics change. Steps to follow at this stage include:

- library or computer data base research
- interviews with existing members of the channels of distribution
- interviews with suppliers—yours and the competitors'
- interviews with publishers/writers of trade magazines
- requests for competitor catalogs
- visits to appropriate trade shows
- debriefing sales people

One of the most important questions to address with research is price knowledge. The more people know about prices, generally speaking, the narrower the range of pricing options. A second key question is the degree to which people perceive differences between the product being tested and its competition. The greater the perceived differences, the more flexible the price. Also, it is important to consider the "Expanded Product." Test not only the value of the product itself, but the value associated with the product/service distribution system, packaging, advertising, and so on.

To measure price knowledge and product differentiation, more sophisticated research should be used. The best approach is generally to research users and potential users. A variety of methods exist for doing this including surveys, controlled experiments, and statistical methods.

Surveys. Well-designed mail, telephone or personal interview questionnaires can be used to identify past purchase activity, future purchase intentions and overall opinions. When asking questions, emphasis should be placed on understanding the perceived benefits, awareness of price, and amounts purchased. It is also possible to ask about amounts that would be purchased at different price points. This will provide insight into demand (units desired at different price points). Profitability analysis can then be done to assist in price setting (also, elasticity will be more clearly understood).

Many trade journals also conduct market surveys on a regular basis. Contact editorial offices of trade journals related to your product/market and ask what information they have available. Often this information is free.

With personal interviews, products can be shown (services described) along with examples of advertising and descriptions of warranties and channels of distribution. Respondents can be asked how much they would pay for the item. The greater the range, the more price flexibility and/or less price knowledge. Combine this information with the demographics of heavy users, the last price paid (or value of the problem), and likely competitive response, and solid insight into appropriate alternative prices will be evident.

Controlled Experiments. Doing tests with actual products can help fine-tune the pricing decision. These tests can be performed by setting up a lab experiment and having customers come to your facility. You may want to show new catalogs with alternative price sheets and evaluate buyer reactions. Another alternative is a field experiment such as a discussion of different prices at a trade show. Both approaches can be very beneficial in honing pricing decisions.

Statistical Methods. Statistical methods, normally conducted by specialized firms, offer the opportunity to model and test alternative prices. These include computer modeling of sales at different prices (electronic test markets) and econometric modeling (developing demand equations based on observed variables which might include price, geographic location, cost of alternatives, and so on).

The smaller manufacturer has many research alternatives to choose from. The best approach is to first identify what you want to learn from your research and then evaluate methods for obtaining this information. Often the methods are inexpensive and can quickly yield valuable insights that contribute to a profitable pricing strategy.

Richard Nagele
Nagele & Associates

The Macro Perspective

The overall pricing strategy of any business involves how the company defines its business. Typically, this is expressed in terms of the product it manufactures, the markets it serves, its channels of distribution, and its expressed quality level. The macro pricing strategy must fit in with this definition. Obviously, it would not make sense for Curtis Mathis, positioned as a high quality TV manufacturer and retailer, to sell product at a lower price than a comparable Zenith unit. Nor would it make sense for an IBM PC clone manufacturer to sell its product at a higher price than IBM.

In a smaller manufacturing company, determining the business definition is often a function of trial and error. Success with one product generally leads to focusing on that product or the market in which it is sold. In this way, companies naturally develop their product and market niche. The Table 3 indicates characteristics that may help decide what macro strategy is best

Table 3 Macro Pricing Strategies:
Pricing Level Relationship to Company
and Market Characteristics

Pricing Level	Typical Company Characteristics	Typical Market Characteristics
Premium Pricing	Superior quality, service, delivery	Absence of/or limited competition
	Unique product or technology	Absence of alternative products or technology
	Unique distribution	Scarcity of resources
	Market perceives high value in product or company name	Scarcity of capacity
		Well informed consumers willing to pay for perceived quality
Average Pricing	Acceptable quality, service, delivery	Substantial competiton
	Reasonable manufacturing cost	Alternative products available
	Established distribution system	Adequately informed consumers on price/value relationship
	Well-defined geographic market	
	Advertising and promotion expenses high	
	Differentiated product features	
Lower than Average Pricing	Acceptable quality, service delivery	Substantial competition
	Economic order quantity lowers total manufacturing cost below average	Alternative products available
	Uses existing distribution system	Consumer very cost sensitive or perceive no benefit in higher priced alternatives
	Markets complimentary products	
	Access to cheaper raw materials than competitors	
	Ability to lock out competition	

suited for your company. By matching company and market characteristics, you can determine the potential for a premium, average, or below average pricing strategy.[4]

Premium Pricing

For many smaller businesses, a premium pricing strategy is desirable. In high technology, for instance, smaller companies often offer a unique technology or product unavailable elsewhere. Companies are wise to seize the opportunity to make a higher than average return on investment. These profits can then be put back into the company to finance new product development, increase manufacturing capability, and so on.

CYPLEX is a small, high-tech firm that designs and manufactures sophisticated communication products used in factory and warehouse automation applications. One market that CYPLEX has identified as a good match with its technology is the Automated Guided Vehicle (AGV) market. AGV's are used to move materials between work areas in large factories. The CYPLEX communication system allows a host computer to have continuous two-way communication with each of the vehicles. This is accomplished by transmitting data over the vehicle guide wire buried in the factory floor, a process CYPLEX has patented.

The primary competition in this market has been radio communication systems. However, as the number of vehicles per installation has been increasing on average, the lower data transmission rate of radio systems is no longer acceptable in many instances. CYPLEX feels that additional competition is unlikely to enter the market due to the relatively small number of vehicles manufactured annually and technological obstacles.

CYPLEX is well positioned to take advantage of a premium pricing strategy. It has identified a small but potentially profitable market where the company has a unique technology that is in demand. In addition, the company can use the profits made in this market to penetrate other niche markets to which the same technology can be adapted.

Smaller companies have another advantage in that they are able to react quickly to market opportunities. New products can be developed and brought to market faster by small companies than by large companies. Initial pricing may remain high until competition enters. By this time, market share has been captured and the smaller company has an established reputation and customer base. The company may then drop prices and compete based on other features and benefits. As testimony to this, consider the hordes of software houses that sprung up to meet the needs of IBM and Apple PC users in the early 1980's. Neither IBM nor Apple could develop software fast enough to satisfy demand for the many applications for which personal computers were used. Initial pricing was very high and has since dropped dramatically for both software and hardware.

Average Pricing

Other smaller companies select an average pricing policy and compete primarily on the basis of differentiated features and associated benefits. This differentiation applies not only to a specific product, but to the company as well. This is especially true in smaller companies. A reputation for quality or on-time deliveries will carry beyond any one item. Understanding your cost structure is even more important here than with a premium pricing strategy. Profit margins are lower and there is less room for error.

Geography also plays a major role when it comes to average pricing in smaller companies. Many smaller companies limit the size of the market they participate in to a region where they feel they can maximize the use of their resources. These resources would include their salesforce, advertising budget, repair capability, ability to provide technical support and so on.

OK Relay is one of 1400 manufacturers of relays in the United States. Purchasers of relays are very price conscious and there is no room for a premium pricing strategy in the market. Two of OK Relay's prime competitors are divisions of very large corporations. However, OK Relay, with sales of less than $10 million, has been able to post a profit every year for the last 15 years.

The president of OK Relay feels there are three reasons for the company's success. First, an OK Relay is a quality relay. Second, the company has never tried to expand beyond the area it could serve well, New England. In fact, 90 percent of OK Relay customers are within a two-hour drive of the Massachusetts headquarters. Their modest advertising budget is spent on regional advertising which it has always yielded good results per dollar spent. OK Relay sales and service people can travel to any customer on a day's notice, providing excellent service. The third reason is low overhead. With all the various functions of the business under one roof, costs are easier to monitor and control.

The OK Relay example reinforces several points discussed earlier. The company has differentiated itself by being a quality provider of both goods and service. It has been successful in doing so by recognizing the limitations of its resources and applying them effectively. It didn't bite off more than it could chew. In addition, OK Relay kept overhead low and carefully controlled their costs. This low overhead cost has offset the cost of goods sold advantage enjoyed by competitors with higher volumes, thus enabling OK Relay to be profitable with an average pricing strategy.

Lower than Average Pricing

Smaller firms can use a lower than average pricing strategy for a short duration to penetrate a market. Trial use is encouraged and the company hopes to earn profits on future sales to repeat purchasers. The smaller company must ensure it has adequate resources available to cover expenses incurred during this time of exceptionally low profit margins. As a long term strategy, the smaller company must be especially careful. Absolute knowledge of all costs is essential. This strategy is successful only under certain conditions and the company must benefit more from this strategy than adopting a premium or average pricing strategy.

Kon-Tact is a seven-year-old manufacturer of spring loaded probes used for testing printed circuit boards. The world market for these probes is small—about $15 million annually. When Kon-Tact was founded the owner had identified a niche market for high-quality gold-plated probes that sold at premium prices. This strategy was adopted for three years and was moderately successful. Sales had risen to $750,000 annually, and a healthy profit was being made.

During this time, all operations were performed by hand and direct labor was approximately two minutes per probe. The president realized that to expand the business and remain profitable, a more cost-effective manufacturing process must be developed. Over the course of the next year, she worked on designing a microprocessor-based machine that combined four manual operations into one automatic operation. Her efforts were successful, and direct labor per probe was reduced to less than ten seconds. A new pricing strategy was developed after a careful analysis of the new cost structure and market conditions. The analysis revealed that the company could lower prices to ten percent below current market prices and maintain the same level of historic profitability. Any increase in market share would boost profits.

The strategy proved successful. Within two years the company had gained nearly fifty percent of the market and profits had increased by a factor of ten. In addition, several smaller manufacturers ceased production and no new competitors entered the market.

Lower than average pricing for a smaller company is a difficult alternative to manage effectively. With the rapid changes occurring in costs and technology, it is tough to stay on top of the fine line between profit and loss in a low-margin business. In addition, smaller companies are less likely to have the complimentary, and profitable, product lines larger companies often have to justify this strategy. Could Kodak justify marketing their low-cost line of cameras if they weren't also the world's largest seller of film?

Before selecting a macro pricing strategy, compare how management's objectives will be met by each of them. Then ask yourself: With the company's present cost structure, does the strategy make sense? Are the resources available to successfully support it? How will the competition react? Does the proposed pricing strategy complement the image the company is trying to project? Evaluate these questions on both the short and long term.

Conclusion

Developing a pricing strategy for a smaller manufacturing company is both a challenge and tremendous opportunity. Success is based on:

1. *Knowing where you want to go.* Identify what the company management really wants to achieve with its pricing strategy.

2. *Understanding your cost structure.* Know both indirect and direct costs and their relationship to sales activity.

3. *Allocating your costs realistically.* Make sure you are effectively using your human and material resources.

4. *Looking outside at competition and market changes.* Conduct market research and stay on top of what's going on outside of your company's walls.

5. *Selecting the macro strategy with the right "fit."* Your pricing strategy has to be appropriate for your overall business plan.

By consistently following these guidelines, the smaller manufacturer will be in a better position to develop and implement a successful pricing strategy.

Endnotes

[1] Washburn, Stewart A. 1985. "Pricing Basics: Establishing Strategy and Determining Costs in the Pricing Decision," *Business Marketing.* July.

[2] Klasnic, Jack. 1983. "Determining the Total Internal Costs of Running Your Business in a 'Nut' shell—and Accordingly," *American Printer*, April.

[3] Heesterman, A.R.G. 1971. *Allocation Models and their Use in Economic Planning.* (Dordrech-Reidel).

[4] Monroe, Kent B. 1979. *Pricing: Making Profitable Decisions*, (New York: McGraw-Hill).

Recommended for Additional Reading

Oxenfeldt, Alfred R. 1975. *Pricing Strategies,* (New York: AMACOM).

Sawyer, Malcolm C. 1983. *Business Pricing and Inflation.* (New York: St. Martin's Press).

Symonds, Curtis W. 1982. *Pricing for Profit*, (New York: AMACOM).

CHAPTER FOURTEEN

PRICING THE PERFORMING ARTS

OLIVER CHAMBERLAIN

OLIVER CHAMBERLAIN

Oliver Chamberlain is Executive Director of the Center for the Performing and Visual Arts at the University of Lowell, Massachusetts, where he manages a performing arts series in addition to overseeing all aspects of the Center. He holds graduate degrees in Arts Management from American University, in Music History from Brandeis University, and in Choral Conducting from the New England Conservatory of Music. In addition to teaching, conducting, performing and managing, he has also designed computer programs for break-even analysis and revenue projection as a consultant in arts marketing and management.

CHAPTER FOURTEEN

The purpose of this chapter is to discuss, from the perspective of an organization presenting the performing arts—music, theatre, and dance—various aspects of the pricing process. The first part of the chapter discusses the considerations of cost, demand and competition and their application to pricing the performing arts. The second part then gives data from a survey of arts presenters regarding the extent to which they used these considerations in their management practice. The third part discusses pricing management as an aspect of both financial and marketing management. It is not the intent of the author to show a "best strategy" or to give a particular technique for developing prices and revenue projections. Rather, the reader will see that pricing the performing arts product requires many different approaches, often based on the application of a range of pricing strategies for the particular local audience as might be most appropriate. In each instance, the decision maker must take whatever information has been gathered about the audience and determine which of the pricing strategies and tactics will best apply.

Problems in Pricing the Performing Arts

Arts organizations attempt to achieve the best possible performance with the least expenditure of financial resources. Typically, they meet total operating costs with some ratio of unearned income, obtained through grants and donations, and earned income, obtained through ticket sales and other services. Earned income, as derived from carefully set pricing policies and procedures, has become increasingly important to the survival of the arts organization. When the growth rate of unearned income is slower than that

317

of artistic, production, promotion and administrative costs, the increasing gap must be closed by raising ticket prices.[1]

Two pressures create problems in pricing the performing arts. The first is the perishable nature of all performing arts events. Seats must be sold either in advance of the event by subscription or within a very limited time span to single-ticket buyers. As performance time approaches, there is less likelihood of selling any large number of seats, especially if sales have not progressed steadily beforehand. Live performances with many empty seats cast a pall on both performer and audience, diminishing that characteristic and necessary interaction which is part of the excitement available to the performing arts patron.[2]

Each alternative solution to this problem has negative aspects. Seats remaining available in the last thirty minutes or so before the performance can be put on "rush" sale at a high discount (much as the airline industry does with "standby" ticket sales). This policy may prove self-defeating to the improvement of earned income, however, as over time more customers simply wait for the bargain rate. Therefore, the "rush" seating area or the sale of "rush" tickets might be limited, for example, to students only, if "rush" tickets are part of the audience development plan.

Another option is to "paper" the house in advance by giving away blocks of tickets. While this might appear to be a method of audience development if done selectively with different groups, experience shows that what is not paid for is often perceived as something of little value and therefore does not bring about consumer loyalty to the presenting organization.[3]

Still another route is the judicious use of complimentary tickets. Given in exchange for volunteer tasks of value performed for the organization, they represent a form of "payment" and are held to be of value. Given in order to attract certain patrons who might be influential in the development of the organization, they represent "perks" which, although the patron might easily pay for the ticket, make that person an insider in the work of the organization.

The second pressure on presenters is the expectation that the arts should be equally accessible to all potential patrons.[4] In the commercial marketplace, this expectation may be fulfilled at one time and place through the competition of different brands at different prices, or of different models of the same brand. For the presenting organization with a single performance at a given time and place, the implication is that the price range should be wide enough not to deny entrance to any potential audience member. This means that the presenter would have to make available some seats at below cost. Careful scaling of the house to meet this demand can fulfill the presenter's social responsibility. At the same time, however, some remaining seats must be priced well above cost to balance the total earned income for the performance.

Pricing Goals

At least three different pricing goals might be considered by an arts organization. These include (1) providing for the recovery of some percentage of the costs of production, including artist fees, (2) providing for some percentage of the costs of production and administration, including promotion, (3) providing for a surplus over costs in order to expand services or promote further audience development.

These pricing goals, of course, must be considered in relation to the overall goals and objectives of the organization. They also have to be balanced against other elements in the marketing mix. One of these elements is the position of the arts product in relation to its competition—whether it should be priced below, equal to, or above the competition. Another element is the attractiveness to patrons of the place where the product is delivered, that is, whether the auditorium or theatre is beautifully appointed, or is perceived as a social meeting place. Finally, the level of promotion which will be expended to communicate the event to its potential audience will have an influence on the pricing. To achieve these pricing goals requires careful consideration of the essential pricing procedures concerning cost, competition and demand.

Pricing Procedures

Pricing for the presenting organization consists of setting specific price levels and allocating a certain number of seats to each, a practice described as "scaling the house." (See Figure 1.) The price levels and house scaling may be changed within the bounds set by the general price goal selected and as the marketing environment changes over time. This means pricing (1) to achieve the break-even point between income and costs, (2) to meet the volume of demand for an event or series, (3) to recognize value as perceived by the organization's patrons, and (4) to maintain a position relative to what the competition is asking. Each of these points should be looked at in regard to the basic pricing considerations of cost, demand, and competition.[5]

Cost-Basis Pricing

Cost-basis pricing refers to setting ticket prices based primarily on the levels of fixed and variable costs connected with the production of an event. Fixed costs are those which continue if there were to be no performance. They include administrative costs such as office rent, utilities, phone, and annual salaries and benefits for staff. Variable costs would not be incurred if there were no performance. They include artist fees, production costs such as hall rental and costs of setting and running light or sound equipment for the performance, and promotional costs such as advertising.

A central part of cost-basis pricing is figuring the break-even point; that is, determining the percent of house seating capacity that must be sold to cover costs. Since the performing arts usually are labor-intensive (high in artistic costs in relation to the number of performances produced), a large number of tickets must often be sold to cover the costs of the performance. In some instances, ticket prices cannot be set high enough to completely cover costs, since demand for tickets would fall, resulting in insufficient revenue along with empty seats. In these cases, unearned income from grants and donations must be combined with earned income

Figure 1   Two-, Three, Four- and Multiple-Price Levels and Patterns of Scaling the House.

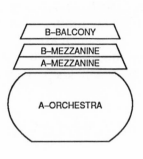

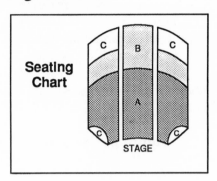

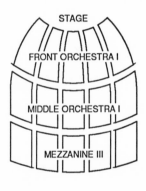

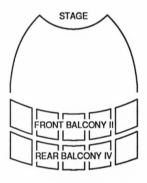

Location	Gourmet Pops 6 Fridays or 6 Saturdays	Judy Collins Special
Parterre Box	$140	$26
Orchestra	126	22
Side Orchestra	64	18
Loge (Rows AA–E)	126	23
Mezzanine I (F–M)	100	17
Mezzanine II (N–T)	74(60*)	15
Balcony I (A–F)	61	11
Balcony II (G–M)	48(40*)	8

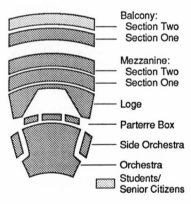

from ticket sales in calculating the break-even point. Figure 2 provides a model of this situation, which is the basis for figuring the break-even point for many arts organizations.

Figure 2 also illustrates the dilemma faced by the organization: while grants and donations may rise on an annual basis, both fixed and variable costs tend to rise faster. The increasing income gap that results places a strain on the organization's ability to increase ticket prices and sales at a rate that will keep pace with costs.[6]

Figure 2 Break Even with Expanding Income Gap

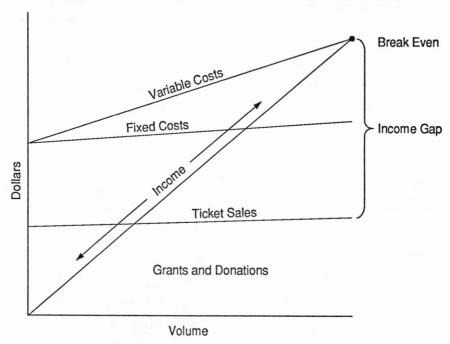

Some arts organizations run at a deficit, especially when artistic goals outstrip available resources. But they cannot continue this practice long and survive. A better approach is to contain costs at the level of available sources, thereby creating a balance between managerial and artistic interests. An alternative strategy would be to produce, through careful pricing and scaling of the hall, a surplus over costs, which would provide for the growth of artistic aspirations while meeting financial and audience needs. Ticket sales then would be projected at some desired percent above the break-even point.[7] In order to accomplish this objective, the organization must estimate the demand for tickets at each price level and adjust the number of seats at that price to meet demand.

Demand-Basis Pricing

Demand-basis pricing places primary consideration in setting prices and scaling the hall on an analysis of past and future demand for tickets to a particular arts product. If the product is a subscription series, then demand levels for both subscription- and single-tickets to each event need to be projected to cover costs.

Defining price range will be a matter of local concern, depending upon what prices are asked for area arts products and the demand level in response to those prices.[8] A possible exception to this projection would be in the case of presenting a very well-known artist, where demand may be such that response is inelastic over all price ranges, with little resistance to higher prices. Highest priced seats would then sell first and most, medium priced seats would sell next, and lowest priced seats would sell last. The trick to making this work is to estimate the amount of demand at each price point, then scale the hall in response to that demand, so that the audience fills in the seats from the front to the back of the hall without large gaps between price levels. Obviously, such scaling/pricing patterns cannot be changed at whim for each new performance or the audience will be confused as to the relative value of different seating locations. But in reviewing the past season before setting prices for the next, it is worthwhile to consider the patterns of demand for each price level as seen in the previous season's seating charts.

This observation still needs to be examined in four areas of consumer demand known as demand-differential pricing.[9] Here, one product—the performance—is sold at several prices that do not proportionately reflect a contribution to total costs. Each ticket buyer sees and hears the same performance, not a larger or smaller version of it, although each paid a different price for the ticket.

The first area of demand-differential pricing, known as "prestige pricing," is setting price on a customer basis. This strategy recognizes that different customers are willing to pay different prices for the product, especially to receive benefits usually associated with the upper range of prices. The strategy relates to scaling the house. The seats farthest from the stage or at extreme side locations will obviously command lower prices. Some arts organizations, however, do not capitalize on the desire of some patrons to pay a differential premium for what they perceive to be seats in a prime intersection of aural, visual, or social axis. If the spread between ticket price levels is $2.00, then seats at the front of the balcony (loge) or front of the floor (orchestra) may command a greater differential, perhaps $3.50, as illustrated by a price range and spread of $15.50, $12.00, and $10.00 Often, the higher the ticket prices, the greater the differential—as for example tickets to a Broadway show priced $45, $35, $30 and $25.

The second area of differential pricing has to do with the perceived value of one hall over another in terms of acoustics, decor, convenience, as a social gathering place, and in relation to other halls in the area. It is often possible to identify such a price leader in an area by reputation. Events in such a hall may command a greater differential over other performance space in the area presenting similar events.

Third, the presenter needs to be aware that setting a time of day, day of the week, or week within the season may promote or constrain the price range. An evening performance, because of its usually greater potential audience base, commands higher prices than matinees for the same performance. In many places, weekend performances are similarly higher priced than weekday presentations. Many organizations attempt to develop a sufficient audience through employing a variety of price levels on a time-differential basis. On the other hand, management of the Boston Symphony a few years ago decided that any performance of the orchestra was the same product and therefore should be priced the same, regardless of the day of the week. For a season, subscriptions sagged slightly, then returned to near sold-out status.

Finally, an arts organization may present the same work with a different director or featured performer, thereby substantially increasing or decreasing demand for seats on a product-version basis. Thus, perceived value plays an important, possibly central, role in pricing procedures for the performing arts. It is especially here that knowledge of the relative value of different performances, of the range of pricing procedures available and the make-up and preferences of the local market, are essential to the setting of arts prices.

Competition-Basis Pricing

Competition-basis pricing refers to setting prices principally in relation to the prices charged for surrounding area arts or entertainment events. Here the presenter chooses to maintain a price range as higher, equal to, or lower than the competition against whom market position may be measured. The greater the product differentiation among organizations, the greater, of course, may be the latitude in price range. If, however, the competition changes price, then the organization must consider adjusting its price to maintain its relative price position.

Some arts presenters may employ exclusively one of these approaches to pricing, most often, that of cost-basis pricing. Many others combine them in a variety of ways, weighing the components according to their knowledge of their own market. In addition, other factors may be weighed in the balance of decision making. These include the role of a board of advisors or directors (especially as regards a finance or marketing committee), other sources of information about the economic sense of the community (such as business and social contacts) and market research (such as audience surveys or box office reports). Still another factor, often valuable to the presenter, is information distributed through arts service organizations, such as the Association of Performing Arts Presenters, the Theatre Communications Group, the American

Symphony Orchestra League and others, which shows what is being done in the field across the country and identifies trends in marketing the arts.

Survey on Pricing the Arts

Twenty-six arts presenting organizations were surveyed in regard to pricing questions.[10] Respondent data are found in Table 1. Column one gives the level of expenditure for artist fees during a season. Column two represents the number of fixed seats in the principal hall used by the presenter. In some cases additional seats may be placed in the hall and other halls may be used. The principal hall seating, however, provides the clearest picture of the potential size of the audience. Column three reflects the number of events presented during the season. This includes, but is not limited to, one or more subscription series. Column four gives the total number of performances presented during the year. In the case where theatre and dance are presented, this often represents multiple performances of the same event. Finally, column five gives the high and low single-ticket prices for the year for the premier series. This does not include single events like special benefit performances that would have special price considerations. Series subscription discounts are dealt with as a reduction from the series single-ticket prices. Where no price is indicated, the series was offered to the public without charge.

The respondents are all nonprofit presenters of the performing arts. They may also be grouped as arts centers, colleges and universities, orchestras, arts councils and others. Arts centers responding included halls operated by an association or foundation, such as historic theatres. Colleges and universities range from two-year undergraduate through undergraduate and graduate institutions. The orchestras were all classified as metropolitan. "Other," as a category, included three organizations neither similar to each other nor to those in the other categories.

The survey asked a number of questions relative to the three pricing bases presented in the first part of this chapter—cost, demand, and competition. The responses to these questions and several additional considerations will be discussed next.

Table 1 Survey Respondents Ranked by Artist **Fee Level**

Fees	Seats	Events	Performances	Price	Range
$315,700	2,897	194	245	$18.50	$9.50
260,000	3,061	14	18	25.00	4.00
198,000	1,471	30	30	35.00	10.00
189,000	1,250	15	41	16.00	8.00
100,000	3,000	70	70	10.00	7.00
65,000	1,308	13	33	17.50	12.50
62,000	2,579	8	8	9.00	5.00
56,000	984	9	12	9.50	7.50
50,000	3,000	14	14	4.00	2.00
40,500	3,000	6	6	10.00	6.00
40,000	170	6	109	7.50	5.00
33,500	2,750	19	43	12.00	5.00
27,500	1,160	3	3	7.00	7.00
24,100	1,471	7	7	15.00	6.50
23,500	1,400	6	9	12.50	2.50
20,000	660	7	19	6.00	2.00
12,600	427	13	13	8.00	8.00
10,500	850	13	69	4.50	2.00
9,300	400	8	9	5.00	3.60
8,100	493	5	5	5.00	1.75
6,000	541	6	36	25.00	3.00
5,500	1,000	5	7	7.00	2.00
5,000	484	5	20	—	—
4,600	150	24	24	—	—
1,800	300	8	9	3.00	3.00
1,500	80	12	12	—	—

Cost Considerations

The issue is which costs to include in the break-even analysis as you do a revenue projection based on the number of seats, number of price levels, and number of performances in the season. Should only variable costs such as artist fees and production costs be included, or both variable costs and fixed administrative costs? This will depend on the sources of funds and the method of budgeting employed. Total costs, in whatever categories, will be divided by total potential revenue, in whatever categories, to figure the percent of capacity necessary to break even. For example:

Assume that your hall seats 1000, you will present 12 events, and the average ticket price is $11; your total potential revenue (1000 × 12 × $11) will be $132,000. If total variable costs = $100,000 and total revenue from ticket sales = $132,000 then break-even point is at 75.8% of hall capacity, or, you have to sell 758 series seats to achieve break-even.

Of the survey respondents, 65 percent figure at what point they will break even. Of these, 19 percent consider break even on artistic fees for each event, and a similar percentage consider break even on artistic fees for the series. The survey showed that 23 percent include fixed costs in the break-even analysis, and 46 percent include subsidies, grants, and other income in break-even analysis. The model of Figure 1, showing break-even points including grants and donations, was the approach most often taken.

The flip side of cost considerations is revenue production. Several basic aspects of how a season's revenue will be produced can be seen in Table 1. The number of seats available for a performance is the least variable aspect of revenue production. The number of performances is somewhat more variable, and the price range is even more variable.

Although care should be taken in making price increases, this avenue of support ought to be considered first in building a financial base, rather than looking only to more grants and donations. An alternative to increasing prices, however, may lie in finding other ways to present an artist. Booking several performances can offer a reduction in cost per performance while increasing the number of performances available for sale and thus increasing revenue. These additional performances need not be in the principal hall. They could be sold by the presenter to area schools, clubs, or associations for special programs that might also promote the main performance in the hall. Such performances also could be in the form of master classes or workshops to colleges or universities. These are only several of many possible ways to produce revenue through additional services.

It is also interesting to compare, in Table 1, halls that have similar seating capacities with the relative number of performances offered and price levels. In a number of instances, either the level of performance activity or the level of prices or a combination of these shows a correlation to the level of artistic costs. While representing many different situations regarding the size of the potential market, the type of artist, the capacity of audience, and the total producing budget, these three variables—seats, performances, and price range—most clearly define the level of earned income that an organization can project. Manipulating these three variables provides several avenues of achieving pricing goals set by the organization.

Of the survey's respondents, 19 percent set as a goal the recovery of artistic costs. An additional 12 percent attempt to recover production costs. Only 12 percent indicated that they wanted to increase revenue, while even fewer, just 8 percent, said that they set a pricing goal of reaching a surplus over costs. A small number indicated that they wanted to increase audience attendance as part of their pricing goals. Audience development is, of course, one possible means of financial development. Rescaling the hall and changing the price structure are additional means, together with looking for other ways to present the artist. Asked whether they had met their pricing goals, 23 percent of the respondents indicated that they had met their goals, while 35 percent said that they had not. Others did not respond to this query.

Asked if they had set specific pricing and scaling strategies, respondents listed the following means for reaching their objectives (not presented in any rank order): (1) set group prices, (2) lower student series prices, (3) broaden publicity, (4) rescale house, (5) increase subscriptions, (6) adopt all reserved seating, (7) cooperate with local arts council to more closely target mailings, (8) become more aware of pricing techniques, and, (9) acquire technical assistance in developing marketing plans. While they are not exhaustive, these strategies indicate considerable thought devoted to finding ways to meet costs for the coming season.

Demand Considerations

Sixteen presenters, or 62 percent, responded positively to the survey question asking whether they considered the relative demand for the number of seats allocated to each price category in scaling the hall. The remaining 38 percent indicated this question did not apply, or did not respond. Of those responding, 50 percent said they reviewed box office reports or seating charts for similar events. Only 19 percent said they try to allocate the largest number of seats to the highest price level. In addition, 31 percent of the respondents said they used more than one scaling pattern during a year, especially for single events and benefits or for additional series.

Queried about whether they had determined price elasticity (that is, measured the responsiveness of demand for seats to a change in ticket prices), 22 presenters responded. Of these, 36 percent indicated that they had measured elasticity, while 59 percent said that they had not. Of those who responded positively, none indicated that they had determined the exact change in demand for seats in response to a particular level of price change. Given the widely variable nature of one artistic event over another, of differences such as performers and works to be performed, it is little wonder that presenters find difficulty in attempting to measure price elasticity. Perhaps this is an area in which knowledge of an audience, based on experience and guided by demand levels from previous seasons, will best project response to change.

Table 2 shows the spread between prices employed by respondents to the survey. It can be seen that on the high end of

Table 2 Price Spread and Discount Rate

| Single Ticket Spread | | | Series Discount | | |
High	Medium	Low	High	Medium	Low
$3.00	$3.00	$3.00	10%	10%	10%
3.00	2.00	2.00	36	30	29
3.50	—	4.50	12.5	10.4	10
1.00	1.00	.50	—	—	—
2.50	—	2.50	—	—	—
1.00	1.00	1.00	—	—	—
1.00	–	1.00	44	33	11
—	2.00	—	50	—	50
2.00	—	2.00	50	33	20
.50	.50	1.00	—	—	—
2.00	—	3.00	12	—	14
3.00	—	.25	25	—	—
2.00	—	2.00	25	—	—
—	—	—	25	—	14
1.50	—	1.00	—	—	—
1.00	—	.40	20	—	10
1.50	—	1.25	25	15	10
—	—	—	—	—	—

ticket prices, the spread ranges from $3.50 down to $.50. The average price spread is just over $2.00. In the median range of ticket prices, the spread is reduced by $.50 at the top, but the average price spread is just over $1.50. At the low end of ticket prices, the spread ranges from $4.50 down to $.25, and the average spread is $1.90.

Under "Single Ticket Spread" in Table 2, three dollar-values in the columns indicate that there were four or more price levels given by respondents. Two dollar-value indicates three price levels. Dashes indicate that there was only one price level of general admission seating or that no admission was charged; this response applies to 28 percent of respondents.

Discounts shown in Table 2 represent those offered from high, medium, and low ticket price ranges, defined in terms of the particular pricing scale of each presenter. Discounts offered by respondents range from 10-50 percent off single ticket prices. Discounts are offered for series subscribers in adult, student, senior citizen, and group categories. Series and single-ticket purchasers are also offered discounts as members of an arts association or as faculty or staff of a college or university. Additionally, some organizations offer group discounts for single sales of ten or more tickets at one time. Such group discounts generally range from 10-25 percent off single-ticket prices. While discounts offer an incentive for patrons to buy a series well in advance of the season, many now recognize that another strong incentive for early purchase is the ability to obtain a reserved seat in a specific desirable location in the hall, at the same time making a commitment in advance to certain social and artistic events during the year.

Table 2 shows that respondents to the survey used differential pricing in their single-ticket prices. Twenty-four percent of respondents employed a greater differential for the spread between higher priced seats. These presenters recognize that patrons will pay proportionately more for what they regard as the best seats, especially to events of perceived quality. Twelve percent of respondents employed a greater differential for the spread between lower priced seats. These presenters recognize that some patrons may be unable or unwilling to pay the amounts asked in the higher price levels, so they extend the price range lower in order to meet the needs of this segment of their audience. Another 24 percent of these presenters use the same spread between each price level. These presenters may recognize that all seats are relatively priced in terms of the distance from the stage and other factors such as sight lines and acoustics being equally good throughout the hall.

On a time-differential basis, 19 percent of presenters indicated that they charge less for matinees, while 8 percent charge less for weekday performances. Asked whether they charge differently for single events as opposed to series events, 27 percent said that they ask higher prices for single events, while 15 percent ask lower prices. When asked why they charge differently for single events, 23 percent said they had to cover their costs. Another 19 percent said that the demand for seats is greater for single events. Twelve percent felt there was a higher perceived value by the audience of the single events they offered, while only four percent said they charged differently because their competition did so.

A survey query asked what assumptions were made in projecting ticket revenue. Of 18 organizations, or 69 percent of respondents, no one indicated that all seats sell in equal proportion. It was assumed by 39 percent that the highest priced seats sell in the largest number; 11 percent assumed that medium priced seats sell the largest number; and four percent assumed that lowest priced seats sell the largest number. Of the respondents, 32 percent indicated that they estimate the demand separately for each price level. Thus, about one-third project ticket revenue closely for the coming season. None said that they use a computer in performing demand analysis or projecting ticket revenue.

It is indeed pleasant for both presenter and artist to have a sold-out hall for a performance. It is important to earned income, therefore, to be able to project the demand for seats at each price level. Too many seats at the highest price, if not sold, create a visible sea of emptiness. The objective in scaling the hall is to sell out seats progressively from higher to lower price levels. If seats remain at the lowest price, the lost income is not so great as if they were to remain in higher price categories.

Twelve presenters responded to a survey question asking whether high,- medium,- or low-priced seats sell out while seats in other categories remain available. Forty-six percent indicated that they had sold out one or more seat categories. Of these, 83 percent indicated that highest priced seats sold out, often before other price levels. Medium-priced seats sold out for 33 percent of those answering, including one respondent who only sold out this price level. One respondent sold out only the lowest priced seats. In this instance, it may be necessary to consider repricing and rescaling the hall. It may also be necessary to do some market research on audience preferences to determine why the demand takes this particular twist.

Competition Considerations

Survey respondents varied widely in estimations of their primary and secondary competition for the performing arts market.

Primary competition is defined here as those organizations with whom the respondents might directly compete for much of the same audience. Secondary competition includes those organizations with whom they compete for some of the same audience. For the presenter, these audience members may be difficult to identify in absolute numbers. Identification of an organization's primary and secondary competition, however, will help the presenting organization find its own place in the market. Respondents considered primary competition to come mainly from other arts groups. Single responses also indicated that some consider athletic events, television, and other events in general as competing for the patron's leisure time. Secondary competition continued to be considered as coming from other arts organizations, although the distance increased geographically from one group to the other.

Asked whether they consider competitor's prices when setting their own, 42 percent among 24 responses indicated that all of their competitors influence their own price setting, while about 14 percent indicated specific competitors against whom they measured their price range and share of the market. When queried about where their own prices stood in relation to those of their competitors, 22 percent of 22 respondents indicated that their own prices were higher than their competitors; 9 percent said their prices were the same; and 59 percent said they were lower. Of those whose prices where lower than their competition, 18 percent felt that their prices should be the same as the competition. Thus, the downward pressure on arts pricing was felt by a large percentage of respondents, although they also felt the need to change. Only one-third of respondents saw themselves as price leaders in their area.

Twenty-four organizations responded to a question asking if they did market research that affected ticket pricing. Of these, 33 percent indicated that they had done such market research. From this number, 21 percent had done the research by mail survey, eight percent by phone. One respondent did market research through the box office. The research had been done from three months to two years previously and overall did not seem to change other considerations about ticket pricing. This may indicate the importance arts organizations place on informal information gathering and sources other than market research in setting ticket prices.

Other Factors Surveyed

Asked to rank a number of considerations they felt most influenced the price they could charge for their premier series, presenters surveyed on the average gave the following order: (1) prestige performers, (2) hall location, (3) hall acoustics, (4) hall reputation, (5) seat sight lines, (6) social visibility, (7) convenient parking, (8) seat comfort, (9) convenient restaurant, and (10) receptions. Additional responses included moving into a new hall, an unusual location for performances, and patrons receiving special attention in selecting seat location. These show several considerations, besides the principal artistic performance, that presenters feel influence ticket prices. Patrons also respond to secondary offerings in the marketing package, such as the availability of restaurants and receptions, to complete a social event.

To a question on whether ticket prices have kept pace with their costs, only 15 percent of respondents said yes, but not every year. Another 15 percent said they regularly raise their prices, while 35 percent indicated that their prices did not keep pace and they have to raise more money. Only four percent said that they actually cut costs. Other ways of closing the income gap included finding concert guarantors and getting a bite of the city tax pie. In all, this remains a problematic area, one where few presenters feel they can regularly meet the challenge only through increased ticket prices.

Respondents gave the following levels of how they attempt to reach their audiences: (1) targeted mailing list, 81 percent, 92) targeted publicity releases, 77 percent, (3) targeted advertising, 73 percent, (4) targeted promotion, 65 percent, (5) special ticket price offers, 65 percent, (6) untargeted general audience appeals, 19 percent, and (7) selected additional ticket outlets, 15 percent. Thus, most presenters attempt to define their own audience rather closely and to reach it through carefully chosen channels.

Finally, these arts presenters were asked to evaluate whether they felt their pricing strategies for the past season had been successful. Fifteen percent said they were highly successful; 50 percent felt they were moderately successful; and 8 percent indicated that they were not successful. Nineteen percent felt that they were in need of change for the coming season. Respondents were also asked if they felt their scaling strategies for the past season had been successful. In answer, 23 percent felt they were highly successful; 31 percent said they were moderately successful; and four percent said they were not successful. Twelve percent indicated that they felt that a change in scaling the hall was necessary for the next season.

The preceding discussion is part of a larger management consideration—that is, the management of pricing research, decision making, and communication, which forms the focus of the next section.

Pricing Management

Pricing management focuses on the information necessary to set an appropriate price, the decisions required to build a ticket revenue projection into a budget, and the communication of the product package, including price and discount structure, to attract an audience. Pricing, therefore, is an essential element of both marketing management and financial management.[11]

All too often, pricing management is not given the same consideration as other aspects of arts management. It may be left to the administrator or marketing director alone, and a decision may wait until it is forced by the publication of a season brochure. The need for a systematic approach to pricing has been demonstrated in the survey discussed above; our purpose now is to integrate aspects of pricing theory that apply to the performing arts with organizational communications systems, so as to involve all constituents of an arts organization who might be concerned with the pricing decision and its various outcomes.

The pricing management model to be discussed consists of three phases—information systems, decision processes, and action procedures—each comprising a number of steps. The model will be presented from the point of view of the general manager of the arts organization, the person most likely to confront these problems.

Implementation of the model may be seen as cyclical and continuous. The timeframe during which pricing decisions must be made may be divided into segments (such as fall, spring, and summer). Depending upon the schedule of the performance season, the management of pricing information, decisions, and actions will usually require planning for a future season at the same time performances are being presented during the current season.

For example, those who present or perform during a fall through spring season, might view the model as follows. The administrator would gather pricing information that has influence on the coming season during the previous spring, make pricing decisions during summer, and take pricing actions during the fall. This kind of timeframe would allow for communications between management and all constituents in a timely manner. It would make needed pricing information available prior to marketing decisions that usually occur in succeeding portions of the year. It would also provide revenue projections for the budget as that is being prepared. The timeframe for the pricing system can, of course, be adjusted to meet the needs of whatever schedule controls board or management decisions. An illustration of this approach to pricing management can be seen in Figure 3.

The series of overlapping cycles in Figure 3 represents pricing management at the center of budget and marketing considerations. Since there is usually no person designated "Pricing Manager" in an arts organization, pricing consideration is often not planned in a systematic way, but rather neglected until it is too late to take well-considered action. On the contrary, planning the gathering of pricing information, making timely pricing decisions, and taking well-considered action can all be done systematically, as illustrated.

As will be seen in the following discussion, it will most often be the general manager's duty to assign pricing tasks, and to keep each phase of the pricing system, with its several steps, moving to its necessary conclusion—to provide pricing information in a timely manner for budgeting, fundraising, programming, and marketing. It should also be the general manager's aim to include, as

Figure 3 Pricing Management

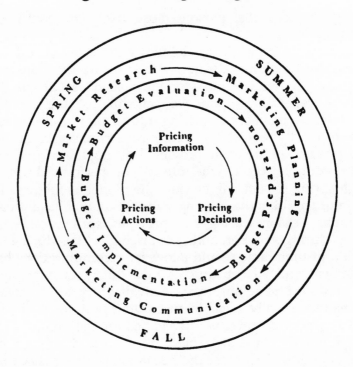

broadly as is feasible, most of the organization's constituents in the pricing decision: audience, artists (if a producing organization), board, management and staff.

Pricing Information

There are two kinds of approaches that can provide information about the audience to the management of a performing arts organization. The first is systematized research about the various publics served by the organization and their interests or concerns. This can be accomplished by direct mail, by a questionnaire in the program book, by a card filled out by ticket buyers at the box office, by organization volunteers or staff developing, administering, and analyzing a probability survey or telephone interview of a judgment survey, just to mention a few research techniques. The second is the informal approach, often utilized by arts managers, of taking note of comments by audience members during intermission, luncheons, or extended discussions.

These two approaches to information gathering provide many possibilities for determining audience interests and concerns regarding price, payment method, seating locations, box office hours, and programming preferences, among others. At the same time, management must communicate with the audience. At close hand, there needs to be the clearest presentation possible of the price and discount structure, perhaps with graphic illustrations of the hall scaling pattern, current special price offers, to whom they apply, and information about how, when, and where tickets may be purchased. At the other end of that communication, management must let ticket sales personnel know all information necessary about special ticket offers, current program information, policies and procedures to best communicate with the public. As is true in restaurants, where the service person represents the whole establishment, box office personnel represent the arts organization, its attitudes and qualities, to the ticket-buying public the organization wants to attract.

Pricing Decisions

The board of directors should be afforded the opportunity to contribute to the pricing decision. Important questions for the board are whether the stated mission of the organization is being met as regards the range of ticket prices offered to the public and the revenue generated by ticket sales. After such overall direction is determined, then prices can be set with clear objectives, as illustrated in Table 3. As discussed earlier, basic financial objectives include attempting to cover part or all of artist fees, production, promotion and administrative costs. Beyond that, if demand for the product is strong, there may be reason to project a surplus over costs, which may be used to provide for the growth of the organization or an increase in services offered to the public.

The constituencies targeted by the board for the organization to serve at any given time should also be decided before pricing the product. Is the organization reaching all age, geographic, ethnic, economic and social segments of the market area that it has the ability to reach or that it wants to attract? The development of pricing, scaling, discount, and other strategies may help to build capacity audiences. Pricing, especially "prestige pricing" if the product has the strength to support it, may help build the product image and thereby attract patrons to support the organization with contributions.

Table 3—Pricing Objectives

Financial	*Audience*
Provide for growth	Enhance product image
Achieve break-even	Attract segments
Cover specified costs	Build capacity

Prior to setting prices it will be useful to review audience research accomplished over the previous year. Demand for seats on a single-ticket basis (that is, once subscription sales are done) will help to show which events have the strongest general public appeal, beyond those loyal to the organization. Seating preferences, as shown by relative numbers of seats sold on seating charts for each event, will indicate what the audience is willing to pay for those events. Market research, if a large enough sampling can be done, may also provide guidance to questions of price, seat location, discount and event preference.

Setting ticket prices should then take into account the factors of competition pricing and discounts, average cost per seat, average revenue per seat, subscription structure and discount, and the projected demand for seats at various price levels. Scaling the hall should consider seat location, sight lines, acoustics, target audience segments, demand for seats at different locations and the pricing objectives.

A revenue projection from ticket sales will then need to be done together with consideration of costs and other income so that, when the projection is completed, there will be a balanced budget or the possibility of a surplus over costs. The variables of price, discount, scaling, demand, and number of performances should all be considered during this phase of the decision process.

A quick estimate to project ticket revenue may be illustrated as follows. It is essential to base all such estimates on the actual number of seats at each price level available for sale. That is, all complimentary seats—those given to press and other guests—must be subtracted before beginning the calculation.

> <u>Potential Gross</u> (avg. price × no. seats for sale)
> × <u>Estimated Capacity</u> (percent of seats sold)
> = <u>Estimated Revenue</u>
> − <u>Estimated Discounts</u> (av. disc. × av. price × no. seats discounted)
> = <u>Projected Revenue</u>

For example:

$$
\begin{array}{rl}
\$15 \times 2500 = & \$37{,}500 \\
& \underline{\quad .65\quad} \\
& 24{,}375 \\
20\% \times \$15 \times 750 = & \underline{(2{,}250)} \\
& \$22{,}125
\end{array}
$$

Alternative projections can be helpful in determining which price/discount strategy will achieve the desired results. The above projection, however, doesn't accomplish the integration of projected ticket revenue and the other budget variables of income and expense. That projection, which will help in the consideration of all aspects of a balanced budget, is shown in Table 4. This outline of revenue projection and breakeven analysis requires that revenue at "Total Estimated Ticket Sales" equals the projected deficit at "Target for Ticket Sales" in order to achieve break even.[12]

In conclusion, the pricing process may take any of several directions, including recommendation by management for board decision, discussion between manager and board committee for presentation to the full board, or direction from the board to the manager as to the course policy should follow. In any instance, since the outcome will have a major impact on the budget bottom line, the board should be involved in a clearly structured manner early in the pricing process.

Table 4 Break Even Projection

Income
  Subsidies
  Grants
  Donations   Total Unearned Income

  Additional services
  Concessions
  Advertising   Total Earned Income   Total income

Expenses
  Salaries
  Utilities
  Supplies   Total Fixed Costs

  Artist fees
  Production
  Promotion   Total Variable Costs   *Total Expenses*
                                             (Target for Ticket Sales)

Revenue from Ticket Sales
  Estimated subscription sales
  Estimated group sales
  Estimated single ticket sales   Estimated Ticket Revenue

Deductions from Revenue
  (Estimated subscription discounts)
  (Estimated group sales discounts)
  (Estimated single ticket discounts)   *(Estimated Deductions)*
                                          Total Estimated Ticket Sales

Break Even: Total Est. Ticket Sales = Target for Ticket Sales

Pricing Actions

Pricing actions, that is, implementation of the pricing decisions, require communication with the public served by the organization, the full board of directors, the management and staff and, especially for an organization which produces its own product, the artists and artistic director.

For the public, several questions regarding pricing may need to be answered before the prices are actually announced in a sales brochure or newspaper advertisement. These include: whether the price will be lowered, remain the same or be raised; whether the hall pricing pattern (scaling) will be significantly different from the previous season; and whether the discount structure will be changed.

These issues may be signaled in a subscriber newsletter or in a general news release explaining the need for change, the objectives and the outcomes which might be expected. For some members of the public served, the issues surrounding pricing, scaling and discount structure appear complex. It is often a good idea to have copy for such a release reviewed not only by management but also by persons not on the inner circle of discussion, in order to have the advantage of their suggestions on the clarity of the intended communication.

For the board, a schedule should be set annually for discussion of pricing research and setting pricing objectives and strategies. Both the board and management may want to consider courses of action, alternatives, outcomes, problems, and the impact of pricing decisions on other organizational objectives. Such discussion should result in a written, measurable pricing objective in terms of revenue and/or number of audience for each program or project. This is a function in which the experience and expertise of board members can contribute to the success of the program.

Management will need to take part in planning the marketing campaign once pricing objectives and strategies have been set. Alternatively, marketing staff might well be involved in the pricing process and the proposal of objectives and strategies from the outset. Planning and coordination will be necessary for the assignment of tasks, due dates, and budgets. An area for staff discussion should be a consideration of what publicity can contribute to the price image of the organization.

Box office procedures and the format of financial reports concerning subscription and single-ticket sales may need review. Also, it should be determined whether the necessary information regarding audience patterns of desired price and seat location for various events can be summarized easily. Is the box office receiving in a timely manner the information it requires to inform the public about events or to explain prices or discounts? Can personnel suggest new ways to promote and sell subscriptions or single tickets?

Perhaps the most difficult step is to plan and implement the evaluation of the pricing process, as regards both the time when tasks need to be accomplished in the next cycle and an estimation of the success of the written statement of objectives. Whether this is done informally or as part of an annual report, it is important to incorporate this step into the actions taken on pricing.

Finally, management of a producing organization may need to initiate communication with the artists or artistic director about the value to be placed on the artistic product. Although an artistic director may be too close to the artistic product to render objective judgment on its public value, such judgment should be sought and discussed. Bringing the artists into the pricing process may increase the commitment to the necessary outcome—the accomplishment of the performance within budget. Is it the goal of the organization to present the best possible performance with the least expenditure of financial resources? If this has not been stated, it may be worthwhile to discuss such a goal. If the pricing structure, and therefore the projected revenue, seems reasonable, there may be more acceptance of the outcome, whatever that may be. It may be helpful to keep artists informed on progress of ticket sales and the income/expense equation. All pricing decisions, after all, begin and end with the artistic product.

Conclusion

Managing the pricing process will require some effort on behalf of the arts administrator who will schedule tasks. Each of the three phases in the pricing management process—gathering pricing information, making pricing decisions, and taking action to communicate those decisions—comprises several steps that must be assigned. The pricing management approach under discussion suggests that communication in the pricing decision process should involve all constituents for the longer term benefit of the organization. The timeframe which can be developed by the organization for implementation of this approach will provide information in a timely manner to other management systems, especially those concerned with budget, fundraising, programming, and marketing. As a central element in both the financial and marketing considerations of an arts organization, pricing deserves careful planning and discussion in preparing to offer the artistic product to the public.

Endnotes

[1] Analysis of the income gap has been given in William J. Baumol and William G. Bowen, *Performing Arts—The Economic Dilema*, part 2 (Cambridge, Massachusetts: M.I.T. Press, 1966), p. 161ff.

[2] See Christopher Lovelock and Phillip Hyde, "Pricing Policies for Arts Organizations: Issues and Inputs," in *Marketing the Arts*, ed. Michael P. Mokwa, William M. Dawson, and E. Arthur Prieve (New York: Praeger, 1980), pp. 241–242.

[3] Regarding the impact of "rush" tickets, see Lovelock and Hyde, p. 241–242; and Neil M. Ford and Bonnie J. Queram, *Pricing Strategy for the Performing Arts* (Madison, Wisconsin: Association of College, University and Community Arts Administrators, 1979), p. 3.

[4] Lovelock and Hyde, p. 242.

[5] Considering these bases for pricing, cf. Philip Kotler and Alan R. Andreasen, *Strategic Marketing for Nonprofit Organizations*, 3rd ed. (Englewood Cliffs, New Jersey: Prentice-Hall, 1987), pp. 462–466; J. Marc DeKorte, "Pricing the Product," in *Presenting the Performing Arts*, ed. Toni Fountain Sikes (Madison, Wisconsin: Association of College, University and Community Arts Administrators, 1984), pp. 1–3; and Ford and Queram, pp. 3, 6, 12–13.

[6] For break-even models, see Kotler and Andreasen, p. 464; and DeKorte, p. 3. On calculating the break-even point, see also Ford and Queram, pp. 13–16. On break even including variable and fixed costs with grants and donations, see Lovelock and Hyde, p. 250.

[7] On calculating break even with a return on investment, see Ford and Queram, p. 15.

[8] For price elasticity models, see DeKorte, p. 2; and Lovelock and Hyde, p. 248. For an estimated demand model, see Kotler and Andreasen, p. 463.

[9] On demand-differential pricing, see Philip Kotler, *Marketing for Nonprofit Organizations*, 2nd ed. (Englewood Cliffs, New Jersey: Prentice-Hall, 1982), p. 312. On "prestige pricing," see Ford and Queram, p. 13.

[10] Results of 1984–85 survey of members of ORACLE, an arts service organization of presenters, artists and managers in Ohio, published in Oliver Chamberlain, "Pricing Theory and Its Application for the Performing Arts," *The Journal of Arts Management and Law*, (Spring 1985), pp. 84–94.

[11] See Oliver Chamberlain, "Pricing Management for the Performing Arts, *The Journal of Arts Management and Law*, (Fall 1986), pp. 49–59.

[12] On a computerized approach to revenue projection and break-even analysis for an arts center or subscription series, see Oliver Chamberlain, "Achieving break-even (with a little help from your friendly computer)" *Case study no. 36.* (Madison Wisconsin: Association of College, University, and Community Arts Administrators), passim.

Recommended for Additional Reading

"Box Office Guidelines," and "Subscription Guidelines," (New York: Foundation for the Extension and Development of the American Professional Theatre, 1977).

Neil M. Ford and Bonnie J. Queram, *Pricing Strategy for the Performing Arts* (Madison, Wisconsin: Association of College, University and Community Arts Administrators, 1979).

Philip Kotler and Alan R. Andreasen, *Strategic Marketing for Nonprofit Organizations*, 3rd ed. (Englewood Cliffs, New Jersey: Prentice-Hall, 1987).

Joseph V. Melillo, *Market the Arts!* (New York: Foundation for the Extension and Development of the American Professional Theatre, 1983),

Arnold Mitchell, *The Professional Performing Arts: Attendance Patterns, Preferences and Motives*, 2 vols. (Madison, Wisconsin: Association of College, University, and Community Arts Administrators, 1984–85).

Michael P. Mokwa, William M. Dawson, and E. Arthur Prieve, eds., *Marketing the Arts*, (New York: Praeger, 1980).

Kent Nakamoto, Kathi Levin and Cate Elsten, *Marketing the Arts: A Selected & Annotated Bibliography* (Association of College, University and Community Arts Administrators, 1981).

Toni Fountain Sikes, *Presenting the Performing Arts*, (Madison, Wisconsin: Association of College, University and Community Arts Administrators, 1984).

PHARMACEUTICAL PRICING:

Strategies in a Regulated Industry

JANE T. OSTERHAUS

JANE T. OSTERHAUS

Jane T. Osterhaus is assistant director of Pharmacoeconomic Research with Glaxo Inc. Research Triangle Park, North Carolina. She received her B.S. in Pharmacy from the University of Iowa, her M.S. in Pharmacy Administration and her Ph.D. in Health Policy and Pharmacy Administration from the University of North Carolina at Chapel Hill. She is a member of the American Pharmaceutical Association, the American College of Clinical Pharmacy, the American Association of Pharmaceutical Scientists and the Iowa Pharmacists Association.

CHAPTER FIFTEEN

The purpose of this chapter is to discuss pricing strategies applicable to pharmaceuticals. As more players get involved in health care activities, decision making is being spread among more people, including the patient, payer, pharmacist and physician. At the same time, purchasing is becoming more concentrated. This creates a dilemma: What group or groups should a product manager consider when developing pricing strategy? The first section of the chapter will describe the environment in which drugs are sold. The second section reviews pricing strategies consistent with the economic structure of the pharmaceutical industry. The final section discusses new approaches to pricing strategies.

A Unique Environment

Pharmaceutical manufacturers are typically divided into "branded" manufacturers who concentrate on research and development (R and D) to introduce new chemical entities (NCEs) to the market; and "generic" manufacturers who concentrate on production, conduct little or no R and D, and basically produce drugs whose patents have expired. Like all producers of goods and services, both branded and generic manufacturers need to be aware of the environmental components that influence their business strategy.

The environment in which the branded and generic pharmaceutical manufacturers operate is comprised of many factions, including patients, governments, other manufacturers, wholesalers, retailers, and third party payers. Each group has a role in the distribution and utilization of prescription drugs; some groups have multiple roles. An example of a faction having multiple roles in the distribution and utilization is the federal government. The federal government, through its different agencies, acts as a purchaser, payer and overseer of drugs. The Food and Drug Administration (FDA) reviews and approves drugs for marketing in the United States. The U.S. Public Health Service and the Veterans Administration are major purchasers of drugs. Through Medicaid and Medicare, the government is also a major third party payer of prescription drugs.

The environment in which pharmaceuticals are developed and sold is highly regulated. The regulations affect the breadth and depth of the marketing mix of product, price, promotion and place. Before marketing in the United States, drugs must be approved by the FDA. Additionally, advertising must be reviewed and monitored to insure that full disclosure is included where appropriate and that all claims advertised are for approved indications. The placement of prescription drugs is also controlled. In most cases, prescription drugs must be prescribed by a physician and dispensed by a pharmacist. *The price of a prescription drug is the only one of the "Four P's" of the marketing mix not under direct government regulation.*

Awareness of environmental changes is a crucial component of sound pricing strategy. Ignoring the changes can have a negative impact on a business venture. The Detroit automakers missed the signs indicating a shift in demand from large cars to small, fuel efficient cars during the 1970's, and consumers turned to Japanese cars.

It is especially important to monitor the environment when it is changing rapidly. Health care expenses have mushroomed in the past 20 years and the steady growth of this sector has presented both problems and opportunities to various health care industries. There have been shifts in the mechanism of health care delivery and in the payment of health care goods and services. These shifts have forced hospitals and other managed care institutions to modify their standard operating procedures and to become more competitive. The health care industry, including pharmaceutical manufacturers, has also been shaken by these changes. While drugs are an important component of health care and have contributed to the advances of modern medicine, there is a general perception that drugs are too expensive. Support of this perception is found in a review of the Producer Price Indexes. The price indexes for prescription drugs have outpaced the general indexes in the 1980's.[1] On the other hand, the cost-effectiveness of several drugs has been demonstrated, indicating that relative to alternative forms of therapy, drugs may be the less expensive option in some cases.[2] Drugs also account for less than seven percent of national health care expenditures. Nevertheless, Congressional hearings on prescription drug prices and the discussion of prescription drug price controls have sent signals to the drug manufacturers about the consumer's increased sensitivity to prescription drug prices.

The drug industry cycles through periods of new drug dominance, when it is viewed as a specialty industry, and generic dominance, when it is viewed as a commodity industry. Currently, the industry has been attempting to emerge from a period of generic dominance. This interval has been characterized by declines in significant new drug introductions and patent expiration of existing products. During this stage, price pressures are great because new drugs are not available to replace older drugs whose patents have expired. Markets are more crowded, and share taking is a predominant strategy because unit growth is flat. As the generic era unfolded, not all managers made the transition to promoting their product on the basis of economic criteria (e.g., price, service, reliability). Some ignored the change; others assumed the change was not an important shift.[3] Even as the industry shifts from the commodity to the specialty sequence, the environment has become more cost-conscious. Price will still be a concern, even for unique, new chemical entities.

Environmental changes can affect the way any product is evaluated and the way purchase decisions are made. As gasoline prices increased, people began to include fuel efficiency as a parameter by which cars were evaluated. Similar changes helped to alter the basis on which health professionals evaluate a drug for use. As drug prices continued to increase, pharmacy and therapeutic committees in hospitals, in HMOs, and in some communities reacted by becoming more aggressive in promoting the efficient use of drugs in their settings. Drugs now have to be safe, effective and economical. One approach involves minimizing the number of chemical analogues ("me-toos") on a formulary by considering both cost and efficacy when making drug therapy decisions.

As formularies and other attempts to control drug therapy costs continue to proliferate, the importance of price relative to product value becomes obvious. The more value a drug adds to the market, the greater its price flexibility. New products offering only marginal advantages may be rejected by the market. Key Pharmaceutical's reformulation of theophylline (Theo-Dur®) is an example of a modification the market judged as adding value. Hoffman LaRoche's reformulation of diazepam (Val-Release®) is an example of a modification the market determined was of limited value. Product line extensions, such as prefilled syringes, patches and other unique dosage forms have also been well accepted in certain therapeutic categories. Product managers who fail to consider the price value relationship when developing their market niche will lose price flexibility.[4] The relationship needs to be considered in terms of the target(s) being addressed: the patient, purchaser, pharmacist and/or the physician. A sustained release version of a product that allows the patient to take a drug once a day instead of three or four times a day may seem like a boon to the patient, pharmacist and the physician because it is more convenient and may increase compliance, resulting in a healthier patient. But the purchaser may disagree if the daily cost of the drug is more than the daily cost of the original drug the patient had to take four times a day. The product manager who considers the perspectives of different players will have a better idea of how those players might respond to a product's price. If third party payers are expected to view a product as a budget buster, it would be sensible to consider a strategy to counteract that criticism, perhaps in the form of cost-effectiveness studies.

Drug product selection legislation, pressure on health care prices, increasing costs of new product development and decreasing numbers of significant research breakthroughs have placed pressure on pharmaceutical manufacturers' prices and pricing strategies. A cost-conscious coalition of health care consumers and government regulations have altered the stability of the pharmaceutical industry's environment. The changing environment should signal drug manufacturers to re-evaluate their pricing strategies. The changing environment requires that the "consumer" be redefined. Pharmacists, nurses,patients, third-party payers (including corporate purchasers) and physicians are the new consumers and are all players in the game. When developing a pricing strategy, all of these consumers should be considered. Pricing strategies have to be developed with some recognition of the cost-containment environment, of the increasing concentration of purchasing power for prescription drugs, and of the company's long-term plans to be responsive to their shareholders by generating an acceptable return on investment.

Pricing the Product

The transformation of theories into applicable techniques occurs via pricing policies and strategies adopted by the firm. Price, therefore, is the expansion of strategic policy. Pricing policy should define the image a firm wants to project. The company should develop a strategy or multiple strategies to achieve its marketing objectives in the target market. Developing strategy involves defining the initial price range and planned price movement through time. Cost, demand, and competition should be considered in pricing. Many firms, however, tend to focus more heavily on one element than others. Costs (of raw materials, research and development, product liability, and so on) may or may not be consequential to establishing price. Pricing decisions are sometimes based on their expected impact on the firm's market position and/or on the manager making the decision. Pricing may be based on the firm's financial position if the corporation needs sufficient internal funds to achieve long-term investment goals (i.e., firms with high fixed costs, such as airlines; or research-intensive firms, such as pharmaceutical manufacturers).[5]

Pricing strategies are important to all firms but are most applicable and of greatest interest to firms operating under conditions allowing the establishment and adjustment of prices independent of outside influence. Firms selling commodities do not need to spend a lot of time developing pricing strategies because the market sets the price. Successful firms which have differentiable products and/or services, however, should devote as much time to pricing strategy as to other marketing components.

Manufacturers of branded products are more likely than manufacturers of generic products to develop definitive pricing strategies because they have more factors on which to differentiate their products. The fact that the products have a brand name allows them to be differentiated. Branded manufacturers are also more likely to rely on forms of competition other than price, such as extended dating, new formulations, new credit or discount terms and professional services such as drug information centers or consumer hot-lines. Generic manufacturers have no major differentiating factors between them and therefore must compete on the basis of price. "Branded generics," multi-source drugs produced by research and development oriented companies, differentiated by a family brand (e.g., Lederle, Parke-Davis), are lower in price than the original branded product but, are more expensive than most of the "pure" generics. Branded generics present an image of a less expensive but high-quality product.

The major competition a drug faces lies in the therapeutic category in which it is grouped. Within a therapeutic category, there may be three segments of intra-group competition: brands, generics, and branded generics, based on price and other factors. Within the category there may be little or no inter-group competition. Food products such as ice cream or peanut butter can be differentiated in the same manner. Jif® and Skippy® are branded competitors, A&P,® Harris Teeter,® and Spartan® are house brands. There are also generic versions. Price bands are a useful way of viewing the groups within a therapeutic category. Price bands are created by plotting the unit price of a product against unit or prescription volume. Generic product prices are grouped together and are usually significantly different from the branded products' prices (see Figure 1). Price bands exist because of the imperfections in supply and demand. On the demand side, imperfections include brand loyalty, purchasing power, and lack of price

Figure 1

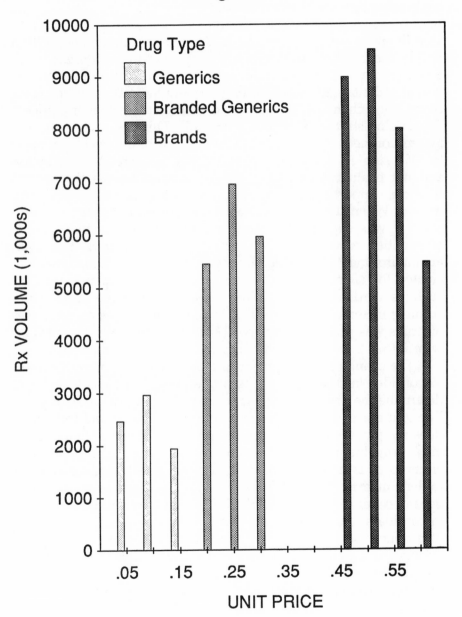

visibility. On the supply side, these imperfections include differences among competitors and in competitive intensity (size of firm, market mix composition, and so on). Pricing strategy may aim to shift the price band, to alter the firm's relative competitive position within the band, or to position the product in a different band. This may involve changing the product through reformulation, expanding the target market through a new indication, or changing distribution channels, in addition to or instead of, changing price.[6]

Pricing strategy should not be static. This is especially true in an environment changing as rapidly as that of the health care sector. If a single pricing strategy is adopted at a product's inception and not evaluated or altered as the product travels through its lifecycle, opportunities to meet marketing objectives may be missed. When drug product selection laws were passed in every state, it was expected by some industry observers that generic competition would derail the branded manufacturers. However, an environment favorable for drug product selection was not created for all products. Drugs with narrow therapeutic margins such as cardiac glycosides or anti-epileptics were rarely substituted; in some cases, substitution of specific drugs or categories of drugs was prohibited by law. *The perceived risk was not worth the price difference between the branded product and the generic product.*

The changing environment has created more potential targets to consider in developing a pricing strategy. The challenge is to determine the primary target market of the drug in terms of price. The ultimate consumer doesn't choose the product and frequently does not pay the entire cost of the product. The physician decides on a drug but that may be subject to change if the pharmacist elects to or is mandated to drug product select, if there is a formulary in existence that applies to the situation or if the payer doesn't cover the drug prescribed. Strategies need to be developed in consideration of the group that is the most influential in terms of product use and how that group is expected to react to price. Pricing strategies are separated into different categories based on the elements of cost, demand, and competition. The following pricing strategies may be considered by product managers of prescription drugs as they consider their different target markets.

Cost-Oriented Pricing

Cost-oriented pricing may include *percentage markups* and *target pricing*. A percentage markup is simply pricing the product at a certain percentage over costs. With target pricing, the price is established according to the firm's targeted rate of return. In the unlikely event that price does not influence unit volume and unit volume can be estimated, target pricing can help managers achieve the targeted return. But the manager is trying to consider the company's needs rather than market demand. Because prescription drugs are somewhat inelastic, price does not affect unit volume to a great degree in some markets. A cost-oriented strategy might appear to be appropriate for a drug or a product line. Market position could be protected after patent expiration by lowering the product's price to marginal cost, but the revenue loss would weaken the firm's capacity to conduct research; therefore the research-oriented pharmaceutical companies are unlikely to use a cost-based approach.[7]

Demand-Oriented Pricing

Demand pricing strategies include *perceived value pricing* and *differential pricing*. Charging consumers their expected value of a product based on market research is known as perceived value pricing. Focus group interviews are often used to determine the utility a group of patients has for a specific treatment of a disease The patients' willingness to pay for a treatment that may cure a disease or lessen the symptoms is assessed. Focus groups are a useful technique, provided the patient group is representative of the market of interest. If, for example, a disease's presence can be mild, moderate or severe and most patients have the mild form, information generated from a focus group composed of severely diseased patients might overestimate the value of a treatment for the general population. The severely ill may be willing to pay more to treat the disease than the majority of patients with a mild form of the disease. It is also important to consider the actual payor's willingness to pay, the physician's willingness to prescribe and the pharmacist's willingness to dispense. Tissue plasminogen activator (TPA), Genentech's drug that dissolves blood clots, was expected to be a blockbuster product. However, many institutions have balked at the $2,000 price tag associated with each use, so anticipated growth may not be realized.

Differential pricing involves charging different market segments different prices that do not reflect marginal cost differences. Prices are established based on the different segment's price sensitivity. Airline tickets are priced using the differential method. Under differential pricing, the price is established by adding or subtracting appropriate amounts to specific bases. The base used may vary depending on the pricing decision at hand, and includes producers' costs, competitors' prices, past prices, or distributors' costs. Differential bases may be geographical, temporal, vertical, horizontal, or internal.[8] (See Table 1).

Horizontal price differentials are important in a price-competitive environment. For instance, hospital and community pharmacies are on the same horizontal purchasing level because they both provide products to the ultimate consumer. Hospital pharmacies, however, are able to purchase some pharmaceuticals at lower prices than community pharmacies. Differential pricing allows companies to compete in the more price-sensitive hospital market without having to maintain lower margins in the retail sector. As hospitals expand their pharmacy practices to outpatient clinics, and both hospital and community pharmacies enter the home health care arena, the hospital and retail market borders have become less distinct.

Manufacturers are under pressure to curtail differential pricing because it has alienated many purchasers. Further pressure to control differential pricing exists because it has been associated with drug diversion.[9] To avoid these problems, some companies have reverted to single price policies.

Competition-Oriented Pricing

Competition-oriented prices are established based on the price rivals are charging. This market-oriented approach seems most

Table 1. Selected Bases Used to Establish Differential Prices

Geographical	Charge different prices in individual local markets.
Temporal	Prices different at different times (daily, seasonal, rates).
Vertical	Prices vary through distribution chain (wholesale price different than retailer's price).
Horizontal	Different prices charged to different buyers at the same distribution level.
Internal	Different prices charged for individual items in a product line.

compatible with the drug industry. There is no rigid relationship between cost and price in this situation. A manufacturer may decide to price at the market, below the market, or above the market depending on the product, the competition, and the target market. Competitive pricing is common in homogeneous markets and oligopoly-type markets. A "me-too" product with no unique characteristics would most likely be priced at the market level. As markets become saturated, pricing below the market level would be expected. To set a price above a saturated market, the product would have to be easily differentiated in terms of cost-effectiveness or provide some unique attribute.

Entering the market with a low price to establish market share and long-run profitability is known as *penetration pricing*. Other firms are discouraged from entering the market because of the initial entrant's low prices. This approach is used in price sensitive-markets when either lower costs over time or the learning curve is expected to discourage actual and potential competition.

Branded manufacturers would not be expected to use penetration pricing in normal retail markets because of the inelasticity of product demand. Demand for a new drug is generated by the number of people with an illness for which the drug is intended and by the availability of substitutes. If the product is for a life-threatening illness or is unique in its mechanism of action, its price may be relatively inconsequential to the demand for the product. When AZT was introduced to treat patients with AIDS, it basically had no competition in the form of an FDA-approved drug and its initial cost to the patient was approximately $8,000-$10,000 per year. Burroughs Wellcome received much criticism for the product's price, but felt justified because of the resources they dedicated to get the drug approved so quickly and also because they knew it would not be without competition for long given the many firms involved in AIDS research. A low penetrating price would neither generate more demand nor discourage entrants who could differentiate their product.

A modified form of penetration pricing is used by generic manufacturers when they enter a market with a drug that has recently lost patent protection. These firms compete among themselves on the basis of price. A manufacturer with the first generic version of patent-expired drug may set a low price in order to minimize the number of generic competitors entering the market and maximize the number of initial purchases of that generic house's product. When the patent for Valium® expired, generic manufacturers' initial prices changed rapidly as the companies were adjusting to their own competition.

Price skimming takes an opposite stance. A producer first on the market will charge a very high initial price to quickly recoup all investment costs. As competitors enter the market and as patent expiration approaches, the pioneer will either lower the price, drop out of the market, or lose market share (assuming the product is homogeneous).

When a new drug introduction creates a new therapeutic category, like cimetidine (Tagamet®, Smithkline), the drug maker may have a near-monopoly on the market, depending on the availability of substitutes. Antacids and surgery were alternative therapies for the treatment of ulcers, but neither were perfect substitutes. As other H2 antagonists entered the market (Glaxo's ranitidine and later, Merck's famotidine), the pioneer's market share started to decline. Initially, the market was still expanding, allowing the pioneer's sales and unit volume to continue to increase. As the market reaches the saturation point with additional products and fewer new patients, sales will start to decline. When

Smithkline's patent for cimetidine expires, generic versions will enter the market. The generic versions will be lower in price than the branded version. This will further reduce the branded product's market share. It would not make sense for the pioneer to drop out of the market completely because the product will still generate revenue. Research-based companies typically price themselves out of the market after patent expirations by continually raising their prices, which leads to constantly decreasing sales. In many cases it does not make financial sense for the pioneer to decrease the price of their product to compete with generic versions. In the current environment, total revenues generated will be higher if the price is kept higher because not enough additional unit volume will be generated at a lower price to compensate for the lower unit profit. This may change as purchasers become more price-sensitive. If third party payers and corporate purchasers become more influential, they may be able to exert enough pressure to dictate a revision in price strategy.

In general, it is important to consider the company's pricing policy and the environment's signals when developing strategy. There are many pricing strategies that could be adopted singly or in various combinations for prescription drugs. No company uses the same combination of factors to generate price policies and strategies because the same situations affect each firm differently.

When considering strategies, it is important to consider the lifecycles of the industry, therapeutic category, and product. Acute and chronic drugs may require different pricing patterns because chronic users of maintenance medications tend to be more price-sensitive than the rare user of an occasional antibiotic. A drug's safety and efficacy profile and the degree of consumer demand for generics are other important considerations in the strategy decision. A manger also needs to be aware of changes that indicate a drug is falling into disuse. A change in prescribing habits, for example, may negate any positive impact of a price change.

The Future

The current and (expected) future structure of the health care system dictates that new types of information are needed to aid in the determination of price and pricing strategies. If prices are to be raised continually, especially in the cost-conscious environment in which health care is operating, scientific data will be essential to justify the price of a drug and provide it a valid niche. Cost-effectiveness analysis (CEA) and other similar evaluation tools should aid in the development of pricing strategy. The cost effectiveness of drugs will have to be demonstrated at levels that recognize the importance of the patient, payer, and health care system. Multiple perspectives should be evaluated because the costs and benefits associated with a therapy do not necessarily accrue to the same people. For instance, if the use of Drug A permits a patient to be discharged from the hospital three days earlier than if Drug B is used, the savings generated (e.g., in terms of reduced nursing time and reduced housekeeping time) is a factor the pharmacy director should consider in addition to increased inventory costs when evaluating the drugs for addition to a formulary. If the patient is to be targeted, side effects, convenience, and variables previously considered intangible (like quality of life) may be of interest.

When should these studies be undertaken? If they are to make a contribution to the pricing strategy of a drug, some studies would have to be undertaken in Phase III clinical trials before FDA approval. Obviously, such trials have a controlled intervention period, but some preliminary data could be collected that might indicate the appropriate niche and strategy for the drug once approval is gained.

Not only must new information be considered when developing strategies; so must new players. Corporate benefits and managed care administrators are likely to bargain based on their purchasing power. Pharmacists generally decide which brand of multi-source product to dispense. They may also work with physicians to interchange drugs that are considered therapeutically equivalent. (One second generation cephalosporin for another, for instance.) Pharmacists also feel and face the effect of pricing strategies more than any other health professionals since most prescriptions are still dispensed in community pharmacies. Such individuals tend to question prices and are less accepting of an emotional appeal for a product's use. These new players should be targeted with CEA information, but they may also have to be educated about how to evaluate and interpret the studies.

Prescription drugs contain multiple dimensions of quality and value. But for the normal consumer, the dimensions are difficult to visualize and appreciate. These dimensions may serve to sensitize or desensitize consumers to the price of the drug.[10] The value of an anti-hypertensive may not be apparent, for example, because people with high blood pressure rarely feel sick. In such a case, the unit price has great influence because it is a quantifiable and visible factor. The value of an antibiotic in treating an acute bacterial infection is easier to appreciate because symptoms such as fever and pain go away when the drug is taken. If price is going to represent the total value of a drug, all important dimensions must be made concrete so people appreciate the full value of the product.

A Final Summary

The current position of the drug industry in its market lifecycle, coupled with the changes in the health care environment, have destabilized the pharmaceutical industry. If a company plans to actively participate in this environment, its current pricing strategies should be reviewed and perhaps revised.

Drugs are often referred to as cost-effective therapy; however, the general public is not fully aware of this claim and the campaign for public understanding of the point should continue. As the purchasers of health care goods and services become more concentrated, price is going to be of greater interest. Prices and price changes do not only affect current sales, but are far-reaching. Indeed, price increases are not without costs. Such changes can generate consumer anger, government investigations, and aggressive competition. Price increases of branded, multi-source drugs provide an incentive to select the generic versions.

Pricing strategies must tread a fine line between shareholder obligation and marketplace requirements. The current marketplace, in which generics and viable therapeutic substitutes predominate, will most likely respond to strategies based on scientific data that demonstrate economic reasons for the price of a product.

Endnotes

[1] U.S. Bureau of Labor Statistics. *Producer Price Indexes.* Washington D.C.: U.S. Government Printing Office, 1980-1987.

[2] Fineberg H. V. and L. A. Pearlman, "Benefit and cost analysis of medical interventions: The case of cimetidine and peptic ulcer disease." *The Implications of Cost-Effectiveness Analysis of Medical Technology,* Background paper #2, Case Study #1. Washington D.C.: U.S. Government Printing Office [OTA-BP-H-9(11)], 1981.

[3] Paul L. M., "Drug Pricing—what the market will bear." *Pharmaceutical Executive,* 5(0) (October 985), pp. 75, 77.

[4] Crossen D. K., "What's happening to pricing's marketing clout?" *Pharmaceutical Executive,* 6(8) (Aug. 1986), pp. 54, 55, 58.

[5] Eichner A. S., *The Megacorp and Oligopoly.* Cambridge: Cambridge University Press, 1976.

[6] Ross E. B., "Making money with proactive pricing." *Harvard Business Review.* 62(6) 1984, pp. 145-155.

[7] Von Grebmer K., "Competition in a structurally changing pharmaceutical market: some health economic considerations." *Social Science and Medicine.* 5 (1981), pp. 77-86.

[8] Oxenfeldt A. R.,"The differential method of pricing." *European Journal of Marketing.* 13(4) (1979), pp. 199-212.

[9] Rankin K., *Drug Store News.* August 5, 1985.

[10] Sampson R.T., "Sense and sensitivity in pricing." *Harvard Business Review.* 42 (6) (1964), pp. 99-105.

Recommended for Additional Reading

Bond R. S. and D. F. Lean, *Sales promotion and product differentiation in two prescription drug markets*. Report to the FTC. Washington D.C.: U.S. Government Printing Office. 1977.

Drummond M. F., G. L. Stoddart, and G. W. Torrance, *Methods for the Economic Evaluation of Health Care Programs*. Oxford: Oxford University Press, 1987.

Gould J. P. and S. K. Sen, eds. "Pricing Strategy. Proceedings of a conference" Sept. 24-25, 1982. Supplement to the *Journal of Business*, 57 (No.1, part 2, Jan. 1984). Chicago: The University of Chicago Press.

Kotler P., *Principles of Marketing*. 3rd ed. Englewood Cliffs NJ: Prentice-Hall, 1986.

Nagle T., *The Strategy and Tactics of Pricing*. Englewood Cliffs, NJ: Prentice-Hall. 1987

Oxenfeldt A. R., "A decision-making structure for price decisions." *Journal of Marketing* 37 (1973), pp. 48-53.

Von Grebmer K., "Pricing medicines." In *Health Economics: Prospects for the Future*. ed G Teeling Smith. London: Croom helm, 1987

Warner K. E. and B. R. Luce, *Cost-Benefit and Cost-Effectiveness Analysis in Health Care, Principles, Practice and Potential.*. Ann Arbor, MI: Health Administration Press. 1982.

PRICING IN SMALLER SERVICE FIRMS:

Cassette World, Inc.

JOHN Y. LEE

JOHN Y. LEE

John Y. Lee is Professor of Accounting at California State University, Los Angeles and a partner at McKay Business Systems, an Artesia, California, consulting firm that specializes in process improvement for companies in the service sector. He is the author of two books and numerous articles on cost systems in top business and accounting journals and is currently the Western Regional Director of the Management Accounting Section, American Accounting Association.

CHAPTER SIXTEEN

Small companies in service industries face very unique problems in their pricing decisions. The problems are due to their small size and the nature of their business—providing service rather than producing and selling products.

This chapter discusses the particular pricing problems smaller service firms must cope with, and suggests how to make successful pricing decisions on a consistent basis. A pricing system that has actually been employed by a small service firm will be used as an example to facilitate understanding.

Then follows an examination of the pitfalls of relying on the firm's cost data generated from the conventional cost accounting systems as the basis of pricing decisions. These result from the inequity and inaccuracy of the traditional cost allocation methods practiced by most firms. Since reliable cost information is especially important in making pricing decisions for service firms in their application of full-cost pricing methods, this coverage is meaningful to many service firms.

Unique Pricing Problems of Smaller Service Firms

Service firms do not carry significant inventories; often they carry no inventory at all. The work is usually labor-intensive, and it is difficult to measure the amount and quality of services, especially after the time a particular service has been rendered. In the case of service firms, non-human assets are not important as compared to manufacturing firms. *People* are the most valued assets. Accordingly, pricing methods such as the target ROI pricing are not appropriate. This is because the physical "assets employed"—used for ROI calculation—are not meaningfully related to the prices of the services provided.

This fact emphasizes the importance of full-cost pricing in service firms, although constant attention to the competitive situation and prices in the market is essential to ensure that the cost-based price stays reasonable. The full absorption cost will serve as the lower limit in pricing. The difference between the price quoted and the absorption cost is markup. Different markups should be applied when different business segments are involved in order for the firm to stay competitive.

If a particular service firm has established a reputation for high-quality services, then the firm may be able to charge prices that include markups representing certain predetermined earnings expectations. The majority of small service firms, however, can not apply their full-cost formula as they wish. They should be flexible enough to adjust the markup percentage according to the competitive situations they face.

Small firms experience difficulties in determining the costs of rendering services to use as the basis of pricing because record-keeping of costs incurred to provide service and accurate cost allocation among different services can be overwhelming. Their pricing decisions, therefore, tend to be heavily influenced by the prices prevailing in the area—that is, if the information is available.

These limitations of small service firms force them to resort to a trial-and-error approach to pricing, which can hurt their long-term growth and sometimes threaten their survival. Developing a sensible pricing system that is rigorous enough to reflect the many complexities of implementing pricing theories yet simple enough to be employed within a small service firm is essential. The case example used in this chapter, Cassette World, Inc., serves the purpose of illustrating how such a sensible pricing system can actually be developed by a small service firm.[1]

Cassette World, Inc.

The Firm

Cassette World, Inc. (CWI), located in Southern California, is a small service company with major operations comprised of duplicating audio and video cassettes, recording conferences on location, and cassette program development involving seminars and publications. The three divisions performing these operations are described next.

The Duplication Division comprises a major part of CWI's business. Materials used for the majority of duplication jobs include the audio/video tapes, custom-designed labels, and those for packaging options. In addition to the duplicating process itself, this division also does tape mastering, editing, labeling, and packaging. Duplicating may be done in-cassette, or out-of-cassette, in which case an additional process of loading raw tape into cassette shells has to be performed.

On-site Conference Recording is a bit of a hybrid service. Services in this division combine the duplicating services of the Duplication Division with the custom-design services of the Program Development Division. Cassette tapes of individual conference sessions are duplicated and labeled for on-site and mail-order sales. Additionally, full-conference or 16-tape sets are offered in a custom-designed, vinyl, cassette-tape album. Conference sponsors receive a royalty on conference tape sales. As the conference recording service is highly competitive, prices and royalty percentages are fairly well established in the industry.

The Cassette Program Development Division offers the cassette program author a complete line of program development services that include: program mastering and editing, duplicating, labeling, album cover and label designing, packaging, copywriting, marketing and distribution. The program author also receives a royalty from the sales of the program.

All three divisions offer various packaging options. Individual cassettes, for example, can be packaged in soft-plastic boxes; a hard, clear-plastic Norelco box; or in a single-cassette binder custom designed for use as a cassette program or multi-media presentation. Albums, or binders as they are often called, can be designed to hold from 1 to 16 cassettes, with or without a booklet pocket or three-ring binder capabilities, as well as a variety of cassette holder placement designs within the binder. Additionally, any of these packaging configurations may be shrinkwrapped.

There is a limited degree of standardization of production materials between the three divisions. Some configurations of tape albums are very popular and might be used in both the Conference Recording and Cassette Program divisions. Audio and video tapes share a few popular tape lengths between all three divisions. Since the materials standardization is minimal, it is impractical to carry large inventories of production materials. Materials are usually ordered according to the specifications of each job as it is received by CWI.

Growth Stage

CWI has annual sales of about $400,000. It is run by a sole proprietor. Growing from a one-man operation, CWI is presently in a transitional stage. Up until the start of 1986, labor requirements beyond the capacity of one person were fulfilled on a contracted, per-job basis. The company is now switching gears from a single-person mentality to a 'semi- corporate' mentality. This mentality shift is regarded as vital to the continued growth of the company.

Present personnel include:

1 full-time production worker,
2 full-time administrative/production workers,
1 part-time marketing employee, and
4 on-call personnel (mostly for production functions).

With this personnel configuration, it is still possible to have a high degree of personal observation of production by the company president. The practicality and efficiency of the president's personal involvement in day-to-day production, however, has decreased, and will continue to do so.

CWI is still not large enough to maintain specific personnel to monitor and evaluate an elaborate mix of control systems. The majority of control and monitoring responsibilities are still carried out by the company president. *The current size and growth stage of CWI requires a fairly simple pricing system.*

Marketing Factors and the Company Image

Long-range goals of CWI include the development of numerous cassette program and conference recording revenue accounts. The Duplication Division fills a role complementary to the other two divisions, as well as being a profitable division in its own right. In addition, it plays a major role in increasing CWI's short-run profits, as duplication jobs help utilize idle capacity, smoothing out production highs and lows.

The majority of the company's sales involve a two-stage customer configuration. Stage 1 consists of cassette program authors, conference sponsors, and business clients requesting duplication. Stage 2 is comprised primarily of the final product users and consumer duplication requestors. The emphasis on business-to-business marketing highlights the need for non-price competition.

CWI strives to differentiate its services by producing the highest quality products with distinctive copywriting and graphics while maintaining quick turn-around cycles. The company offers 24-hour service whenever necessary. Products are distributed primarily through the mail, which makes distribution cost easily attributable to each customer's job. Overall, these characteristics of CWI call for a pricing strategy which does not emphasize price competition.

Managerial Characteristics

If management feels uncomfortable with a system's operating requirements, or isn't supportive of the system, then the system is doomed to failure. This aspect should be evaluated before a detailed design of the system is undertaken.

The following is an assessment of CWI's managerial characteristics:

- Management has a general desire for and understanding of the importance of a formalized pricing system. However, previous attempts to implement rigorous systems have failed because CWI did not follow up on the necessary operational details.

- Management has no taste for a system requiring extensive calculations and paperwork that demands management's attention. If the tasks of accumulating and manipulating system information could be spread among a handful of people, the system would not be perceived as a production impediment. Management could then concentrate on the task of applying the information to the pricing process, instead of on system mechanics.
- Management likes to stay with traditional costing methods.
- Management wants to retain significant flexibility in pricing alternatives.
- Management wants a pricing system that recovers all costs that have been incurred—the costs specifically traced to the job as well as those considered general in nature for the overall business.
- Management wants to have the capability to analyze whether specific jobs are profitable in the short run, considering temporary idle capacity.

In summary, the implementation of a successful pricing system should depend on whether the system can accommodate the managerial needs and preferences listed above, as well as the needs arising from company and industry characteristics discussed in prior sections.

Accounting and Pricing Characteristics

CWI uses a cash basis accounting system, and is expected to do so for some time. The company prices on a per-job basis. Elements of a job have been priced based on rough estimates of current cost plus desired markup, which were estimated using "gut feeling." Up until now, a market-based pricing approach was appropriate as CWI was trying to establish itself in the market and had no historical costs to base its pricing decisions on. For job elements for which little market information was available, management used a cost-plus approach.

A major materials element of most jobs is the charge for cassette tape. The purchase cost of cassette tape is somewhat flexible since a lower-quality tape can be substituted. This flexibility, nevertheless, is limited by the high-quality image CWI wants to project. Standard costs could be used for cassette tape, assuming that the tape quality can be controlled. Tape is priced according to its time length.

The Conference Recording Division operates in a very competitive environment, and market-based pricing will be mandated for the time being. At successful conferences, the market price for conference cassettes will be sufficient to cover all conference expenses and contribute to profit. The pricing analysis presented here does not affect this division.

The Cassette Program and Duplication divisions both require pricing for duplication, the price of which varies with the tape length and the order size, and other support services. The pricing analysis presented in this chapter covers CWI's attempt to price accurately the core duplicating function, as well as the support services—graphics, design, typesetting, labeling, and so on. The pricing of these support services have thus far been a guessing game.

Implementation of a formalized pricing system will allow CWI to cover the full costs and earn the desired profits on these services. CWI's services, as is true with most other service firms, are labor intensive. Accordingly, the labor element of the final price will be a key component. Determining the hourly workers' cost is easier than that of the indirect personnel such as the president, who receives no definite salary to be applied to the pricing.

Pricing Problems Highlighted

An appropriate pricing system, if properly implemented, will alleviate the following problems:

1. Previously, no pricing analysis existed to identify the various job elements for pricing of individual jobs.
2. For major and support services no cost figures were actually developed for use in pricing.

3. Problems related to incomplete invoicing have been frequently reported.

4. No formalized procedure of determining an adequate level of markup exists. This was not a serious problem in the beginning stage of the company, but, given the present growth, a formal system deems to be cost effective.

5. There should be a proper way to calculate special order prices. Special orders won't affect the normal operations while smoothing operation peaks and valleys.

6. The pricing of incoming jobs should be performed in a relatively hassle-free way, so that the established procedures could be used without frustration.

7. The company currently cannot price jobs if an employee works on multiple jobs at the same time to take advantage of machine loading capabilities.

8. Management cannot tolerate a lot of paperwork.

The Pricing System

The pricing system of a small service firm like CWI should be designed with adequate consideration given to its growth stage, operating characteristics, and managerial preferences. An effective pricing system must also incorporate factors such as cost information, competitive strength, client preferences, and so on. Given the size of CWI, the company needs a pricing system that is as simple as it is effective. Management control systems such as cost accounting and pricing systems should be able to grow with the company. CWI is still too small to afford a full-time staff member to monitor and administer management control systems. Thus, the company needs a system that can "flow with the natural flow" of its operations.

Pricing Method Selected

CWI needs to consider the full costs of being in business, not just the product costs, in its pricing decisions. It is through the revenue generated by appropriate pricing that the company meets all current expenses and provides the means for continued operations. It needs pricing benchmarks to guide it in pricing decisions so that the company's needs are addressed. CWI needs a very basic, easy-to-use approach that will give it a starting price range for a job, without having to price each job element from scratch in each case.

The system selected for CWI is a hybrid cost-plus approach with a job-order costing process. The cost-plus figure provides the company with a minimum long-term price to be adjusted for marketing and general economic conditions. CWI's costs are defined and handled according to the traditional absorption costing approach; materials costs are traced to job orders. Direct labor and overhead costs, variable and fixed alike, are applied as processing costs to job orders.

Total Costs Charged = Materials Costs + Processing Costs

Processing Costs = Direct Labor + Overhead Costs

Allocating fixed overhead costs to the respective jobs is in line with the pricing objective of this small company: it should cover all the costs of doing business.

There are some other reasons for adopting the absorption costing approach for overhead. Management of CWI, like most other small company owners/managers, prefers to stick with the traditional cost accounting methods. Since absorption costing is also the method required for tax purposes, and most banks that CWI has dealt with expected total costs in the financial statements submitted with loan applications, absorption costing made a lot of sense to CWI.

Being a small company, CWI's needs were met by the use of average costs for overhead items, as well as for direct labor. The company can "get away with" using average costs without too much concern over "fair allocation" of overhead costs. The average cost concept is easier for CWI people to understand and use compared to other more rigorous concepts such as contribution approach. A typical small business, CWI does not have responsibility center managers who will fight over unfairly allocated overhead costs, as is the case with larger companies.

CWI management also espoused a unique sense of fairness to its clients by the use of the average cost concept, because the company can avoid penalizing any particular client by charging for inefficiencies in any specific operations.

The Pricing Process. The actual costing and pricing processes rely heavily on the forms developed for daily use, as explained in a subsequent section. The forms will be used to calculate the incurred costs for a given job. The overhead allocation is done on the basis of the expected actual activity for the year, not the full capacity. [This is because full capacity is not yet realistic.]

$$\text{Overhead Allocation Rate} = \frac{\text{Estimated Overhead Costs}}{\text{Expected Activity Level (in Hours)}}$$

The use of the full capacity as the allocation basis will make the per-job overhead allocation rate lower, which in turn will lead to an under-applied overhead. This, of course, will make the full-cost coverage objective difficult to be accomplished.

The price quoted on a typical job will be based on the following components:

1. Materials cost
2. Processing costs which include direct labor and overhead
3. Selling, general and administrative expenses
4. Commissions and delivery costs
5. Markup desired

Materials and direct labor costs are based on average actual costs. Overhead costs are allocated based on the formula presented above. Selling, general and administrative expenses are charged based on the processing costs, since it seems logical to link SG&A to processing (value-added) costs considering their labor-intensive nature. Commissions and delivery costs can be calculated easily.

The markup is determined by the management considering the average percentage and competitive conditions.

The difference between the total costs incurred and the costs charged is isolated and available for periodic evaluation by the management. Work hours spent on each job are recorded on each production record for costing as well as for monitoring purposes.

Special Order and Other Contingent Procedures

For the purpose of evaluating whether or not to take a special order for a below-full-cost price, CWI must use a relevant cost approach. When there is idle capacity, the relevant costs are the incremental costs incurred by taking the special order. Management is cautioned against thinking that all variable costs are relevant and all fixed costs are irrelevant. Individual cases must be evaluated on a per-order basis. For a small company like CWI, the use of the following type of analysis is suggested:

- Look at the total revenue increase from the special order.
- Compare that to the total cost increase caused by taking the special order.
- How do you like the difference?

The company is advised not to be concerned with the unit revenue and cost figures in that particular decision-making process.

CWI can sometimes accept special orders at a price below their minimum long-term price, provided that the special price is at least higher than the incremental cost of producing and selling the order. This decision may be warranted if it helps CWI get its foot in the door with a desirable client, or gain the exposure to a new market segment represented by the special order.

Quantity Discounts and Other Evaluations. When a vendor grants a price cut for the purchase of cassette tapes, CWI, under the company policy to be a flexible and innovative service firm, passes the savings on to their clients. This is realized as a decrease in the materials cost used in the pricing scheme of CWI.

If there need to be other evaluations on the incremental effect of pricing—for example, for a profit-volume analysis—CWI can augment the full-absorption costing approach by dealing in totals and in directly traceable costs for those evaluations.

Forms

The primary vehicles used in implementing the pricing system are forms. The two major forms used by CWI are the production record and the work order. The forms are adapted to the full- costing system.

The Production Record (Figure 1) is a complete record of all work performed. Materials, labor, and overhead are all charged to this form. The job number assigned is the control number for a specific job performed for a client. Direct labor hours are recorded to the nearest tenth of an hour. Total cost for all work performed and all materials used are compared to the amount actually charged on the form to isolate the difference for subsequent evaluation and calculation of markup.

The Production Record, (although the record shown in Figure 1 is not illustrated in such detail) is structured to a sectional approach to coincide with the work order in order to facilitate costing and the followup analysis. The sections are designated: studio, duplication, graphics, materials, assembly, delivery, and accounting. The sectional approach helps the company make sure that invoicing, costing, and pricing are done properly, accounting for all the elements that have been put into a particular job.

The Work Order (Figure 2) uses a job numbering system that has been improved from the previous system in which no systematic assignment of numbers was done. The new system assigns job numbers according to the date of job entry in order to make it compatible with the recordkeeping and cost accounting procedures. This improvement will help CWI track cost data across costing, financial reporting, tax, and pricing records.

Figure 1

Production Record

JOB NUMBER: *FB605*

SHIPPING DATE: *4/16/88*

CLIENT *CREATIVE PRODUCTS, Inc.*

JOB TITLE/DESCRIPTION *3 CASSETTE PROGRAMS DEVELOPED*

Please record below a complete record of all work performed, materials used and costs incurred in the performance of this job. Hours necessary to complete job should be recorded to the nearest tenth of an hour. Do not fill in shaded areas.

DATE	QUANTITY	WORK PERFORMED/MATERIALS USED	HRS	UNIT COST INCURRED	TOTAL COST	AMOUNT CHARGED	DIFFERENCE
1/88	1	PROG. MSTRNG	7	50	350	420	70
3/88	2	DUP. LABLNG	11	60	660	800	140
		UPS/OTHER					

GRAND TOTALS:

Figure 2

Work Order

Job Number: *FB605*

Due Date: *4/10/88*

Finished Quantity *3*	Job Title/Description *CSST PRGR DEVELOPED*	

Client name *CREATIVE PRODUCTS, INC.*

Address *14114 HUNTINGTON DRIVE*

| City *PASADENA* | State *CA* | Zip *90047* | Contact / Telephone *D. MURPHY* |

Studio ☒ Remastering / Bin Loop ☒ Editing ☒ Recording
    Initials / Date *7L* *1/10/88*

Duplication ☒ In-Cassette ☐ Out-of-Cassette
    Initials / Date *DP* *2/17/88*

Graphics ☐ Inserts ☐ Lables ☒ Other
    Initials / Date *3F* *3/3/88*

SEE THE INSTRUCTIONS ATTACHED.

Materials
    Initials / Date *CYN* *3/21/88*

☒ Tape *17-60 MINUTE*
☐ Albums
☐ Printing
☐

Assembly Date needed by: *SMOOTHING*
    Initials / Date

Delivery ☐ Pick up ☒ Deliver ☐ Ship via _____
    Initials / Date

BE SURE TO DELIVER TO D. MURPHY.

Accounting Terms ☐ COD ☐ Net 10 ☐ Other _____ Pricing: ☐ STD ☒ Other

☐ Paid	Amount $	Initials / Date	☐ Invoiced	No.	Initials / Date

Forms that work sensibly are vital to a pricing system of a small business, because small firms cannot maintain a sophisticated system of costing and pricing, and depend instead on convenient mechanisms such as forms. The accumulation of cost and job information through forms is the primary basis for allocating costs for pricing purposes.

Pitfalls of Relying on Conventional Cost Data

In the case of Cassette World, Inc., we observed how a small service firm can rely on a consistent pricing system. However, when companies use a full-costing method of pricing, as most service firms do, they must rely heavily on the cost data generated and supplied by the cost accounting area. If the cost data provided are inaccurate or determined on the basis of unfairly allocated costs, then the validity of the resulting pricing decisions should be questioned. The concern here is that in many services, as well as in manufacturing, industries, the cost allocation process contains serious flaws.

This section examines the pitfalls of relying on the cost data generated from conventional cost systems as the basis of making pricing decisions.

Cost Allocation Based on Business Volume or Revenue

At many service firms, the allocation of indirect or support service costs is based on the contribution margin, profit, revenue, or other business volume of each operating department (major production departments) which use the services of support departments. This practice of allocating indirect costs is by far the most widely used today; nevertheless, it produces pricing and profit results that may be totally distorted from reality if they are applied to a firm that is larger and has more complex operations than CWI. The following example illustrates the ramifications of this situation.

Benedict Finance Company is a small financial service firm located in Orange County, California. The company extends medium- and long-term loans to individual and commercial customers through its two loan departments—Individual Loan Department and Commercial Loan Department. These two operating departments handle marketing and loan administration functions. There is also a Credit Department that supports these two revenue-generating departments. The Credit Department processes customer loan applications forwarded through the two loan departments until the loan is approved. The processing functions include checking the credit and financial information contained in the application; confirming the information through internal and external sources; analyzing the credit worthiness of each customer; and writing a credit memo (recommendation for approval or rejection).

The support costs of the credit department had been allocated to the two operating departments based on the contribution margins until 1986. Table 1 summarizes the 1986 operating results.

Table 1 Cost Allocation Based on Contribution Margin

	Individual Loan Dept.	(Thousands) Commercial Loan Dept.	Total
Interest and Fee	$376	$745	$1,121
Direct Cost	144	190	334
Contribution Margin	$232	$555	$787
Indirect Cost*	84	201	285
Net Earnings	$148	$354	$502
Earnings Contributed	29.5%	70.5%	100%

* Indirect cost includes administrative support costs other than credit department cost.

The practice of allocating indirect cost had been continued until 1987, when a new manager took over the commercial loan department. The new manager objected to the allocation method used by the company, claiming that the profit contribution by each department was grossly distorted by the allocation method.

The supporting argument was as follows:

"Allocating indirect cost based on each department's contribution margin is unfair and also outdated as a practice. Why should the department be charged on the basis of the profit (contribution margin) it made? It should be based on the amount of services each department receives from the support areas. According to my calculation, my department's share of indirect cost should be $132,000 (instead of $201,000) and contributed earnings amount to $423,000 (instead of $354,000), accounting for 84.2% (instead of 70.5%) of the company earnings."

The president of the company, upon hearing this argument, instructed his assistant to analyze the situation further. The analysis revealed the facts presented in the following section.

Cost Driver Approach to Indirect Cost Allocation

After the study, the president's assistant concluded that the argument that had been made by the new manager of commercial loan department was legitimate. Although the amount of contribution margin and the size of loan portfolio reflected the ability of the commercial loan department to absorb the allocated indirect cost, he agreed that the more appropriate method, proposed in recent cost accounting literature as the cost driver approach, should employ the amount of actual service they received as the basis.

The amount of actual service should be determined on the basis of the time the credit department staff spent on each department's loan packages. Although a time study was not undertaken formally, credit department analysts seem to agree that individual loans, with the average loan amount of $25,000, take almost as much time as commercial loans, with the average amount of $87,000.

For the year, there were 30 individual loans processed (53.6%), compared to 26 commercial loans (46.4%). Accordingly, if the number of loan packages processed is used as the basis of indirect cost allocation under the cost driver approach, the individual loan department should share a higher portion of the support service costs.

Table 2 shows the 1986 operating performance under the new approach.

Table 2   Cost Allocation Based on Cost Drivers

			(Thousands)	
	Individual Loan Dept.	*Commercial Loan Dept.*	*Total*	
Interest and Fee	$376	$745	$1,121	
Direct Cost	144	190	334	
Contribution Margin	$232	$555	$787	
Indirect Cost*	153	132	285	
Net Earnings	$ 79	$423	$502	
Earnings Contributed	15.7%	84.3%	100%	

* Indirect cost includes administrative support costs other than credit department cost.

The cost driver approach, which has recently gained a significant acceptance among major U.S. companies, is not an entirely new approach. It emphasizes the inequity caused by using arbitrary overhead cost allocation bases such as direct labor hours, direct labor dollars, machine hours, and so forth, in calculating product cost for performance measurement and pricing purposes. The approach suggests the use of true cost drivers, the factors that cause the overhead cost to increase, as the bases of allocation. Examples are the number of purchase orders processed (rather than purchase volume) in allocating purchasing department cost to manufacturing departments and the number of engineering change orders to allocate production engineering department cost.

The importance of using cost drivers has been discussed largely in the context of manufacturing firms' costing processes. The same principle and practice applies to the service industry. As can be seen from the Benedict Finance Company example, the impact of introducing the cost driver concept into the cost allocation process will be enormous for many service firms. The pricing decisions incorporating the costs allocated on the basis of true cost drivers are more informative and realistic.

Although the simple case example used here to illustrate the implications of this approach does not deal with a pricing problem directly, the allocated costs, as discussed in this chapter, become part of the full absorption costs used in pricing decisions. We can visualize the impact by thinking that the credit department of Benedict Finance Company could charge "prices" for their services for the two loan departments. Of course, there is a big difference between the prices charged on the basis of the two different allocation methods. The changes will eventually lead the company to charge different loan(and other service) fees to individual and commercial loan applicants. Accordingly, different prices result from the different cost allocation methods.

Summary

This chapter has examined the various pricing problems smaller service firms face and has presented some examples of how better pricing decisions can be made. The pricing methods used should be reasonably accurate and flexible, but at the same time the methods should not be too complicated to be applied by small businesses.

The first example, Cassette World, Inc., illustrates how an easy pricing system can be applied by small service firms using forms. Although service costs may be more difficult to calculate than manufacturing costs, they nevertheless should be traced and accounted for, to assure that full costs are covered. Since it is too expensive for smaller service firms to devise and maintain formal pricing systems, it makes sense to design and rely on forms (such as those shown in Figure 1 and Figure 2) to track and calculate actual costs for full-cost pricing. The task of accumulating and manipulating cost information can be assigned to some staff members so that management can be relieved of the daily task. Careful-ly designed forms will make this possible for smaller firms. The full absorption cost, accounted for in this manner, should be used as a benchmark for the minimum price that a firm can live with. To be competitive, a service firm must be flexible in pricing its services. It must also know where the bottom line is in order to show profit.

The second example, Benedict Finance Company, discusses how cost allocation can be improved by a firm that, while still small, has more support service departments that provide services to other departments. This approach does not need to be applied if a firm does not have many service (support) departments that operate as responsibility centers. As in the case of CWI, the average costing method can be used without any problem. Never-theless, when there are responsibility centers whose managers fight over overhead allocations, the cost driver accounting ap-proach discussed above should be considered. This is necessary in order to reflect the proper costs, allocated on the basis of efforts and contributions, in pricing services. If direct charging of costs to jobs (services) can be made easily, then the firm does not need to be concerned with the cost driver approach; average costing can be used. Whatever pricing method may be selected, a firm should recover total actual costs incurred by tracing the costs to specific jobs (services); relying on forms can be very practical in this regard for smaller service firms.

Endnotes

[1] The case discussed here has been adapted from Lee, J.Y., "Develop-ing a Pricing System for a Small Business," *Management Account-ing* (March 1987), pp. 50-53. Permission granted by *Management Accounting*, copyright © 1987, by the National Association of Accountants.

Recommended for Additional Reading

Haynes, W.W., "Pricing Practices in Small Firms," *The Southern Economic Journal* (April 1964), pp. 315-324. A survey of small businesses regarding their pricing practices.

Lee, J.Y., *Managerial Accounting Changes for the 1990s.* (Reading, Massachusetts: Addison-Wesley Publishing Company, 1988). For more information on the problems of conventional cost accounting and recent changes in cost accounting of U.S. industry.

Possett, R.W., "Measuring Productive Costs in the Service Sector," *Management Accounting* (October 1980), pp.16-24. A discussion of determining productive costs in a service firm, using a financial and insurance service company case.

CHAPTER SEVENTEEN

PRICING IN TODAY'S HAIR CARE INDUSTRY:

Who's In Charge?

DEBORAH FERRO

DEBORAH FERRO

Deborah Ferro is a Marketing Manager at L'oreal, a division of Cosmair Inc. in New York where she specializes in the development of comprehensive marketing programs, financial spreedsheet analyses, and the restaging of hair care products. Before joining the marketing group at L'oreal, Ms. Ferro was a product manager at Colgage-Palmolive in charge of several national brands. She is a graduate of The University of Rhode Island with degrees in Marketing and Finance.

CHAPTER SEVENTEEN

Twenty years ago, the average consumer could choose among two, three—with luck maybe five—products in most consumer goods categories. Certainly, the quality of the product, the packaging, advertising, and perhaps the product claims influenced the final purchase decision, but just as likely the price of the product was the ultimate deciding factor. Of course, there were and still are many brand-loyal consumers who stand by their favorite brand no matter what the price, the advertising message of the product claims; however, the numbers of brand-loyal consumers has dwindled over the years. In a Needham, Harper, Steers study in 1975, 75% – 80% of consumers said they try to "stick to well-known brands." In 1981 only 60% made the same claim. This indicates that more consumers have become brand switchers, and therefore are motivated to buy a product because it is on sale or the advertising is appealing. Reaching this type of consumer and influencing his or her final purchase decision can be extremely difficult, especially today when the choices in a single product category have grown dramatically and the competition is spending millions of dollars on various consumer programs, price-offs, and trade allowances.

The competition for the consumers' dollar is particularly intense in the hair care products industry. Not only are consumers bombarded with multiple brand choices, and switch constantly from one to another, they are inundated with advertisements, coupons, refund offers and other promotion vehicles. These media have become an expensive cost of entry for hair care manufacturers. In addition to these issues, there is the difficulty of developing pricing strategies and tactics in an industry in which power has shifted from the manufacturer to the retailer. The notion of "Suggested Retail Price" is obsolete. Instead, the environment requires a manufacturer to discard the traditional linear approach to pricing—from production and cost accounting estimates to grand marketing strategies. Instead, manufacturers have had to shift their attention away from wholesalers and consumers to the dominant member of the distribution channel—the retailer.

The primary focus of this chapter is on an approach to formulating a pricing strategy in a retailer-dominated industry using the shampoo and conditioner category as an example for analyses. As a background to the proposed pricing analyses, a general overview of the hair care market will be discussed along with further insights into the characteristics that define this industry.

The Hair Care Market

Brand Proliferation

Who would have imagined that the average woman would use more than five different products on her hair as part of her daily cleansing/styling regime? The number of products and different forms of the same product is staggering. The extent of brand proliferation that has occurred over the past 10 years has created a fierce competitive arena for manufacturers of hair care and styling products. For instance, in the Mousse portion of the styling segment, the number of stock keeping units (sku's) has grown from about 10 in 1984 to almost 500 (including private label brands) in 1988. The size (total) of the current hair care market exceeds 9,000 sku's and represents approximately three billion dollars in sales volume. The market is composed of four categories: shampoo/conditioner; styling aids (includes mousse, gels, lotions, and non-aerosol styling sprays); "traditional" aerosol hair sprays; and treatment/repair type products. The major competitors in these segments are Revlon, Clairol, Helene Curtis, L'Oreal, Faberge, Proctor & Gamble and Jhirmack.

Given the extensive brand proliferation, manufacturers have attempted to create unique product positioning and niches in order to stand apart from competition. Most companies aggressively support their brand with advertising, consumer and trade promotions in order to reinforce the selling position and insure volume objectives. In many cases, especially in the past five years or so, all of the major manufacturers have restaged their brands with packaging, formula and positioning improvements. For example, Revlon has recently introduced another four sku's into the already huge shampoo and conditioner category, under the brand name *Clean 'n Clear*. The unique feature of this new brand is the product positioning which conveys "purity" since the formula resembles water. The packaging is unique in terms of the shape and "see-through" quality of the plastic. The launch of this brand has been supported by TV, print, consumer and trade promotions totaling over $10 million. With this level of activity and spending, the retailers have given major in-store support for the *Clean 'n Clear* launch, which has resulted in strong share gains in the introductory period.

Channels of Distribution/Classes of Trade

The distribution system that has allowed Revlon to so successfully push *Clean n' Clear* onto the store shelves is quite different than it used to be. A few decades ago, the primary channel of distribution was wholesalers and secondary distributors such as rack jobbers. Today, most of the volume is sold directly to the account warehouses (e.g., Walmart) and some directly to the retail stores, as is the case with K-Mart. The third and smallest channel is the wholesaler, which once was the primary means of distribution for hair care products. This change came about over the years due to the extensive growth and proliferation of hair care businesses. When the wholesaler was channel leader, the manufacturer was in "control" of the selling process and focused its dollars and efforts to reach and convince the consumer to buy their brand among the limited number of products that were available. There was no need at that time to spend money on the trade since they had no choice but to stock the brands that consumers were demanding. In fact, trade allowances, another cost of entry in today's environment, were practically non-existent; "token" allowances were given to the accounts for stocking the products. Now that the direct warehouse/retail accounts are the dominating channel, the power has shifted to the individual classes of trade—drug, food, and mass merchandiser. The accounts in each class have become so powerful because of the multitudes of brands to choose from, and the sophisticated use of computers and scanners that enable retailers to make selections based on actual brand performance. The manufacturers have been forced to spend significant dollars on allowance incentives, sometimes known as "slot allowances," that pay for the limited retail space available, thus shifting dollars away from the consumer. In fact, overall industry data across many products indicate that companies are now spending 10 times as much on trade deals as on coupons.

Not only is the trade powerful as a "whole," but the emergence of different types of accounts within the classes of trade has allowed the retailer to become even more influential and powerful. For example, specific to the drug class of trade, the "deep discount" chains (e.g., Drug Emporium) have created major competitive pressures on the other accounts because of their low pricing strategy. Also, strong national/regional chains like Walgreens, Kroger and K-Mart are dominating the field in terms of their impact. In fact, for most hair care companies, national/regional accounts probably do well over 50 percent of the company's sales. Since these accounts are very powerful, coupled with the fact that they generally compete on price with each other, the pricing structure in the hair care industry has become segmented.

Industry Price Structure

Another concern for the manufacturer is the nature of the pricing structure that has evolved in the industry. Basically, strong bipolar price points exist for most of the product forms in the hair care/styling market—a price/value and premium segment. A middle tier also exists, but the brands who compete in this area have been relatively unsuccessful compared to the price or premium entries. This type of segmentation is particularly true for shampoos and conditioners. Brands like *Suave*, *Ivory*, and *Flex* have been very successful with limited support but low prices and so have *Finesse*, *Pantene* and *Jhirmack* who compete in the premium category and have major support to "justify" their high prices. The constraint in having tiers of pricing levels is the fact that there is a maximum price "cap" in each segment, or a pricing band within which the manufacturer is forced to operate.

Given the two basic constraints of profit margin guidelines and maximum price points, pricing a new or restaged brand must be approached in a unique way. The standard "cost plus" method becomes a secondary consideration. Instead, product proliferation, retailer strength and the industry price structure requires a different approach to price setting. One such approach is a two-stage process that essentially forces the marketing manager to "back into" a strategy based upon competitive analyses. Stage One begins with an outline of competitive trade prices and allowances along with pricing tier "caps" to generate profit margin guidelines. Stage Two translates the proposed pricing strategy into a P & L statement for profitability analysis.

Sizing Up the Competition

Using shampoo and conditioner category data, it is important to first identify the brands of primary focus—i.e., the ones that are in the same market tier in terms of price and support levels. The following series of examples and analyses will assume that a price/value brand is approaching a restage and is re-evaluating its marketing elements. All of the information, therefore, focuses on brands within the price/value segment.

The first step is to outline competitive manufacturer costs and allowances to understand the terms by which competitive companies are dealing with the trade. Table 1 provides the basic data from which further analyses can be drawn to help determine the optimal pricing strategy for "Brand X."

From the data in Table 1, three further analyses can be conducted: (1) everyday margin guidelines, (2) feature margin guidelines, and (3) allowance structure.

Table 1: Manufacturer Costs and Allowances

	Everyday Cost/Unit	Off Invoice Allowances	Net Cost/Unit	Performance Allowance/DZ	Dead Net
Brand A	1.28	8.5%	1.13	2.50	.92
Brand B	1.25	10.0%	1.13	1.50	1.01
Brand C	1.25	13.0%	1.09	2.00	.92
Brand D	1.34	7.8%	1.24	.50	1.20
Brand E	1.45	8.2%	1.33	1.00	1.36
Brand F	1.72	12.5%	1.51	1.75	1.36
Brand G	1.79	10.0%	1.61	2.00	1.44
Brand H	1.79	0%	1.79	6.00	1.29

Everyday Pricing and Margins

In order to calculate the everyday margin guideline of the brands (A – H) listed in the previous table, the retail prices of those brands are necessary. These data should be obtained by a salesforce survey or an outside supplier service rather than from Nielsen information, since Nielsen combines everyday and feature pricing due to the methodology of their audits. Table 2 shows the basic calculation of the everyday retail margins of the key brands in the segment.

As Table 2 reveals, the margins in the price/value segment range from 21% to 33%. This range, in effect, sets the limits for Brand X's restaged price. That is, the $2.39 price point is the maximum cap in this segment and is strongly enforced by the retailer. The manufacturer's selling price to the trade, consequently, must be "backed into" since the other key variable, retail price, is controlled by the channel. Fox example, if the maximum retail price objective for Brand X is $2.39 and the trade margin range is 21% to 33%, then the everyday selling price (to the trade) must be between a $1.88 and $1.60 respectively.

Selecting the everyday cost between $1.60 and $1.88 then becomes a matter of Brand X's current status in the marketplace in

Table 2: Everyday Retail Margins

	Everyday Cost	Everday Retail Average	Margin %
Brand A	1.28	1.57	22%
Brand B	1.25	1.85	32%
Brand C	1.25	1.70	26%
Brand D	1.34	2.00	33%
Brand E	1.45	1.99	27%
Brand F	1.72	2.39	28%
Brand G	1.79	2.28	21%
Brand H	1.79	2.28	21%

terms of market share levels and trade acceptance of the restage of Brand X. Also the 28 cent spread between the low and high side of the everyday range could represent significant dollars for Brand X especially when determining the feature price strategy.

Feature Price and Margins

Referring back to Table 1, it is evident that most companies in this category give significant trade allowances off-invoice. This type of incentive allows the account maximum flexibility when setting feature prices; however, the manufacturer loses control over these dollars since there is usually no proof of performance requirements. Therefore, in many instances, the consumer does not benefit from lucrative trade deals because some of the money is pocketed by the account and not reflected in the retail sale or feature price. In fact, it has been estimated that two-thirds of all total allowances are not passed through to the consumer. Another type of allowance commonly used to avoid possible misuse of funds, is the bill-back allowance. This requires that the account perform certain activities set by the manufacturer before receiving the allowance. This allowance is usually used for purchasing advertising space in an account circular or for in-store merchandising/display activity. Many companies offer advertising/display allowances, off-invoice as well as bill-back, but for this example it is assumed that proof of performance is required prior to receiving the allowance, and therefore, is of the bill-back type.

Even though the bill-back allowance is typically used for advertising/display activity and the off-invoice nets the everyday cost down to competitive levels, sometimes the entire amount is used to obtain the lowest possible cost or the "dead net cost." This type of dealing, due to an extremely competitive pricing environment, has forced the trade margins on a feature basis down to the range of 7% to 15%. Table 3 illustrates this observation.

Table 3: Comparative Trade Margins

	Dead Net Cost	Average Feature Price	Margin %
Brand A	.92	.99	7%
Brand B	1.01	1.19	15%
Brand C	.92	1.09	15%
Brand D	1.20	1.39	14%
Brand E	1.25	1.39	10%
Brand F	1.36	1.49	9%
Brand G	1.44	1.59	9%
Brand H	1.29	1.39	7%

Focusing on the feature price of the brands (A – H) in Table 3, it is evident that the "hot" price points range from .99 to 1.59. These price points, coupled with set margins of 7% to 15%, dictate the possible range of manufacturer "deal selling prices" which can be calculated.

$$\frac{\text{Feature Objective}}{\text{Margin \%}} = \text{Deal Selling Price}$$

$$\frac{.99 - 1.59}{7\% - 15\%} = .92 - 1.35$$

Now that the competitive environment has been analyzed for everyday and feature pricing and profit margin guidelines, a possible allowance structure can be formulated for Brand X.

Allowance Structure

As was previously discussed, the two basic types of allowances, off-invoice and bill-back, are used to determine the complete pricing structure of the brand. Using the figures previously generated and the assumption that when restaged Brand X should be positioned among the brands at the top portion of the price/value tier, a $2.29 everday retail price point is set as the objective. This corresponds into a manufacturer selling price of $1.60 given a 30% margin—a generous margin given the category range. Further, the feature price should be at most $1.59, which translates to a $1.35 deal selling price, using 15% as the target profit margin. Given these very specific pricing objectives, the pricing structure of Brand X can be determined. Table 4 shows two options that achieve the same everyday price objective and dead net costs, but have different implications to the trade and potentially to the bottom line for the brand.

Table 4: Pricing Options

	Option 1	Option 2
Everyday Cost	$1.60	$1.60
Everyday Retail Objective	$2.29	$2.29
Margin %	30%	30%
Off-Invoice Allowance	10%	5%
Net Cost	$1.44	$1.52
Performance Allowance	$1/dz	$2/dz
Dead Net	$1.35	$1.35
Feature Objective	$1.59	$1.59
Margin % (off Dead Net)	15%	15%

In Option 1, the off-invoice allowance of 10% generates a lower net cost than the 5% in Option 2 allowing an account to feature the brand at a better price when using just the off-invoice dollars towards achieving a feature price point. If the objective of a promotion, however, is to obtain advertising or display activity, then the $1.00 per dozen bill-back allowance may not be enough to pay for the event. Since performance allowances of this type are accrued over the number of dozens sold, an account would have to buy 5,000 dozens to accrue $5,000—or enough to pay for an advertisement. Option 2, therefore, may be a better scenario since the advertising allowance of $2.00 would require only 2,500 dozens purchases to pay for the same $5,000 advertisement. Certainly, there are other sources of funds like co-op dollars, but not all brands benefit from these funds, especially if other brands within a company have priority.

Since funding is always a consideration and the sources of those funds are limited in most companies, it is essential to subject all the elements of the brand, not just the pricing considerations, to a profitability analysis.

Profitability Analysis

The final stage of the price analysis translates the pricing options into a P & L statement for profitability analysis. For the example currently under consideration, the analysis would include a direct comparison of Option 1 and Option 2. Table 5 illustrates a typical profitability analysis.

Both options have similar P & L implications in terms of bottom line profit on a percent-to-sales basis, but Option 2 generates over a million dollars more in revenue. Since sales volume, and the percent of sales each element of a P & L represents, is a critical measure in most companies, then the percentages in Option 2 will be more favorable for expense items, but will suffer when calculating profit dollars off a "larger" sales base. In contrast, Option 1 will generate $60,000 more dollars to the bottom line.

Table 5: Profit Considerations

	Option 1	Option 2
Total Units	20,000	20,000
Net Sales[1]	$29,120*	$30,560
Total COG's[2]	14,000	14,000
% Sales	48%	46%
Total Advertising & Promo[3]	2,500	4,000
% Sales	8%	13%
Marketing Contribution[4]	7,620	7,650
% Sales	26%	24%
Brand Profit[5]	$2,620	$2,560
% Sales	9%	8%

* In thousands.

[1] This is calculated as an average of the number of units sold using the off-invoice (90%) and the balance as turn business at the regular cost of $1.60.

[2] It is assumed for this example that Brand X's total COG's is $.70/unit

[3] This includes the performance allowance at $1.00/dozen in Option 1 and $2.00/dozen in Option 2. A consumer promotion budget of $1.0 million is also part of the total.

[4] Brand allocation of $5.0 million has been deducted from sales. This allocation includes packaging, selling materials, trade co-op, and so on.

[5] Brand profit is net of allocated fixed overhead expenses for the company estimated at $5.0 million.

As is evident, the difference between the options is not significant. In this instance, other considerations and objectives must be carefully reviewed since it is the needs of the brand "at retail" which should drive the pricing program. Specifically, if the objective of the brand is to obtain the lowest possible price, then Option 1 should be implemented. It should be realized, however, that this option uses all available funds towards "lowering the price" at the expense of advertising support. This scenario *pushes* goods on to retailers' shelves, generally in larger quantities. The manufacturer and the account are banking on the "hot" feature price to attract customers. In the case of a brand that needs awareness and advertising activity to help *pull* this product through the channel, Option 2 becomes more attractive. In this scenario, retail price is not the only consideration—in fact, the advertising dollars generated with the high bill-back allowance becomes an important factor. The tradeoff in these two options is the attempt to find the right balance between price and promotion.

Conclusion

Tom Vierhile, executive editor of the *Product Alert Journal* in Naples, New York, reports that 15,000 new food and consumer items—most of them mere variations of existing brands—will be introduced this year. By most estimates, roughly 80 percent of them will fail, usually within six months. In addition, retailers have merged, leading to a more concentrated interface with the consumer. And finally, retailers have begun using technology to generate up-to-date product information gleaned from such sources as checkout stand bar code readings. In such an environment, it is only inevitable that retailers start to flex their muscles. One inevitable outcome has been the administering of an industry price structure based upon products' performances. Another outcome has been the additional pressure on manufacturers to support a brand through advertising and off-invoice allowances. Both factors have resulted in a price competitive environment that leaves little margin for error. The consequence has been that manufacturers have begun to place continually greater emphasis on non-cost variables in conducting their price planning. In fact, the standard P & L analysis must now be preceded by a comprehensive review of competitive trade practices and the calculation of various margin guidelines. Then, and only then, can the pricing decision be reduced to a discussion of contribution, sales, and profits.

Recommended for Additional Reading

"Effects of Competitive Context and of Additional Information on Price Sensitivity," by Joel Huber, Morris B. Holbrook and Barbara Kahn in *Journal of Marketing Research*, vol. 23, August, 1986.

"Making Money with Proactive Pricing," by Elliot B. Ross in Harvard Business Review; vol. 62, November-December, 1984.

CHAPTER EIGHTEEN

PRICING IN THE NEW HOSPITAL MARKETPLACE

JACK ZWANZIGER

Views expressed in this chapter are the author's own and are not necessarily shared by RAND or its research sponsors.

JACK ZWANZIGER

Jack Zwanziger is Resident Consultant in Health Policy and Economics at the RAND Corporation and a lecturer at the School of Public Health, University of California, Los Angeles. He is studying the responses of health care organizations to an increasingly competitive environment. Dr. Zwanziger has Ph.D.'s from the Rand Graduate School and Cornell University and an M.B.A. from McGill University.

CHAPTER EIGHTEEN

The hospital industry is undergoing a dramatic change as governments and private industry struggle to contain healthcare costs. As a result of this increasingly competitive environment, the pricing of hospital services is changing from a routine revenue raising exercise to an important component of overall hospital strategy. Hospital managers will have to develop quickly the knowledge and experience required to price their services effectively. This chapter will suggest some approaches to pricing hospital services and present three case stories.

An Evolving Industry

Since 1965, the proportion of GNP allocated to health care almost doubled, growing from 6.1% to 10.9%, with total spending increasing at a 12% annual rate. Expenditures on hospital services has been the most rapidly growing component of the total. Governments and private payers have been trying to develop strategies to slow down the growth in the cost of health care services. One of the cost control approaches that is increasingly popular is for these payers, directly or through their insurers, to organize plans that negotiate contractual agreements with hospitals that channel beneficiaries to them in exchange for a reduction in price. The pressure to reduce prices would be particularly severe in areas with many competitors and/or substantial excess capacity. Providers in such areas are more likely to agree to accept lower fees and increased oversight or risk being "locked-out" of a substantial portion of the market. The growth of such plans—Health Maintenance Organizations (HMO) and Preferred Provider Organizations (PPO) has introduced price competition to the hospital industry.

The development of price competition has been particularly dramatic for the hospital industry because until recently, hospital managers have not had to pay much attention to the pricing of their services. Since almost all of their patients were insured and since most insurance either paid the rates set by the hospital or computed costs of providing the service, these decisions were usually delegated to a relatively low level in the organization. Individual revenue generating departments set prices for a multitude of individual charge items (so much for a bandage, an aspirin, a blood test and so on) so as to generate the required revenue.

The profit margin for each service was unknown and largely irrelevant. Hospitals could be confident of fulfilling their revenue requirements. Demand for hospital services seemed to be limitless as "first-dollar" hospital insurance became more widespread and a stream of new medical procedures were developed to treat a wide variety of diseases. This happy state of affairs had the expected effect. Hospital costs skyrocketed leading to the search for a means to control their rate of increase.

The pressure to contain healthcare costs will not disappear. It will probably intensify as the primary payers, governments and employers, struggle to reduce their healthcare expenditures. Governments are faced with chronic budget deficits, an aging population and increasingly costly medical technology. Employers, adjusting to an increasingly competitive environment, are trying to control the cost of health insurance. As a result, two needs are increasingly being expressed in the market for healthcare services:

1. reduce costs, and
2. reduce risk/increase predictability.

The organizations best able to satisfy these needs while providing high quality care will flourish; those unable to respond will eventually disappear.

From Physician to Payer Centered Marketing

In the past, hospitals have oriented their strategies around marketing to physicians since they largely chose whether, where and how long to admit their patients and what services and procedures were needed. Sophisticated equipment was purchased and medical office towers built to attract medical staff in the expectation that the physicians would reciprocate by filling the hospital's beds.

The physician's ability to control the demand for hospital services has been reduced by two trends. First has been the shift towards a surplus of physicians and hospital beds. Hospital beds and physicians are both in plentiful supply; it is patients who are in short supply. Payors and employers are discovering the market power associated with control of this increasingly scarce resource. The second source of power is more subtle. A variety of organizations now have the capability to calculate hospital cost differences and to trace their origins. Hospitals and physicians must face increasing scrutiny of their decisions. Sometimes this power is used purely to demand discounts; at other times, utilization review techniques are used to review whether the services provided were really medically necessary. In either case, the power to control the system is shifting increasingly to the party writing the check rather than the one in the white coat. Hospitals are going to have to reorient their marketing strategy to emphasize the factors important to the third-party payers and the employers. Both of these parties are price conscious. Payers, able to provide given coverage at lower cost, will be at a competitive advantage, as will employers better able to keep control of health insurance benefits.

Pressure from payers is transforming the hospital industry by pursuing four changes in the methods used to pay for hospital services:

1. Changing the basis of payment from a hospital controlled rate (cost- or charge-based) to rates that are mandated, in the case of Medicare, or negotiated, for HMO or PPO contracts.

2. Repackaging the "product" being paid for to one that is much closer to what the buyer and the patient are really interested in.

3. Reversing the time frame from retrospective to prospective. Hospitals are increasingly being paid at a rate specified before the provision of services.

4. Shifting much greater financial risks to hospitals.

For example, one of the strategic decisions made by William Guy upon being appointed the "Czar" of California's Medicaid program was to require hospitals to compete for a Medicaid contract by by quoting a price per patient-day (per-diem). This step made it easy to compare the bids of competing hospitals. Furthermore, by committing itself to treat patients for this fixed rate, hospitals had to accept a substantial risk.

These changes are placing novel demands on hospital administrators. Pricing hospital services, once primarily associated with meeting departmental revenue requirements and justifying unit costs, has now become a critical aspect of strategic management.

Let us consider an increasingly typical pricing decision: An HMO is offering a contract to provide services to its subscribers. A per-diem rate is specified in the offer. What is the usual response? The hospital will try to make a more or less informed estimate of what the per-diem costs are—possibly these are broken down into variable and fixed costs. The price that is finally bid is in the neighborhood of the expected average cost, less where competition is intense, more where few alternative hospitals are available.

Now what is wrong with this approach? Primarily, that the hospital has resigned itself to a passive role in the market. It has accepted the rules formulated by the buyer, and even allowed the buyer to define the product it sells. Now this criticism is not intended to downplay the importance of the knowledge of hospital costs. In fact knowing product costs are an essential prerequisite to any pricing strategy, but focusing only on costs will divert hospitals from a consideration of how this particular offer fits into the hospital's overall strategy. Winning this contract may be crucial in which case an unprofitable price may be called for. On the other hand, winning the contract might even be harmful in the long run if it detracts from the hospital's core business or interferes with its most promising opportunities.

The rapid rate of change that hospitals are experiencing has invalidated many of the traditional rules of thumb that hospital managers have acquired. This chapter will suggest ways that managers can adjust to a price competitive market by defining four generic pricing strategies and selecting two particularly effective pricing tactics that can be used. Finally, other factors to be considered in developing an overall strategy will be discussed and then three brief cases integrating these elements will be presented.

Pricing Strategies

This section will define four "generic" pricing strategies for hospital services. They are generic in the sense that they express fundamentally different views of the objectives of the hospital and of the competitive environment in which it find themselves. No hospital is likely to want to use any of these generic strategies. Most hospitals will price using a "mixture" of these "pure" approaches. For some services one strategy may be most appropriate, for others, another.

Public Enterprise Pricing

This form of pricing is common for organizations that produce politically sensitive goods and face demand that is not price sensitive. Such organizations, public utilities and hospitals are examples, set prices to cross-subsidize politically desirable services.

Although not rate regulated, until recently hospitals were blessed with a market which was relatively insensitive to price. As a result, they had the latitude to provide socially desirable services like indigent care, medical education and research and financed these through "cost-shifting" practices, raising the rates to privately insured patients. With the growth of competition, the hospital may have to reduce or eliminate these cross-subsidies or else be at a competitive disadvantage. Cross-subsidies, then, can be sustained, but only to the extent that the hospital is able to generate profits from some service areas where it has some competitive advantage, such as lower costs or enhanced demand. Therefore, a hospital which sets as its objective the provision of these socially desirable but unprofitable services must identify either external or internal sources for such funds.

Cost-Based Pricing

This approach has the virtue of simplicity. It, or its variants, is the pricing strategy used by most hospitals. However, its internal focus makes it most suitable to a slowly changing environment. When change is both rapid and significant, the rigidities inherent in cost-based pricing is likely to lead to serious problems.

Several different pricing methods are in fact contained in the general "cost-based" category. What they all share is that product price is solely dependant on cost. Beyond that commonality, these methods differ in the way they relate price to cost.

The "full-cost" approach consists of finding the direct costs of production and of then distributing a variety of "overhead" costs, including capital costs, over the firm's products using a somewhat arbitrary set of allocation rules. The price of the product is then the "full" cost of its production. A more sophisticated variant is to establish a target rate of return on the capital investment required. The price has a profit margin built which, over the planning life of the product, will generate the required return. Retailers have often used "mark-up" pricing, with the price a fixed multiple of the cost of the item. Finally, economists favor pricing at the incremental cost, theoretically, the cost of producing the last unit sold. More often this cost is the average over a convenient number of "last" units.

Cost-oriented methods have four great virtues:

1. They are conceptually simple; just calculate the product's cost and turn the crank.

2. They are easy to defend in public—"no price-gouging, just covering the service's cost"—an important factor for as sensitive an area as hospital services.

3. They focus management's attention on operating costs. In the long run, any hospital not able to at least cover its costs, will not survive unless it is the recipient of a continuous stream of outside subsidies (even goverment hospitals that do receive annual subsidies face a limit to their size, so revenue must be linked to cost).

4. They are based upon data that are routinely collected for budgeting and payment purposes, although the "costs" that are generated from these accounting systems may bear little resemblance to the service's actual costs.

Costs are important, but, in a competitive environment, pricing must be more flexible. Prices may have to change over the life of the product. If the hospital is able to offer a much demanded service before its competitors—lithotripsy is a good example—then the hospital can charge premium prices while it has the field to itself. Further, the hospital may have to consider the market power of the plan it is negotiating with and/or the viability of the threat to use one of the competing hospitals in setting its price. Such factors can be incorporated in simple rules of thumb linking prices to costs if the environment is relatively stable and benign. But this approach to pricing is likely to lead to disaster when conditions become more competitive.

Competitor-Based Pricing

This approach is easy to understand and hard to do. The hospital must maintain an awareness of its principle competitors, their prices, objectives, strengths and weaknesses. It must consider their likely reactions to any change in price that is being considered. This strategy is most useful in a market with a few major competing hospitals whose actions can potentially have a substantial impact on the demand for the hospital's services. In such an environment, it is crucial to maintain an awareness of prices demanded by competing hospitals and to gauge their likely reactions to any price changes being considered.

In a market with many competitors, price may be an important factor in determining each hospital's market share. Pricing also expresses the competitive relationship the hospital wants to establish with its competitors. One of the classical patterns for this pricing strategy is one where price plays an important "positioning" role, locating each competitor relative to each other. Some hospitals would provide basic services and try to attract the Medicaid market, another might provide many amenities with their service and orient themselves towards patients with private insurance.

These tasks are very complex, requiring a substantial investment in time and money. Hospitals, novices at competing on a price basis, are just beginning to learn the basic skills involved, "reading" and "signaling" to their competitors properly while not colluding in fixing prices.

Market-Based Pricing

In some markets, there is no need to know the prices charged by individual competitors because there are so many competitors, at least for that particular service, that each hospital can only price in a narrow range or each hospital sets its prices relative to the dominant hospital in the market.

Even in highly competitive markets there is some discretion in pricing. There are some price differences even for homogeneous commodities. Hospital services are far from commodities so that prices are likely to vary substantially even in fiercely competitive markets. Hospitals will be able to price at the high end of the range as long as they can provide a service that buyers value more highly. Two examples for different types of buyers: the hospital may increase the value of its services to payers by sending them claims in a form best suited to their data processing service; more mundanely, a hospital may provide adequate patient parking for outpatient services. The ability to price at the top of the range results in a long-run competitive advantage providing the hospital with the financial resources to continue to invest in enhancing the value of its services.

PRICING TACTICS

Pricing strategies are intended to provide a coherent framework for hospital pricing over an extended period of time; pricing tactics are a response to an immediate problem or opportunity. Two of the tactics that arise most often in pricing hospital services will be described in this section.

Choosing the Appropriate Cost
("Know Your Direct and Indirect, Variable and Fixed Costs")

Hospitals provide a multitude of services. Most of these services share personnel, space and equipment so that it is impossible to assign the cost of these resources to a specific service. But a detailed knowledge of a hospital's cost structure is essential in pricing its services. Different costs are used in estimating the break-even price for a service depending on the circumstances.

1. *Short-run direct cost.* Those costs that would be incurred provide an additional unit of a service. For example, the direct costs of the reagents used for a lab test, the additional time that the lab technician worked to perform the test and the clerical time involved in recording it. This cost would be the price floor should a neighboring hospital or clinic need temporary spillover laboratory services.

2. *Long-run direct cost.* Those costs that would be incurred provide an additional unit of a service were needed for a period of time that would allow the method of providing the service to be changed. For example, in the short-run, an additional patient in a ward will result in little or no increase in the number of nurses on the floor since staff requirements are fixed well in advance of an individual admission. Each nurse will work a little harder and the patients will receive less attention and a slower response time. Such a situation, however, is not viable in the long

run as nurses will leave and patients will complain. In the longer run, a hospital will have to hire additional nurses and/or redesign its staffing to deal with the additional patient. The long-run direct costs for treating that patient must include these additional costs.

3. Average service cost. These costs are the total cost of all the resources identified as being used in the provision of that specific service divided by the number of units of the service provided. For example, the costs of obstetrical services could be built up in that way by finding the costs incurred in operating the labor and delivery rooms, the costs of the newborn nurseries and so on. But the costs of the backup resources needed in case of an obstetrical emergency would be included only if any additional resources were required purely to serve obstetrical patients.

4. Fully allocated average service cost. This cost is the most inclusive. Not only would it include all of the service's direct costs, the cost of all of the resources used in its provision, but it includes the costs of all of the resources consumed in "overhead" activities.

The costs increase in size from the first to the fourth as the costs of more and more resources are ascribed to the provision of a particular service. In the long run, all of the hospitals services must be priced so that they at least cover all of its costs, or their fully allocated costs, but the other costs provide useful guidance when facing a particular pricing decision.

Service Bundling

Bundling is the offering of two or more services and/or products at a single price in order to enhance the overall value of the package to a target market. Examples of bundling include the collection of features which are standard equipment on a car, provision of a service contract at reduced rates to the purchaser of household appliances, and vacation packages that include airfare and hotels. As the last example suggests, bundles can be combinations of goods and/or services provided by distinct sellers.

Bundling will be effective strategically when:

1. the act of assembling the package itself adds value, by reducing the buyer's search effort or risk, or

2. standardizing the package reduces costs or risk to the seller(s), or

3. the package, by reducing the effective price for the additional element(s), appeals to a market which would have bought one or the other product separately, or

4. the seller(s) wants to use the packaging to shift their quality or price image.

Hospitals have many possible bundling options, especially when offering managed care services. "Vertically" related services, such as between hospitals, skilled nursing facilities (SNF), and home health agencies (HHA) could easily be bundled, so that both inpatient and after care would be offered at a single price. A hospital could negotiate a contract with a home health agency, for example, to combine the inpatient and outpatient costs of stroke. Hospitals have rarely undertaken to bundle vertical services because of the great variations in costs required to treat such disease categories and because of the complexities in pricing services provided by different organizations (there may also be legal complexities since some hospital may face antitrust challenges to such arrangements). Some vertically bundled combinations appear to be a promising area to investigate, however, because some of these combinations should have additional value to purchasers. The hospital-SNF or hospital-HHA combinations, in particular, appear attractive since they reduce the anxiety involved in the choice of post-hospital care.

"Horizontal" bundling involves the offering of a group of inpatient hospital services at a single price. Such bundling often involves some transfer of risk as well. For example, a hospital may bundle the multitude of individual service items they provide into a few global rates—a rate per day for medical/surgical services, another for mental health and for specific services such as normal deliveries, by-pass surgery and burn care. In setting such a rate, the hospital assumes the risk that the mix of services provided to these patients will average out to the quoted rate (they, of course, stand to profit if they can reduce the intensity of services provided to their patients). Another aspect of such horizontal bundling involves the breadth of services covered by the rate. The hospital may attempt to extract higher prices for areas of particular expertise by excluding them from such global rates, while pricing other services competitively. Or, it may force buyers to purchase the other services at a somewhat higher rate by only offering a bundled product that included the desired services. Hospitals are currently exploring such bundling options especially in areas with substantial PPO and HMO activity.

Case Stories: Three Pricing Problems

To integrate the discussion of pricing hospital services, three brief case stories will be presented. They are intended to evoke some of the general problems facing broad categories of hospitals.

1. The University Hospital

Background. This 500 bed hospital is a teaching hospital associated with a prestigious medical school. It is located in a major urban area where it competes to a greater or lesser degree with over 30 hospitals. The community is substantially overbedded and to a growing extent over-doctored. Within the past two years both HMO and PPO penetration has increased dramatically to the point where they insure over 30 percent of the area's insured population.

This hospital has a reputation for the provision of state-of-the-art, technically excellent, if somewhat impersonal, medical care. Its medical staff has developed particular expertise in the performance of a variety of highly specialized procedures, and are respected in both the general and the medical communities (indeed many are its graduates). This medical staff also has the reputation of being arrogant, of not returning patients to referring physicians and of making life difficult for community physicians who admit patients into "their" hospital.

The hospital has suffered a decline in its admissions and average length of stay, but to a far lesser extent than most of its competitors. In addition, its financial performance has benefitted substantially from some features of Medicare's payment for the indirect costs of medical education. With this payment due to be cut, and a rapidly growing HMO and PPO sector, a significant decline in revenue may be in the offing.

A basic consideration in the hospitals's strategy is its educational mission, requiring the admission of patients with a cross-section of diseases. This constraint prevents the hospital from the straight-forward strategic choice within the framework of becoming the technological leader. The hospital must price at least some of its product offerings in order to ensure a steady stream of normal deliveries and fractures. Its generally higher cost structure preclude it from trying to be the low cost provider in the market. So the hospital has essentially chosen a hybrid strategy of encouraging the provision of services to the Medicaid population, thereby ensuring access to a patients with the entire spectrum of diseases. But the hospital is able to isolate this since it is relatively easy to justify differential treatment of this population, in particular, charging different prices to Medicaid than those it demands from private insurors.

The Pricing Problem. The problem the hospital is facing is the pressure from HMOs and PPOs to "cherry-pick" its services, contracting for coverage for those specialized services unobtainable elsewhere while directing the more routine cases to cheaper hospitals. In particular, should the hospital try to match the discounts offered by its competitors, or risk the loss of a substantial part of its admissions?

Discussion. The hospital's pricing decision can really be broken down into tactical and strategic components. Tactically, given the number of empty beds in the market and the wide spread availablity of a full range of sub-specialists, the hospital's primary short-run need is that it be able to spread its fixed costs over enough patients, to prevent its average costs from ballooning. It can do this by discouraging "cherry picking," combining high prices in contracts for specialized services only, with a willingness to price services below average costs for some of the third-party payers with enough market share. (This does not eliminate the need to ensure that these costs are as low as possible). In addition, plans that wish to contract only for a narrow range of services should be required to reveal this fact in their promotional material.

Strategically, however, the hospital must not lose sight of the fact that it does not compete on price but on quality. The public's awareness of the high quality of the medical care it provides must be strengthened in the context of an admission that this level of quality does cost more. Strengthening this "demand-pull" will raise the price, that plans would have to pay in lost subscribers if they attempt to exclude this hospital. On the other hand, plans that do include it would then be able to charge a higher premium. In the long-run the hospital should try to develop stable relationships with those plans which have targeted those individuals willing to pay a premium price in order to be sure of receiving high quality care. The hospital's pricing structure should reflect its differential advantage having much larger profit margins for those services which it has an effective monopoly than for those where a competitive market price exists.

2. The Community Hospital

Background. This hospital is a 250 bed general hospital in a relatively small city, far enough away from other urban centers to ensure that almost all the patients from the city are treated by the five hospitals sharing this market. The population and the local economy have grown steadily, if relatively slowly, and there is a general sense of stability.

This stability has extended to local hospitals, characterized by a rare degree of service rationalization. Hospitals compete in the provision of basic services, but those which are more specialized, such as neonatal intensive care and a burn center, are provided by individual hospitals. With one exception, hospital administrators have known each other for a long time and there is a good deal of mutual respect; these relationships are secondary, of course, to their commitment to their institution and its success. The lone exception to this stable pattern of relationships is a new administrator installed when one of the not-for-profits, City General, signed a management contract with a private hospital chain. Medical staffs tend to be loyal to their primary hospital admitting almost all their patients there. There are several local HMOs which have established relationships with the local hospitals.

The prevailing stability in referral patterns has made it easier for administrators and boards to turn down medical staff proposals for the provision of new services and investment in new equipment. As a result, the hospitals in this community have been able to keep the fraction of empty beds and their costs down, and are now being rewarded financially through the Medicare PPS program. Hospitals generally have low debt loads and have stable profit margins. The one exception is City General, located in a deteriorating part of town, which has consistently been losing volume.

Several trends are threatening to disrupt this peaceful situation. Average length of stay has fallen steadily. This combined with a slight fall in admissions has left hospitals with some excess beds. As elsewhere, local physicians are growing in number and are increasingly specialized. PPOs are starting to make their presence felt, as the national employers with local branches, push to restructure their health insurance benefits. In fact, close to ten percent of patients at this community hospital originate in some managed care plan.

The Pricing Problem. Several PPOs have approached this hospital demanding discounts. The hospital is concerned that granting these discounts will only lead to corresponding price cuts on the part of its competitors and will not generate any additional volume. On the other hand, refusing to negotiate if the other hospitals do agree to discounts, could lead to being shut out of this growing part of its market.

Discussion. The main point of this case is that pricing decisions can have major strategic implications. The issue here is not the relatively small revenue loss the hospital would suffer if it agreed to the PPO demands, rather it is that this action would signal the end of the era of cooperation, and the beginning of the new game of hospital competition.

In considering its response, the hospital should consider the following factors:

1. In the long run, hospitals will become more competitive. Certainly the new administration of City General is likely to see this as an opportunity to reverse their decline. Of course, this hospital's spare capacity could accommodate less than half the PPO patients admitted to all the other hospitals so that PPOs would still have to reach some accommodation with at least one of the other hospitals.

2. The plans are in a relatively weak bargaining position especially given the stability of referral patterns. Freezing out a hospital would also make it difficult to sell the plan to the patients of physicians referring to that hospital.

3. It would be relatively easy to identify a hospital which adopts an aggressive price-cutting strategy. Retaliatory responses could then be made.

4. Explicit agreements between competing entities are subject to anti-trust scrutiny. So that the hospital must be able to justify its actions as furthering its commercial interests.

The hospital could then conclude that there was little reason for it to offer discounts in anticipation of the action of other hospitals. Two strategic responses are probably called for: one to keep the supply of empty beds low by conversion to non-acute care; the other to shift the focus of PPO negotiation from pure price discounts to other means of reducing expenditures, such as utilization review as long as such activities do not alienate the hospital's medical staff. There will always be an opportunity to retaliate if the need arises.

3. *The Rural Hospital*

Background. This hospital, an eighty bed operation, is the only hospital in its town of 30,000. However, several factors are combining to make it increasingly vulnerable to competition. There are several similar hospitals within a radius of 20 miles with which it competes directly. Two larger hospitals, each roughly 30 miles away, pose more serious threats because they provide a full range of inpatient and outpatient services. As the demand for more specialized services has grown, these two hospitals have gradually restricted the rural hospital to a case mix characterized by OB/GYN, accidents, pneumonia and appendectomies. The hospital has a generally good reputation for the limited range of services it provides, but its main advantage is that it is close and that the town's physicians need it.

The hospital has always found it difficult to keep specialists on staff. In fact it has been this problem which has forced it to concentrate more and more on the provision of basic secondary services. It is dependant for the majority of its admissions on less than twenty physicians. Most of these heavy admitters are over fifty years old. One of the problem in trying to attract and hold specialists has been to define "turf" in a way which satisfies these generalists, and yet generates enough income for the specialist.

Hospital administrators have prided themselves on running a tight operation. As a result costs are low, and most years show a modest operating surplus. The net result of a slight windfall from the Medicare PPS and the loss from cutbacks in state Medicaid rates have largely cancelled out. Although its balance sheet is healthy, its physical assets, both plant and equipment are old. It will have to renovate and expand the hospital within the next five years. Financing this investment will require a substantial infusion of capital, the source of which is unknown.

Occupancy rate has been falling steadily, reaching 50 percent last year. As occupancy has fallen, the hospital has adjusted its operations to keep costs down. Nurses and other staff have been reduced, professional services are contracted out and fixed costs in particular are closely examined. Cost which management feels are really fixed now constitute slightly less than 40 percent of the total. The one item that was purchased was an improved data processing system, essential for the efficient management of both Medicare and Medicaid claims.

An IPA model HMO has started making inroads in the Rural Town area. Its current strategy is to sign a contract with a regional referral hospital to provide all the hospital services its subscribers need. The 30 miles distance to the local referral center is proving to be a problem both from a marketing and a regulatory perspective. Subscribers are reluctant to sign up with hospital services so far away, especially since the weather may make travel time somewhat unpredictable. State regulations place limits on the maximum distance HMO subscribers can live from associated inpatient facilities. The HMO has approached the hospital for a bid to treat HMO patients.

The Pricing Problem. What price level and structure should the hospital propose in responding to the bid request?

Discussion. This example illustrates the importance of the strategic perspective in making pricing decisions. The critical long-term issue for the hospital is to increase its patient load and to reduce its vulnerability to its present roster of admitting physicians. This contract is an opportunity to do both. The issue then that should dominate the negotiations is the definition of the market that the hospital will serve, both the geographic and product markets. In particular, the hospital should try to generate enough demand for at least one specialty such as orthopedics or urology, to attract such a specialist to the staff. Price should then be used to make the deal attractive to the HMO and financially acceptable to the hospital. The actual bid will depend on the hospital's evaluation of the value the HMO will place on the bid and on the alternatives it has.

Clearly the simplest choice of price structure is a discount from usual charges. Given that variable costs are 60 percent of total costs, and that private pay revenue roughly covers costs, a discount of even 40 percent is feasible if the additional patients will require no additional investment. Since the HMO is unlikely to generate more than 200 patients over the year, it is unlikely to require an increase in capacity. The additional equipment required to provide the additional services, however, must be written off over the life of the contract since this equipment will have little value if the services will no longer be provided. The less additional investment the contract entails the lower the price, but the less attractive the contract is likely to be for the hospital.

One clear problem is whether the charge to cost ratio is uniform across all services or not, since the hospital's case mix could shift substantially with such an addition to its medical staff. If the HMO is willing to accept this structure then a cost to charge study should verify that this ratio is reasonably constant across the entire range of services the hospital expects to provide. Then after a readjustment of charges where necessary, the actual discount can be negotiated.

If the HMO insists on some measure of risk-sharing then the hospital's next easiest choice is some per-diem rate, with safeguards for case mix changes and outliers. The computation of the cost for such an arrangement is difficult and some consultants should be hired to assist in preparing a bid.

Conclusion

The case stories are intended to sketch some of the considerations that should enter into a pricing decision. The descriptions are not intended to be exhaustive, but to suggest some common pricing problems hospitals are facing. Shifting a few factors may result in dramatically different pricing decisions. For example, if the community hospital had been the one with a deteriorating balance sheet and decreasing volume then the strategic choices it faced would probably require a more aggressive approach. Alternatively, if a hospital has a higher fixed to total cost ratio it is more vulnerable to the loss of patients, and so benefits more from any increase in volume. All else equal, it should be flexible in discounting its charges to retain or increase volume.

Hospital administrators will have to recogize that pricing must be integrated into hospital's overall strategy, and must always be subordinated to the prime mission of the hospital providing health-enhancing and life-saving services. Making price a dominant feature of a hospital's strategy will almost certainly be self-defeating. Health care raises issues of life itself and so cost control has to tread carefully. Beneficiaries are likely to be willing to pay more for better quality care. Pricing can serve an important role for a hospital as long as it remains modest and publically unobtrusive.

Recommended for Additional Reading

"Promotion and Pricing in Competitive Markets," by William O. Cleverly, in *Hospital and Health Services Administration*, August, 1987.

Profitable Pricing Strategies by Stephen L. Montgomery, New York: McGraw-Hill, 1988.

"Pricing Strategy and Tactics in the New Hospital Marketplace," by Dennis D. Pointer and Jack Zwanziger in *Hospital and Health Services Administration*. November/December, 1986.

INDEX